Descent of the Dolls

How well I remember my first encounter with the beast.

Descent of the Dolls

(Part I)

Jeffery Conway
Gillian McCain
David Trinidad

Guest Starring
(in order of appearance)

D.A. Powell • Wayne Koestenbaum • Denise Duhamel • Aaron Smith

BlazeVOX [books]
Buffalo, NY

Descent of the Dolls
by Jeffery Conway, Gillian McCain, David Trinidad
Copyright © 2017

Published by BlazeVOX [books]

All rights reserved. No part of this book may be reproduced without
the publisher's written permission, except for brief quotations in reviews.

Printed in the United States of America

Book design by Geoffrey Gatza
Photos courtesy of Photofest

Portions of this work have appeared in *Coconut*, *Electronic Poetry Review*, *La Petite Zine*,
Limp Wrist, and *Painted Bride Quarterly*.

First Edition
ISBN: 978-1-60964-260-0
Library of Congress Control Number: 2016943904

BlazeVOX [books]
131 Euclid Ave
Kenmore, NY 14217

Editor@blazevox.org

publisher of weird little books

BlazeVOX [books]

blazevox.org

21 20 19 18 17 16 15 14 13 12 01 02 03 04 05 06 07 08 09 10

BlazeVOX

To Jackie and her dolls

"We grow older with this movie."

June 13, 2006 – ?

Table of Contents

Descent
of the
Dolls

I

You've got to climb...

Canto One

Seated in a dark movie theater, their view partially blocked by a mysterious woman in a black wig, Jeffery Conway, D.A. Powell, and David Trinidad are visited by Frank O'Hara, Anne Sexton, and Tennessee Williams, who offer to guide them through this camp classic.

Weird sisters, the way is dark, and in the boughs
of the elm trees a familiar song: swirl of snow and wind
come chiming between thin branches. The house

lights fade and someone perches before us in a wig.
Try to move, to change the point of view
before the popcorn ads and the proffered cig

(you gasp: but this was a different era, too,
before the bigger blight of cellphone chatter
and it was almost sexy to smoke a Kool

or a Vantage with the cherry growing fatter
in the darkened theater rows). The point is *spectacle*,
one of Aristotle's six concerns in drama—that, or

song, which in this case fills the long rectangle
of the screen with something that might pass for dance
if we hadn't already weathered the more respectable

Thoroughly Modern Millie and *Half a Sixpence*.
We *settle* in the broadest sense for tonight's viewing:
another twist on the 3 gal theme, perchance

(DAP)

Three Giacometti figures rising
up from hell, tipped 90° become
shadows of three females before turning

shades of red, blue, yellow; then they succumb,
are changed into "dolls" (Jackie's word for pills).
The camera zooms in on the red one

standing on end; it falls, splits in two, spills
its white contents. Next the yellow pill, then
the blue. Glimmering crystals form little hills.

All of this to the sound of eerie Zen
music; a woman in voice-over gives
directions to Valley of the Dolls. When

waiting for a rush that won't come, it is
overpowering (so she says). Daunted,
we must not abandon our climb—what lives

in the shadows, whether it wear leopard
skin, preen like a lion, sing like a she-
wolf, is worth the two-hour trip. Cut to blizzard.

(JC)

You've got to climb . . . Byron sits at my feet,
positive we're writing a sequel to *Phoebe*.
Are we? Lynn Crosbie (weird sister in absentia)

in a recent email: "How is the new project? Easier
without a nervous breakdown-having pain in the ass?"
Remains to be seen, my dear. This is a film all about

breakdowns, about leaving the way of truth behind,
the dark wilderness you find at the pinnacle, and "dolls,"
the magic tickets to instant love, instant excitement . . .

ultimate hell. "Peaks and valleys," says a drag queen
on one of the DVD extras. Peaks: Everest, Olympus.
Robert Frost's dictum: "There's only room for one—

and that's me, baby, remember?—at the top of the steeple."
Valleys: Skid Row, Neely's alley. Implicit in the climb
is the fall, and I, perhaps the weirdest sister of them all

(*He took the pink pills*), think of Anne Sexton's poem
"The Falling Dolls": "Dolls, / by the thousands, / are
falling out of the sky." First, a Raggedy Ann hits the roof;

several Dawn dolls pelt the window. Then a downpour:
Barbie, Tammy, Tressy, Thumbelina, Pebbles, Betsy
Wetsy, Hedda Get Bedda, Patti Playpal, Penny Brite,

Chatty Cathy, Shirley Temple, Teeny Tiny Tears, Crissy,
Miss Revlon, Rub-A-Dub Dolly, Giggles, the Littlechaps,
Baby First Step, Cheerful Tearful, Betsy McCall, Kissy,

Tippee Toes, Toodles, Liddle Kiddles, Disneykins,
gumball machine trolls in clear plastic capsules—
dolls within "dolls." It is June. I am tired of being gay.

(DT)

Three fates (mother, beau, old auntie) wave us toward the city,
past a darker city of gravestones out of Plath
"I simply cannot see where there is to get to." Wouldn't we

all like to disappear down some melancholy path
if we could wind up on the climb we never meant to take
(already, we're thinking of the affair, the aftermath,

the booze and pills and the death of Sharon Tate)
but we couldn't have foreseen how Lawrenceville
would morph ever-faster into a cycle of love and hate,

further and further removed from Mom, poor Willy
(the boy who pinned me) and the nearly dead auntie
whose performance consists of a series of photographic stills.

In what rough cut will we find ourselves: scantily
clad blue movie actress, Broadway has-been or Gillian Girl,
we choose our roles the way we choose a pair of panties—

but all of this is yet to come, a replication of the world's
oldest plot (think: Judgment of Paris, with its triad of
goddesses, each vying for the title of most beautiful)

and the myriad variations on wisdom, power, love
embodied in the celluloid of yore: *The Hours,*
How to Marry a Millionaire, A Letter to Three Wives,

Since You Went Away, Keep Your Powder
Dry, Personal Velocity, Women with Money,
First Wives Club, The Witches of Eastwick, In Her

Shoes, Three Coins in the Fountain, 9 to 5, Charlie's
Angels, Drowning by Numbers, How to Beat
the High Cost of Living, Come Back to the Five and Dime,

Jimmy Dean, Jimmy Dean, Faster, Pussycat! Kill! Kill!, Three
Daring Daughters, Les Girls, Gold Diggers of Broadway,
Safety in Numbers, 3 Women, Gold Diggers of 1933

(DAP)

Now at middle age, lost in this movie,
I find myself aboard Anne's speeding train
hurled through the outer boroughs, gloomy

winter day, anticipating the pain
of what lies ahead: eventual toll
of years beyond forty is what remains.

Juxtaposition: unbelievable
heat and humidity outside the lake
house here in Minnesota where I'm holed

up for a week—a short break from the Cape
(have DVD, will travel). Dionne sings
the theme as we approach the city, take

the bridge over the river into Queens.
My stomach sours a bit through Brooklyn
knowing a tunnel lies ahead, which brings

childhood memories of Disneyland,
that dreaded ride into the whale's
gaping mouth, or the dark tunnel within

Willy Wonka's factory (the shrill wails
of Veruca Salt). Sufficiently freaked
as snowflakes fall from the sky like tiny sails

(there's some barely visible on the flat
horizon of Pelican Lake—though real),
and feeling on the verge of a big fat

panic attack, thinking *I just can't deal*,
I turn away from the window to see
a man with khakis and white sneakers steal

the seat on the aisle. "Sit next to me,
if you like," I stammer, "even though you
could be a ghost for all I know—it'd be

a relief to have company." "Thank you,"
he replies hoarsely. "I see you're a poet.
She's pretty, isn't she? Such gorgeous *yeux*.

(That's French for *eyes*—but I guess you know that.)
I've watched you since Lawrenceville jotting new
observations in your *V.O.D.* note-

book every few minutes: 'make-up like dew;
brunette wiglet like wow!' I rarely write
now, but once I often did. Lately all I do

is walk into movies and act flippant.
My family is from Grafton, and both my
parents were born in Massachusetts, but

I was born in Baltimore (just to hide
the fact that I was conceived *before* marriage—
oh, those oversolemn Catholics!). Silent

films ruled Hollywood when I was born, the age
before the reign of the talkies began.
Then in the thirties, Garbo was the rage,

Marlene Dietrich, Norma Shearer, Miriam
Hopkins, Mae West, Jean Harlow, Myrna Loy—
we used to worship more than one legend.

Surely you know the poem I wrote?—boy
am I glad to have an interesting
conversation at last!—it was a joy

for me to write to the film industry
in crisis. But tell me," he inquires,
turning his large head set upon his wiry

body to see me better in Miss Welles's
train car, "why are you climbing Mt. Everest
with the girls to reach the Valley of the Dolls?"

"From the way you talk and the poem you just
referenced," I say, straining not to sound star-
struck, "is it possible you are—you must

be—Frank O'Hara? You've traveled quite far
haven't you. But hey, can you tell me how
to get off this train?—I'd be a liar

if I didn't admit that I'm scared now,
this journey could take years!" He is quiet
a minute and finally answers: "Wow,

you're really wiggin'. To find your way, *get
off from this ride*, out of this deep *darkness
visible*, you've got to climb Mt. Everest,

walk through the Valley of Shadows (bless
your soul). Listen to me, if you trust me,
let me guide you on this trip through places

of horror and pain where has-beens even
cry to come back and fade again!" I smile
nervously: "Anything you say—just don't leave!"

At length I ask Frank why he'd jumped aboard
the Anne Welles Express today. "What's the date?"
"July 25, 2006," I say.

"Well," he responds, "it's some cosmic fate.
You see, I was killed forty years ago
today—that damned dune buggy out so late

at night on the beach! That same year, *V.O.
D.* was published; ergo, I had no chance
to see this stinkin' movie when it o-

verdosed on the screen! Why does this performance
of three girls leaving home for lives in New
York unnerve you so? The romance,"

Frank says lighting a cig, "should thrill you."
I have to be honest with Frank, like I
am with my therapist. "It takes me back to

my own first few years in New York, to my
arrival on a brutally hot day
in late summer with one suitcase and five

dollars cash, 'borrowed' credit card, no way
to pay for a taxi from the airport
(I resorted to the subway)—

a street woman high on crack, I'd report
later to a rapt coterie, asked if
she could 'Suck it for a dollar?'—to cavort-

ing with thieves, druggies, drag queens (their wigs stiff
with stolen spray), to my liver's final
surrender to booze and hepatitis."

"Jeffery, this isn't the Confessional,"
Frank drolls, "but up ahead is another
kind of confined dreariness—the tunnel

to Manhattan. Look out your window, there
is some real cool Keith Haring graffiti
sprayed around the entrance, and let's see . . . there!

Read what's painted above the opening:
'Forget ever going home again, for
always there your climber roots are showing.'

Now grip the armrests of your chair before
the train (whose catty wheels chant *go back go
back go back go back go back* just like poor

Mary Haines's train on its way to Reno
in *The Women*!) dives into the dark hole."
I venture my own simile: "I know,"

I say, "the train is singing a solo:
Manhattan Manhattan Manhattan,
like Rosa Moline's train to Chicago

beckons her in *Beyond the Forest*." An
electric surge proceeds our descent
into the murky tunnel. I see Anne

Welles pause briefly at her open compact,
then continue to patch her pancake.
I grab Frank's hand, brace my neck on the headrest.

A big storm has moved in over the lake.
I pause the DVD on the open
laptop—the computer screen needs a break.

(JC)

Three pills topple: a cascade of crystals
serves as backdrop for the title—in Jackie's
signature font: I used to know the name

of it: Times New Roman à Clef? A simple
shake of the snowglobe resilvers Jeffery's
desktop like an Etch A Sketch. Out of this

swirl of micro-flecks emerges a woman in
fur. No, not Kitty Foyle, jejune on her sled,
but the great suburban poetess Anne Sexton,

dead thirty-two years this October, waving
her Salem like the wand of a New England
Snow Queen. Trailing ash-flakes, exhaling

poison in frosty puffs, Ms. Sexton clinks the
ice in her highball, crosses her legs (twice)
and speaks: "David, I know you keep think-

ing you've asked enough favors of me, that
you've outgrown this 'old tree in the back-
ground,' but I'm here once again (remember

the last time I appeared in one of your col-
laborations? In *Phoebe 2002* I spoke to you
through your Ouija board: offered up some

pretty good advice; and believe me, no high
jinks were involved: 'twas me; a performance
one rather skeptical literary critic—I have

forgotten his name—called a 'lame cameo';
never listen to literary critics) and who, I ask
you, is better qualified than I to guide you

through this cinematic mess, this endless
downward spiral of a shooting script, and
ultimately, help you get off from this ride,

off of this merry-go-round forever spinning
—like an image in the opening sequence of
The Twilight Zone: a shattered window, a doll

eye, a ticking clock—through blackest space.
Must I list my credentials? I, your teacher,
from whom you learned your tell-all style?

Well, first, and most obvious: my name is
Anne. Second, I grew up in *Welles*ley, located
fifteen miles west of Boston. I think this counts

for something: Lawrenceville, according to
Susann, was at the start of the Cape, about an
hour from Boston by train. *In Lawrenceville*

*everyone gets married as soon as they get out of
school.* That's what I did. Later I modeled
for the Hart Agency (Gillian Girl), had break-

downs and became addicted to 'booze and
dope' (Neely on the skids, in the nuthouse)
and, post-Pulitzer, was somewhat of a sex

symbol: slinked onstage in skintight halter
dresses, flagrantly blew kisses at audiences,
called up radio stations and dared them to

read 'The Fury of Cocks.' Also like Jen—
I committed suicide! Need I say more? I
climbed. And if you think scaling Everest

in late-fifties Boston, among all those blue
bloods, was easy—there's no air there to
begin with. I had fame, and it got the better

of me. *Valley of the Dolls* was published in
February 1966, the same month I wrote the
last two poems in *Live or Die*, the book that

would deliver me to the summit and, of
course, to the Valley of the Dolls. The poems
were 'The Addict' (it's all about pills: 'two

pink, two orange, / two green, two white
goodnights') and 'Live' (in which I refer
to myself as 'a killer, / anointing myself

daily / with my little poisons' but in which
I also commit myself to 'the sun, / the dream,
the excitable gift'—well, it worked for a while).

I was alive, but I never read that damn book.
'It's a potboiler!' I cried when Max told me
she couldn't put it down. She had to see the

movie when it was released. One night we
drove into Boston. It was a few weeks after
Christmas, 1967: they were lining up around

the block, during a January northeaster, to see
this thing. We crept along in my station wagon
scoping out the crowd: believe me, I spotted

more than a couple highbrow poets shivering
in the cold. Max actually liked the movie: saw
herself in Anne, I suppose: nature girl hiking

through the wintry woods as the end credits
rolled. My friend, my friend, I couldn't tell
you then that I saw you old: crotchety Helen

Lawson tearing wigs off the heads of students
and younger poets. In dreams we are never
eighty. It goes without saying that I related

to sexy, slutty, suicidal Jen." Snow has begun
to fall: a veil of heavy flakes overlays Manhattan;
the skyline tips sideways, glints like the Emerald

City: full of hopeful answers: *How will I learn
who I am? How will I think of my name?* "Starry-
eyed, the poets come to the big city. They claw,

climb, then stand there waiting for the rush of
exhilaration, but. . . ." Sexton's cigarette rasp
morphs into Parkins's mellifluous voice-over.

She stares at headstones from the window of
the train. Which viewed from above, cuts
through the screen as it streaks across snow.

(DT)

And oh, "the wind, the wind," says the figure
standing now before me in his Panama Hat
and a linen suit the color of old amphetamines.

"*Summer and Smoke*," I say automatically,
as if I'm playing the old parlor game of Guess
the Title. "But that line could have been

from anything," says the man in his cottony
Southern speech. "I suppose," says I, turning.
His face, slightly blotched, suggests he drinks

sun-up to sundown, and the flair in his gestures
hints at other forms of debauchery, the way Marcel
first caught a glimpse of the darker side of Charlus

or. . . . Christ, this is movies we're talking about, right?
How about the way Peter Lorre fondled his cane
in *The Maltese Falcon*? *That's* the vibe I'm getting

from this guy in the Tennessee tuxedo. No sooner
have I thought the words than his lips,
like the rosy lips of Edmund Gwenn, expel the words:

"I'm Tennessee. But my friends call me Tom."
Could it be? "I thought you were dead," is all
that I can manage. "Oh, quite. Quite. Terribly poetic,

in its way, like when poor Tallulah mixed up her vials
and instead of eyedrops, doused her cornea with cocaine.
Of course, she lived, poor thing. Whereas I . . .

some great mother of a hangover wouldn't let me be.
Oh, the pounding. Like poor Blanche Dubois
with that damned Varsouviana playing in her head.

Went for the aspirin, and fought with the childproof
cap (invented, I think, just to torture poor decadents
like me). The fool thing misthreaded, so I tried my teeth.

And when the cap came off it lodged in my throat.
That's right, laugh. It would have been a wonderful joke
if it weren't for the fact that I asphyxiated (now *there's* a word!)

Sometimes (as I wrote so long ago) there is god—so quickly."
An angel passes, as they say. "I thought the cap you choked on
was from a bottle of nasal spray."
                              "Well, who would you believe,

me or the goddamned coroner? Don't you think I know
what has and hasn't been in this throat?" He's flushed
and sweating, even though he's only a ghost.

What could possibly bring this trembling mass of flesh
back from the dead to board this train, hurtling like a wig
toward the ominous valley? "Jackie and I shared an editor,

Michael Korda," says Tennessee, reading my unspoken question.
And then, "Poets are always clairvoyant," he says with a chuckle,
happy, I suppose, to have the chance to quote himself.

"And besides," he settles his broad bottom on the arm of my chair,
"who better to show you the back alleys of Broadway? Who else
might know a real Helen Lawson or Neely, Jennifer or Anne?

I knew Carroll Baker when she slipped off to Italy, peddling
her ass in *Orgasmo*. I saw Vivien after electroshock,
so close to being Blanche that the artifice of acting disappeared.

Kim Stanley on booze. Liz Taylor on dolls. If it had been set
in Hattiesburg instead of New York, I could have written
that trashy novel myself. Certainly, I'd have done the adaptation."

The wind is picking up outside and the snow is swelling
and the awful musical score. The feeling that something
will happen is so palpable that even the *terza rima* is failing,

coming in and out of focus the way the camera
gives us the sense of losing our sanity. Instead it is the rhythm
of the train that connects us all, from Desire to Cemeteries

to Elysian Fields—that's the journey we're taking.
Tom: "That was the name of the hotel where I died."
"Martha Washington?" "No, you ass. The Elysee."

(DAP)

"Shhhh! This is the Quiet Car," says my guide
to the others on the dark train. A huge
black wig blocks our view of the screen and hides

swirling snow—it's a synthetic refuge
from the fake storm that'll soon become real.
Under the giant hairsprayed subterfuge

sits Jacqueline Susann, trying to conceal
a bottle of Dom she sneaked in, praying
this viewing will redeem her movie deal.

(JC)

"Snow, / blessed snow, / comes out of the sky,"
says *my* guide: "Today God gives milk / and I
have the pail." (While D.A.'s rolls his eyes,

flicks an irrelevant ash from the tip of his
cigarette holder, and says in his unmistakable
bored-to-death drawl: "Fer Kee-rist's sake!

Don't say nuthin bout *milk*—or the confounded
train it *didn't* come in on. If I was to conjure me
a Snow Queen, she'd look like Ms. Lizbeth

Taylor-Burton in *Boom!*: voluminous white
bead-encrusted caftan and headdress—more
a helmet, really—of ice-spikes and white orchids,

or that brunette hair ratted to high heaven!
[he laughs and coughs] Boom! Ya think those
dumbbells would've known: that's the sound

a bomb makes. Like this thing y'all got me
watchin': a dismal failure, albeit a visually
splendid one.") Thanks, in large part, to

William H. Daniels, the DP who lit Garbo,
Harlow, and Shearer during MGM's golden
years, whose name just flashed—drat, that

woman's wig is in the way—in front of a
cemetery. As did the name of Travilla, who
designed Marilyn's most famous gowns at Fox

during the fifties, and who was devastated
(it reportedly broke his heart) years later
when he ran into her and MM failed to rec-

ognize him—too disoriented from alcohol
and dolls. That, my weird sisters, is where
this journey will end. The light spikes—

like Liz's headdress! Snowglobes shatter:
Heidi's smashed hope of reuniting with the
Grandfather; the blizzard that falls from Kane's

hand and breaks at the foot of his deathbed.
Anne, full of hope (milk), stares out the train
window. Manhattan darkens, is darkly inked in.

And snow, blessed snow, comes out of the sky.

(DT)

Canto Two

To settle the poets' doubts about taking the journey, O'Hara tells of how a blonde starlet appeared to enlist his help. Another blonde, New York poet Gillian McCain, steps in to assist Conway and Trinidad.

Inspirationless in the West Village
—that line lies pendant for over twelve hours,
as doubt and trepidation pillage

my will to go on—this journey of ours
could take years (three months for one canto!—less
than three minutes of film). I turn to powers

greater for help, courage, and guidance:
Jackie sitting a row in front of us, merely
traveling incognito, her annoyance

embowered in her wig's severely
sprayed strands; my New York poet Frank O.—
is he still here in the darkness with me?

Did he leave with a pleasant stranger? O
Muses, O high genius, help me now.
I start: "Poet, you who are my guide . . . oh

let's be real—what the hell, Frank, allow
me to speak plainly—why should I travel
into the Valley, into God knows how

many years of ripping this movie (full
of campy lines) to shreds as one might rip
the wig from the head of a rival?"

"Well, Miss Thing, if I have understood," quips
Frank, "your soul has been assailed by fear.
That we should have *no fear* isn't what keeps

us strong; rather, it's that we should *know fear*.
I'll tell you what went down—why I've come.
A lady called to me, so blessed, so dear,

that I begged to serve at her command from
the moment I saw her top-heavy rack.
She told of a blessed woman who had come

to implore her to go to me and ask
if I'd help you out—and that *she* (said blessed
woman) had herself been sent on this task

by another! Confused? I confessed
that I was too. No biggy though—she was
super nice about it all. She was dressed

in a bloody maternity top, was
filming, she said, a new horror movie.
Give up? Sharon Tate—that's who it was!

And the other two (whose silvery
images embossed screens of yore): Monroe
and Harlow. So with a cast like this, *we*

(meaning you and me) cannot say no."
Dumbfounded, silently nodding to Frank,
to the darkness, I intone "Let's go."

(JC)

Overwhelmed in Andersonville—
it's been how many weeks since JC sent his
"patch" (*Phoebe*se for "passage")?

At least three. Last Saturday, my
desperate email to D.A.: "I can't believe
I haven't written my lines yet . . ."

Litany of excuses: had to finish my
book; had to correct galleys of essay coming
out in next issue of *APR*; teach classes;

read student poems; plan upcoming
trips; etc., etc. "Plus Byron sick in the middle
of it all, cramming antibiotics [dolls!]

down his poor little throat. Enough
of an apology? I plan to write tomorrow; wish
me luck. We'll get this baby moving,

won't we?" The sad thing: now I can't
bug D.A. for *his* lines, having taken this long
to get my own ass in gear. "Not to take

pleasure in your busy-ness," he writes,
"but I'm glad it's you this time causing the slow-
down. I was beginning to feel like the

fat kid on the relay team, slowing
everybody else down." Confession: there were
also those ten episodes of *Medium*

I had to watch (season two's just
out on DVD), not to mention some personal
(distracting) stuff involving a man

I'm getting to know. In the mean-
time, our heroine makes *her* first confession:
she knows not one man in the big

bad city. I wanted to see if there
was anything interesting to say about Martha
Washington (probably not). I

wanted to compare the beginning
of *V.O.D.* (the book) with *V.O.D.* (the movie):
how the former starts with fire

("an unseasonable hot spell") and
the latter with ice: Anne emerging from a cab
in front of the Martha Washington

Hotel (From Wikipedia, the free
encyclopedia: "The Martha Washington Hotel
is a hotel in New York City that

opened on March 2, 1903 as the
first hotel exclusively for women. It is at 30 East
30, and originally had 416 rooms.

As of 2003, the building still contains
a hotel, which calls itself Hotel Thirty Thirty.")
in the midst of a blizzard. (In *Phoebe*

I wrote an elaborate patch about
fire and ice—not to be repeated here?) I wanted
to mention the hotel at the beginning

of *The Bell Jar*: the Amazon—
for women only. And how Plath based that hotel
on the Barbizon Hotel for Women.

But the merry-go-round's spinning
too fast, weird sisters, to even fall down a rabbit
hole of hotels for women. Am I

committed to this? Am I up for
repeating a journey I already acted out in my own
life? Guileless poet moves to

Manhattan, to "live his dreams," only
to become disillusioned by the ruthless careerism
rampant in PoBiz and the Helen

Lawson-esque hardness of bards
at the top. I even met my very own Lyon Burke—
and he was an agent! Well, he

was a publicist and editor first.
I ended up on dolls (Xanax, for fear of flying) and
finally had enough: hightailed

it out of town, found refuge in
the Midwest. Can be seen, as credits roll, strolling
through Chicago snow, swinging

a stick. Wait—my guide wants
to say something. She stands in the street in front
of the Martha Washington, wind

whipping cigarette smoke and
snow all around her. "Since Jeffery stole David's
idea [David: "Actually, I gave JC

permission to use it."] that the chain
of command between Dante's lovely/heavenly
ladies be, in *V.O.D.*, between tragic

blonde screen goddesses [David:
"Anne, I think it was D.A.'s idea to make Beatrice
Sharon Tate."], I'm left, at this

juncture, with little or nothing
to say or do. It's like that poem of mine, 'The Play';
many times have David and

Jeffery had a good belly laugh,
at my expense, listening to that god-awful recording:
me slurring the word 'soliloquies'

and delivering their favorite line
('Many boos. Many boos.') with all the dramatic flair
I could muster. Hell, I was drunk

and on dolls! I was Neely doing the
second act first. I'll spare you the speeches, prayers,
and *soliloquies*. It's better with the slur!

The point—Oh, what does it matter.
It's an existential kind of thing, trust me. About running,
and never catching up. David, take note."

(DT)

Running and never catching up is the number
one cause of doll abuse in North America
having come so far beyond

rest and relaxation ("hackneyed" "dull")
I'd need these to make the climb even without
a Sherpa, let alone an espresso machine

(baton twirl) and here I land
Miss Tiny Tot of Dallas, Miss Autorama,
Queen of the star-spangled sandpile

more on the flag, and what it means, later
how would you feel if you'd grown up
on an army base, high school in Vicenza

(Italy) then hitchhiking Ventura Boulevard
going to auditions, which was fine
once I convinced Daddy I was safe in the city

that was before he went off to Vietnam,
specialty intelligence, so he didn't get
to see me on *The Beverly Hillbillies*

standing in the background, in a black
wig, nine times, over the course of one year
I'd met a man named Marty (not Melcher)

who had agreed to "represent" me
no more Coppertone ads or car shows
in order to make a huge splash

I had to come out of nowhere
(which can only happen in private)
with the help of voice lessons, Pilates

V05 and house arrest, I knew
he was right of course but what
did I know? A nineteen-year-old girl

who was still not accustomed
to people staring ("get used to it, kid")
but I had something more than that,

didn't I? You can't deny that at the end
I was always "Oh, Sharon? Sharon was
such a sweet girl" and Zsa Zsa really *meant* it,

and so did Steve McQueen, and Roger
Vadim *god, I could go on and on*
but I've spent the afternoon suffering

at the hands of the Virgin Megastore
hunting for V.O.D. *on DVD*
after a successful 26th Street

morning: a vintage black & white (*London Mirror*
dead file) Jayne Mansfield has collapsed!

her legs center stage as two Italian
policemen help her up from the ballroom
floor to her left is the pedestal of the statuette

Jayne had just been awarded
for "fostering good relations
between Europe and the American

continent" and the January 1967
issue of *Motion Picture* (35 cents)
". . . Barbara Parkins, with hair pulled

back like Martha Washington, looked
sensational in a blue-and-white tie-striped
double-breasted mini-dress at the opening

of a brand-new dress shoppe
called Paraphernalia, which is smack
across the street from the Daisy Club. . . ."

(GMC)

"Hold on a sec," Frank says. "What happened to
D.A. and Tennessee? Who's the hot blonde
chick who just joined us?" "I'll introduce you—

Frank, this is Gillian, she's coming along
with us into the Valley. And D.A.,
well, he and his guide had to step out—long

story." Frank takes in what I have to say,
gives Ms. McCain the once over twice, then
declares: "Let's get back to this film, Conway."

Anne Welles takes the room key from the old hen
at the desk of the Martha Washington,
then heads to the bar for a sherry, when

a haggard blonde barmaid appears: "Hi hon,
what'll it be?" Anne stares in disbelief.
"Say, aren't you Veronica Lake?" Undone,

the waitress takes a seat. "There's been no relief
since that damn reporter discovered me
here and wrote that story, dispelling belief

in America's sex symbols—I'm free
now, anyway." She lights up, takes a puff.
"I'm writing my autobiography,"

she explains, "and I hope to get enough
proceeds to co-produce and star in a
low budget horror—with Nazi-myth stuff

in the storyline." Anne (appalled): "I'd pay
to see that—what's the title?" "*Flesh Feast*."
Veronica gets to her feet. "Did you say

a sherry?" She shuffles off, arriviste
gone bad, dubbed "The Bitch" by co-stars, *sans*
peekaboo sweep (cut years earlier), artiste

supreme who blew herself up before dawn
in *So Proudly We Hail!* to save fellow
nurses (Claudette Colbert and Paulette Goddard)

from having to perform fellatio
on Japanese soldiers, progenitor
of two Elizabeths the world came to know:

Short (vis-à-vis *The Blue Dahlia*) and adored
Montgomery (*I Married a Witch*). Good-bye,
lovely bombshell, as you begin your

final spiral into hepatitis
and renal failure (at age fifty). Our Anne
is shocked by this tragic metamorphosis.

(JC)

But no less shocked than I
to be back in the proverbial saddle—
how long has it been? Three long months.

Everything happens in threes in this universe
(heroines, collaborators, tercets, etc.),
so why am I surprised. Three days

before the end of January, 2007, I sit at
my computer, snow outside the window,
fingers cold, unable to recall what I wrote

in my last patch, last October. I could
simply scroll up and refresh my memory,
but that seems too easy, somehow.

I've had serious doubts about this project:
first, whether it would take off (and mind you
we started it over six months ago, on June 13,

the day the DVD of *Valley* was released;
I thought that all the planets, like pills, would
be lined up, that that would bring us luck),

whether we could develop, and stick to,
a steady pace; then, when Doug dropped out,
how and with whom we might proceed.

"It's a bit like trying to write a novel in verse,"
emailed D.A., "and I just don't think I'm cut
out to be a novelist." Though this was, JC and I both

moaned, *his* idea. "I keep hearing that voice
that says 'sparkle, Neely, sparkle' and I fear
that I'm no sparkler. Meanwhile, I have a few

other things that are distracting me, and in fact
I've been having to take a few dolls now for this
ongoing problem with my kidneys." Maybe he's

our Judy Garland (originally cast as Helen Lawson,
then replaced, due to pill popping, after filming began).
So be it. We lost Doug, but gained a Gillian Girl!

Welcome, weird sister. (JC and I do have good collab
karma with Canadian chicks!) I lost more than one Doug
since last I wrote: the man, mentioned in my last

patch, that I was getting to know. Hit, after five
months of dating, the proverbial brick wall.
Let's just say, like D.A., he wanted to but

when it came down to it, couldn't. Then,
in the midst of that disappointment, I reconnected
with a friend I hadn't spoken to in eight years.

Instant intimacy: she invited me to visit her
and her husband in Denver. So . . . the day after
teaching my last class of the fall semester, I

boarded a flight. Enjoyed the beautiful pink
sunset during the descent, but knew, upon
meeting my friend in baggage claim, that the trip

was a mistake. I'll spare you the details. Let's
just say it turned out to be my own private
Die! Die! My Darling! in Denver. Then, the day

before my return flight, a blizzard hit. 22 inches
of snow, the airport closed, and me stranded
an additional five days, through Christmas, with

an obsessive-compulsive control freak who,
because I sighed when I heard "The Little
Drummer Boy" one too many times, decided

I was the Grinch sent to spoil her Christmas.
This woman, mind you, owns 200 Christmas
CDs. Oh, I said I would spare you the details.

Imagine me safely at home, piling every-
thing I'd bought in Denver—clothes, DVDs
(all five seasons of *24,* on sale at Best Buy),

and a titian bubblecut (this woman, whom
I met when she was a Barbie dealer, still
has a stall in an antique mall)—in the middle

of my living room and performing a purification
ceremony with a smoldering sage stick. Imagine
smoke circling the doll's body. And imagine

me coming home to learn that Byron, my
beloved Cairn terrier, has a tumor in his chest
and three to six months to live. He'd turned

fifteen the day after Christmas, the day I finally
escaped from Denver, completely shut down,
with four of that woman's mediocre chocolate chip

cookies, which she'd foisted on me the entire
visit, in my carry-on bag. What a thud they made
when they landed in the trash! *Meow!* And what

does any of this have to do with the movie?
Snow is the slender thread I hang this inordinate
weight from. It snows in New York, as Barbara

gets out of her cab, goes on her job interview.
I was supposed to be in New York this weekend,
to read at St. Mark's with Richard Hell and

Eileen Myles, but in shock over the news
about Byron, cancelled my trip. Richard
generously offered to read some of my poems.

Yesterday he emailed a report, said before
he read my work, he tried to describe me to
the audience: "I said you looked kind of like

Johnny Carson but a male model version. Then,
realizing a lot of the crowd might well not ever
have seen Johnny Carson, I said maybe Greg Kinnear.

And that you are a great poet, really great. Further,
that you're way into ALL ABOUT EVE and Barbie dolls."
Richard would be surprised to know that on 12/16/05

I wrote the following in my journal: "Last night I
dreamed I was kissing Richard Hell. He kept insisting
we were 'talking.'" Last night, walking Byron, the

snow looked like glitter as it fell. A few weeks ago,
after learning about Byron's tumor, I dreamed this:
I'm in an auditorium, watching the end credits of a movie.

My name is going to be in the credits and I want
Doug (the one I dated), *who's in the audience, to see it*
up on the screen. Diana Ross enters with an entourage.

Possibly she's going to perform. A woman yells:
"Take your pills, Diana!" I leave, carrying Byron.
As we pass Diana Ross, she meets and pets him.

(DT)

Roman walked out during the credits.
When I got home I curled up on the couch
with Saperstein (our terrier named after

the ob-gyn in *Rosemary's Baby*) & tried
to forget his earlier comment: "Is this
camp on purpose or camp by chance?"

I decided it was time to make some changes:
find a new sublet, settle down, have a baby.
It wouldn't kill me to take some time off.

(GMC)

With my peeps—Frank, Tate, Monroe and Harlow,
DT, Anne, and Gillian guided by
(channeling?) Jen—I've found courage to go

deeper into the abyss, let wigs fly
and fall where they may: hell or bust. Next stop
Bellamy and Bellows, where Anne will vie

for a job (with a beige beret atop
her head). She'll see Miss Steinberg, who laments
Queenie's pregnancy from the stairs of a prop

balcony. She'll meet Mr. Bellamy, since
there's no longer any Mr. Bellows,
just his nephew Lyon Burke—whose presence

is known mainly by the gaggle of does
that gather around the watercooler.
Anne admits to weak shorthand, then follows

Miss S. into the boss's office, her
hat and coat now removed. A one-week trial
is set: starts with contracts to Lawson at theater.

    Bellamy and Bellows
    Law Offices
    Human Resources Department

Competency Definitions
for all Staff
(in alphabetical order)

Accountability:
takes responsibility for remembering everything
and having but one sherry.

Clear Communication:
speaks in a tone appropriate for a B.A.
from Radcliffe.

Initiative:
will work till midnight some days,
have dinner with the boss and prospective clients.

Managing Conflict:
deals effectively with unhappy clients,
offering fountain pens, relaying obscene messages.

Professional Appearance:
tries not to be too good looking,
wears boxy dresses which emphasize droopy breasts.

(JC)

Trope of the day: snow and freezing rain.
It's still winter, still Chicago, and I'm still
crouched at my cold desk. Sunday morning:

scrape of snow shovels outside my window.
Waiting for the water for my second cup of
tea to boil. Already boiling myself. Trope

of the day: the double strike: a friend twice
betrays, ten years apart, in the same way.
This, after two Dougs and the Denver harridan.

Woman can't help herself, must befriend/
defend the monster (her mother) at expense
of male friend (her brother); jealousy, resent-

ment (feels beholden rather than grateful);
too narcissistic to have relationships. Trope:
She of the push-pull. She of the stand-ins.

She of the intimacy falsely professed. This,
during one of the toughest losses of my life.
Yes, Byron died. Three weeks ago yesterday.

He started having seizures, so I had him
euthanized at home, on his bed, under cover
of night. It was peaceful, and not without a

sense of grace. Held his head as he moved from
this plane to the next. I've been bereft. His last
two weeks were amazing: buoyant and

robust, he was a pup again (and he had been
dragging): except for an occasional cough,
I forgot that he was sick. A real gift. No more

walks in the snow (which he liked; I was the
one who always complained about the cold).
A week or so before he died, we came across,

on his morning walk, a pink scarf laying in the
snow. I would have kept it, had it not reeked
of perfume. Tied it to a fence; took a few days,

but someone finally claimed it. What other
colors can I give you? Yellow tulips on my
purple IKEA table. Pink of Byron's portrait

(painted by my father in May '98). Red of
the couch on which B. curled up at my feet.
Anything but the drabness of Barbara's costume:

She of the beige coat, dress, damp mushroom hat.
(Flashback to my first job interview: McDonald's.
I was seventeen, still in high school. Got hired, but

lasted less than a week.) Purple, yellow, blue, and
orange: colors of one of Byron's throw toys. Pink
of that scarf out my window, blowing in the snow.

(DT)

". . . pinks tending to mauve, blues tinged with frost,
greens dabbed with silver, wispy yellows and pale
lavenders . . . shadings slightly out of focus, almost

fuzzy . . . soft, fluid . . . like a line of free verse."
("The Quiet Poetry of the New Spring Pastels"
Ladies' Home Journal, April 1970). In the same

issue: "Along Came Joe" by Jacqueline Susann
("When her famous Josephine died, Miss
Susann vowed she'd never own another

dog. Here she writes about the poodle that changed
her mind"); and "The Sharon Tate Murders" by
Peter Mass ("This savage, senseless crime brings

into sharp focus several unresolved problems
posed by contemporary American life—youth,
drugs and family relationships"). *Two days*

later: Am I being passive-aggressive—
refusing to give up my guest spot? Is that
why I can't seem to finish this? Advice

from Mr. Trinidad—"just jump in and write.
Compose the passage in one sitting. Or like
John Huston said to Marilyn Monroe during

the filming of *The Misfits*: 'Just roll the dice,
Marilyn, that's what you've done your whole life. . . .'"
Okay, here goes: Compare and contrast.

Hometowns: Lawrenceville (Anne), Florenceville (me).
First job in New York: Bellamy and Bellows (Anne),
Smallwood and Stewart (me). Initial residence:

The Martha Washington Hotel (Anne),
The Gramercy Park Hotel (me). And then
of course there's the "Gillian" connection . . .

I was given that name on New Year's Day,
1966, one month prior to the publication
of *Valley of the Dolls*. Florenceville, where

I was born, had originally been called
Buttermilk Creek, but was renamed
after the war, supposedly as a tribute

to Florence Nightingale. With a population
of only seven hundred, anonymity was not
an option, and that, along with a lack of

serotonin and natural light, only contributed
to my melancholy. In an attempt to lift my
spirits, my father would quote Churchill:

*Depression follows me like a black
dog*; and it was true: that depression
followed me all the way to New York,

eventually finding a cure in pills, poetry
and *Please Kill Me*. So get over yourself, Anne—
you weren't the first girl to make it out without

a guide, and you certainly won't be the last.

(GMC)

Canto Three

As Anne Welles enters the Stage Door and is directed to Helen Lawson's dressing room, Conway, McCain, and Trinidad recall encounters with their own Helen Lawson, a famous Beat poet. Conway ponders Helen Lawsonism, the first of the Seven Deadly Sins.

David here, just rolling the dice. . . . What I failed to tell Gillian
was that *The Misfits* was filmed in Reno; one night while gambling,
as she was about to throw the dice, Marilyn said to Huston, "What

should I ask for, John?" Hence his famous (or maybe not-so-famous,
as nothing showed up when I Googled it) reply. What should *I* ask
the dice for? *Inspired lines. A patch that will please my weird sisters.*

Or *Yahtzee*, I call out, as I rattle five red dice in their cup. God knows
my lines are long overdue. Light flurries this morning; it's been a cold
spring. I meant to write several weeks ago, after returning from my

whirlwind visit to New York. All hyped-up on our project, having read,
the day before I left, Canto Two at the Ear Inn: the three of us huddled at
a table beforehand, eating and discussing the future of *V.O.D.*—if that's

even a title that sticks. *Valley of the Dolls* meets Dante's *Inferno*, is how
we described it to the "packed house" on that nascent spring after-
noon. Gillian's funny story, while we ate, about her cab ride to join us:

the driver mean to her for no reason. Which prompted me to confess
one of my secrets: how during my years in New York, whenever I'd
encounter a taxi driver from Hell, I'd leave the passenger door open

as I exited, so he'd have to get out and walk around the cab to close it.
A dirty little trick. Which we laughed about nonetheless. Looks like
Anne has a pleasant enough driver though, as she pulls up to the theater

in a white, yellow, and green Sire (I think that's what it says: picture me
with my nose pressed against the TV, trying to make it out) cab. The
stage door a fitting entryway, don't you think, to the lower world.

(It's no coincidence that we see "FIRE ALARM" as soon as Barbara
comes through the door.) But let me tell you some of the things I did
during my week in New York: dinner with Elaine Equi and Jerome Sala;

breakfast with Denise Duhamel (in town to promote the anthology we
co-edited with Maureen Seaton, *Saints of Hysteria: A Half-Century of
Collaborative American Poetry*, we both booked rooms at the Washington

Square Hotel); lunch with Marvin Taylor, curator of the Downtown
Collection at the Fales Library at NYU, to discuss my editing a collected
poems of Tim Dlugos; *Saints* reading at KGB Bar (hosted by me and

Denise, and featuring Elaine Equi, Joanna Fuhrman, Noelle Kocot, Chris
Martin, Jean-Paul Pecqueur [a hottie], Susie Timmons, Susan Wheeler,
and [a pregnant] Rachel Zucker); dinner afterwards, at Veselka, with

Aaron Smith (we then went to St. Mark's Books where we spent a great
deal of time in the poetry section, dishing and laughing); lunch with
Christopher Wiss, Tim Dlugos's last boyfriend and executor, to discuss

Tim's collected; afternoon visit with JC, at his "Polly Pocket" apartment
on Jones Street (where . . . well . . . I won't discuss it in detail, but someone
from our past reappeared, via an email to me [he'd already reappeared

to JC in person, in Philadelphia, the week before], and JC and I had to
process the strangeness of it all); dinner at Japonica (on the way I touched
[I always do] Frank O'Hara's front door [90 University Place, there's a

plaque saying he once lived there, in case any poets out there are look-
ing for luck]) with Michael Montlack; a day with Elaine (lunch, followed
by a show of Joe's erotic work at Tibor de Nagy [we splurged and took

cabs both ways], followed by cookies and caffeine at Café Loup); another
Saints event at Cornelia Street Café (Denise and I again hosted, readers
included Tom Breidenbach, Guillermo Castro, Ron Drummond, Tom

Fink, Eric Gamalinda, Stacey Harwood, Jacqueline Johnson, Nathan
Kernan, Sparrow, Mike Topp, and Bill Wadsworth); meeting with my
publisher, Jonathan Rabinowitz, to discuss *The Late Show*, followed by

lunch; dinner at Nathan's beautiful loft on White Street (with Nathan's
partner Tom, and Tom Breidenbach and his boyfriend Andy); lunch
with Susan Wheeler (subletting Carol Muske-Dukes's apartment on

Fifth Avenue, the frilly digs of a *literary lady*); cookies and caffeine with
Erica Kaufman; dinner with JC in the West Village; our lunch and reading
at the Ear Inn; dinner and a movie with Anselm Berrigan and Karen Weiser

in the East Village. I had more than one crying jag about Byron in my
room (#717) at the Washington Square Hotel. The walls a pink mauve;
above the bed: framed portraits of Grace Kelly and Lauren Bacall. Solved

a few Sudoku puzzles. Slept a solid eight hours every night. Twice my
guide visited me in dreams. In the first, Lynn Crosbie had purchased
one of Anne Sexton's scrapbooks. It was full of photographs. She'd

bought it from Kayo's second wife, who was moving, I believe, and had
to unload a bunch of stuff. Lynn had paid very little. I was jealous.
"She was selling more of Anne's belongings," Lynn said. She put me in

touch with Kayo's wife and I arranged to buy the black satchel in which
Sexton kept her poems. There were still some loose papers in it. She was
only going to charge me $100.00, and I was thrilled. But she insisted I go

away for an hour (I can't remember why) before I could take it; I was
anxious that the deal would fall through. In the second, Anne appeared
and whispered in my ear: "It's such a big change, you're going to feel

differently about things." That wasn't it exactly; it sounded more profound
in the dream. She must have been referring to Byron's death. That, my last
night in New York. A wonderful trip, during which I relived some of the

excitement I felt nearly twenty years ago, when I was new to New York
and excited to be there, excited to be around poets both living and dead
and to *hear them singing and lying*. Wonderful, except at the end. . . .

Can you guess? The hotel called a car service to take me to LaGuardia.
The driver, a tall Black man in his thirties, took an instant dislike to me
(homophobic?), was gruff and abrupt, talked loudly on his cell phone

all the way to the airport, and when we arrived, instead of dropping me in
front of the airline, stopped on the other of side of the median strip. "Why
are you dropping me here?" "Why do you think!" he screamed, "Over there

is traffic! Why should I get stuck in traffic!" I paid him (no tip), got out,
pulled my bags after me, extended the handle on my suitcase, and walked
away—*you know how bitchy fags can be*—leaving the passenger door wide open

(DT)

Anne's panty-hosed gam exits the taxi, plants itself firmly on the pavement.
The driver waves appreciatively, thankful for the hefty tip. Anne enters
the building and is immediately greeted by a shadow sister, a real live

"New Yorker," brash but personable, a fatty with a heart of gold adept with
directions, which Anne follows, smiling smugly to herself at the wonder
of it all—finally, she is *here*, where she belongs, among "her" people—

beautiful, talented, passionate, temperamental—a netherworld of Type As—
relentless, driven, intense, smoldering. *People who really live.* She will ingratiate
herself into this demimonde, offering herself up as a foil for others to reflect

themselves upon, as a vehicle for transference, an improv partner. *Good,
sweet Anne.* Oblivious to her own banality, her coif brushed in the opposite
direction in order to give it more flow—*and* help hold the lines of her set.

(GMC)

THROUGH ME THE WAY INTO THE GLAMOROUS CITY,
THROUGH ME THE WAY TO ETERNAL FAME,
THROUGH ME THE WAY THAT RUNS AMONG THE BIG TITTIED.

These words—their meaning obscure—flicker like flames
in worn neon above the stage door Anne schleps
her beige self through. Then the last warning from Dame

Astro: IF YOU'RE A CAPRICORN, WATCH YOUR STEP!
Anne, perplexed by this admonishment, walks on
into the tempest, into this busy skep

of ego and drive. She shoos wasps and flies, drawn,
she thinks, to her Aqua Netted hair, which holds
up well to the hurricane-force winds upon

her in the vestibule—winds so strong skinfolds
form on her flawless face. The gate slams behind
her. The whirlwind of the starless air enfolds

the opportunists and outcasts, those confined
to windowless rehearsal rooms where loud cries
echo in the timeless, turbid air entwined

with words: "Why? Why?" "Why!?" "How old are you?" and sighs
of chorus girls to an endless *one two three
four five six seven eight* beat. Leotard thighs

rub together in never-ending deathly
drill team rhythm as shrill wails of young upstart
divas—*Give a little more*—waft eerily

in the tumult reserved for those set apart
from the rest of us because they do nothing
for society.
             "Preachy, preachy!" My heart

jumps—*who's there?* I whisper into a darkening
"Polly Pocket" at 7:06 PM
on this April Saturday eve. "I'm slumming,"

says Frank O., "Don't turn around—write your poem."
Hallucinations, I say aloud, *I knew
they'd catch up with me.* "Oy, always the victim,"

exhales Frank. *Are you smoking? I can't undo
cigarette smoke—this is a small studio!*
"Tiny," says Frank, "but cool. Don't get all imbued

with bourgeois fussiness—what's wrong with homos
these days anyway? Things were so different in
the sixties. Don't freak—I'll open a window."

Frank, I'm feeling a little like Hope Lange in
The Ghost & Mrs. Muir. "Do you mean that
movie from 1947 wherein

lovely Gene Tierney falls for the always flat
Rex Harrison, who is, of course, a phantom?"
Gee, I say to thin air, *do I sound like that?*

*Have I become the snobby older filmdom
queen who rails against TV spin-offs?* "I think
I resent that," Frank miffs. "Besides, you're the one

ranting about actors and dancers who shrink
from their obligations to society.
FYI, methinks that 'society' quite stinks!"

I'm rolling my eyes at the computer screen.
"Meanwhile, what's this? *The Album That Changed My Life.*"
That's my new book, I say, trying to sound serene.

Frank slowly flips through the book; the room is rife
with tension. "How come none of the poems bear
epigraphs by me?" *Clearly an oversight,*

*Frank. I would be honored to use one somewhere
in my next book.* "Well," says Frank, slightly put off,
"I like your poems." (I know—I'm well aware

it'd be a little awkward for him to scoff
at my work. After all, he's sitting on *my*
bed!) *This is kind of fun, sort of a spin-off:*

The Ghost & Mr. C. "Hilarity, thy
name is Jeffery," quips Frank. *When I moved to this
place after my nine-year relationship died*

*over three years ago, I saw this address
—21 Jones—and the apartment number—
7—and zip—10014—as*

good omens (all multiples of the number
7—my lucky number!), so publishing
my first full-length collection while here figures,

in light of such numerological divining.
"Wow," says Frank, "You *are* from California!
Did you say—is this 21 Jones, darling?"

Yes Frank, I just said . . . are you in a coma?
"This is amazing!" I can feel Frank spraying
on the back of my neck as he speaks. "Karma,

major karma! John Ashbery was living
in the basement apartment of this building
in '49, and I stayed here, partying

with him and his roommate. One night, carrying
on, I found a lavender feather boa
and walked outside and around the corner, wearing

that thing like a superstar, and a bona
fide woman with a little boy came up to
me—totally out of breath and all drama—

and said, 'This is my son. Please take him won't you
and show him your ways.' Isn't that just brilliant?
I'll never forget my NYC debut!"

How weird, Frank—that mother could've been an ardent
spokesmom for all Mothers of America
who you address in "Ave Maria"— "let

your kids go to the movies!" Frank rolls across the
bed. "Speaking of movies, aren't you supposed to
be *writing* about *Valley of the Dolls*? Uh!

I'm going now: 'Am I a photo?' Are you?
'I can't remember.'" The room now lit by my screen,
quiet at last. Click *PLAY*: Anne comes back into view.

(JC)

Anne's in. And so her descent begins. The first figure
she encounters is this smoke-breathing "fatty," who utters
a line JC and I have been puzzled by for years: "If you're

a Capricorn, watch your step." Perhaps I can at last solve
the riddle. In the final screenplay of *Valley of the Dolls*,
completed by Dorothy Kingsley on February 22, 1967

(I bought it for fifty bucks on eBay when we started this
project; it has a pink cover and is signed by Lee Grant),
fatty is described as "a fat old woman" who is seated

on a chair reading an astrology magazine. Unfazed by
a "nervous and excited" Anne, who announces her
signature-seeking mission "importantly," the old woman

offers directions and astrological advice, then goes back
to her magazine. Somewhere between writing and filming
the woman became younger, the magazine (she does hold

something, but it's impossible to tell, on my 16" TV, if it's
zodiacal; it looks like a newspaper) was overshadowed
by other business (cigarette and phone conversation)

yet her weight and lines remained the same. And if we
examine fatty's directions—"You go down the hall to the
balcony, turn left . . . it's the first dressing room on the right"—

we see that she misleads our heroine: Helen Lawson's
dressing room is the first room *on the left*. Is fatty our
Charon, the pilot of the boat that transports shades of

the dead—newly arrived from the world above—across
the waters into the lower world? She may as well holler:
"Woe to you, Ms. Beige Ensemble, Ms. Mushroom Hat,

you poor starstruck soul. You're not dead yet (in fact
you're barely pink); I'm trying to spare you, throw you
off. I cannot, in good conscience, ferry such an innocent

as yourself into eternal darkness."
                              Wrapped in her
mother's fur coat (today's May 13th, Mother's Day), my
smoke-breathing guide appears among the throng of

small souls (extras) rehearsing on the shore of the river
Acheron. *Aren't you going to tell them about your dream?*
"Must I?" There's no need for her to answer. She

is here to remind that in spite of *Valley* or Dante, I am
first and foremost an actor in my own autobiographical
play. I dreamt this last month, on another 13th, a Friday:

I was in a used bookstore. The owner had known Sexton;
in fact, Sexton admired his wife's poems. I asked if his
wife had ever published a book; she hadn't. There was

a signed Sexton book (*All My Pretty Ones*?). I looked at
it and noticed that the title page (which Sexton had signed?)
had been torn out—so it really wasn't a signed copy. I

tried to communicate this. The owner was gone. His wife
was there, curled up in an armchair reading, but I couldn't,
or knew not to, speak to her. I tried explaining the torn-

out page to a clerk.
                 Anne: *It was a dream that was not a dream.
And the other two?* "The other what?" *Other dreams.* "You mean
the other dreams that were also not dreams?" *Cute.* In the

first (March 27), Byron was lying on top of me (I was holding
him?) as he fell asleep. I smelled something burning—incense?
(His death/cremation?) In the second (April 22), I come home

(with a woman). Byron doesn't come to greet me—so I know
something's wrong. He's in the bedroom—lying on the bed.
I can tell he's not himself, that he's sick. I lie down on the bed

and he comes over to me—rests his face against mine.
Anne:

Now tell them about yesterday. "What am I, your dummy? Your
Jane Roberts?" *You know not. Just go with it.* OK. Yesterday,

at Columbia College's commencement ceremony, legendary
recording artist Dionne Warwick was awarded an honorary
doctorate degree. During a video tribute, a compilation of

clips of her greatest hits, there were a few seconds of her
singing "Theme from *Valley of the Dolls*": "Gotta get off,
gonna get, / Have to get off from this ride . . ." Other

than reminding me that I promised myself I'd write
my lines this morning (commencement freeing me up for
a whole summer of line-writing!), I was unmoved. Her

speech was brief, unprepared (she read from jotted notes),
her message unexceptional: *It's gonna be hard, but you have
to follow your dream.* That is, you've got to climb. Should

she have warned the graduating seniors what to expect
once they reach the top? Should she have told them about
the Valley of the Dolls? That, after countless hit singles

and gold albums, after five Grammy awards, there'd be
no place left to climb? That in the 1990s her career would
take an unexpected downturn, with only a few moderate-

selling records released and no major singles? That she'd
be best known for hosting infomercials for the Psychic Friends
Network, a 900 number psychic service? That in 2002 she'd

be arrested at Miami International Airport for possession
of marijuana? That Miami-Dade police officers would report
finding eleven marijuana cigarettes inside a lipstick container?

That charges would be dropped when she agreed to complete
a drug treatment program, donate $250.00 to charity, and make
an anti-drug public service announcement directed at youth?

Should she have made such an announcement at commencement?
Some sort of anti-dolls statement, followed by a poignant rendition
of the *Valley* theme? Warwick maintains that the marijuana cigarettes

were dropped in an open bag she was carrying.
DT: That was
exhilarating, Anne. I get it now. *See! Amazing how far a little
willingness will take you. Now tell them about* her. "Her?" *You know*

who I mean. [DT sighs] *The friend you talked about in Canto Two.
She of the . . .* [DT breaks in] She who can only take, who has
nothing to give. What is there to tell. Two days ago, at the end

of a reception for our graduating poetry students, I took the
road less traveled. I knew this would probably be the last time
I saw her before she left Chicago. One road: not say anything,

simply walk away (and let anger choke at my heart). The other:
walk up to her, look her in the eyes—straight into her soul—
and say: "Good-bye." And that made all the difference: I left

feeling empowered and free. A few weeks ago, after a different
event, I saw her flee (rather than encounter me). She was running
towards the exit that was locked, I told JC. To which he replied:

If that's not a metaphor for her, I don't know what is.
An unearthly
wail rises from the souls pressed against the river's edge. Anne
disappears among them: *Let's say no more about her. Walk on by.*

(DT)

CAPRICORN (December 22–January 20) is represented
by the sure-footed GOAT, who owes much of its agility
to its HOOVES, which are cushioned with skid-proof

pads, perfect for climbing to the top of any mountain.
Stable, shrewd, calm, confident, practical, cautious,
responsible, independent & unemotional, Capricorns

are capable of persisting for as long as it is necessary
to accomplish any GOAL they have set for themselves.
Feet planted firmly in what those back home would

call *some godforsaken place*, Anne is convinced
that Operation Helen Lawson is sure to be a cinch
so she pauses on the balcony, takes some time to breathe

in the atmosphere, no need to hurry, it's only
a signature, why she can probably finish
her assignment with plenty of time left over

to stop and return that sweater to Lord & Taylor
before picking up Mr. Bellamy some of that divine
chicken salad she read about in *The New Yorker*

(GMC)

It's Memorial Day on Fire Island.
I'm sitting on the beach at the edge of The Pines,
the approximate scene, along this slim sand

bar, of the accident which *still* maligns
the very nature of art: the spot where Frank
O'Hara was killed by a dune buggy. No sign

marks it; nothing under this overcast blank
slate of gray points the way to the place where one
of the greatest poets who ever lived sank

under the weight of that charging fender some
forty years ago. Frank was taken across
the bay in a police launch so a surgeon

at a second-rate hospital could crisscross
his trampled body with cold instruments to
no avail. He was buried under lush moss

at Green River Cemetery on Long Island. Blue
sea glass—I found a lovely piece not far from
here yesterday as Wally and I walked to

Cherry Grove (where we're staying)—a small gift from
Frank I'd like to think, the rarest, most prized color,
a very "well done" piece, cool, smooth in my palm.

Dear Frank, we who are not dead salute your valor,
thank you for your service in the South Pacific
and Japan as a sonarman on the destroyer

USS *Nicholas* during World War II. Heroic
poet of high and low culture, dreamlike
lyricism, the spontaneous and quick

"I do this, I do that" poems that you'd strike
out on scrap paper, shove into coat pockets
or simply misplace to become ghostlike,

I love that you didn't care so much, had guts,
and absentmindedly left your typewriter
and finished work in train stations. Now inlets

of water are encroaching on the beach—water
rushing in as high tide approaches. Good-bye Pines,
thanks for the place to sit and remember.

A few weeks ago I read Dante's *Inferno*
with my 12th grade English class. When we finished,
I gave a test with a question about Canto

Three: *Why do you think the Vestibule is the worst place to go in hell?*

    I think, based on his life, Dante chose the Vestibule as the worst place to go in
        hell because
    he was exiled in his later life and thought that he'd be unable to contribute to
        society

anymore. He felt that that kind of a life is a bore and terrible. He hated lazy
    peeps.

Because the worst thing a human can do is do nothing with his or her life.
    That type of
person really deserves to be stuck in a hurricane with wasps and flies biting
    their face and
maggots eating the blood that runs out of the wounds, like a very scary
    movie.

I think Dante thought the Vestibule would be the worst place in Hell cuz it's
    not even
the best place to be in Hell—like living in the Bronx when you want to live in
    Manhattan.
He wanted to show that doing something in life was better than sitting
    around watching TV.

We think we are safe because we really didn't, you know, do anything bad,
    but we really
didn't do anything good neither. So what are we? Laziness is a killer. The
    souls in the
Vestibule have to learn that lesson. And the punishment never ends. Like
    science class.

The problem here is that these people in the Vestibule don't even understand
    why they
are there, because in their heads they think "I'm good; I didn't do anything
    bad." But
the problem is they didn't do ANYTHING—good or bad. Wake up people.

God or whatever made humans so we could do good and help others, so
    what if you
were made and lived your whole life in "the waiting room"? No good. You
    should have
to go to the Waiting Room in Hell too. Self-centered people deserve to live
    with worms.

It would be better to do something really bad in life than do nothing at all
    with your life.
So kill someone, well maybe not kill someone, but do some bad things (have
    some fun)
because if you go to Limbo at least you have a chance to get out some day.

The unsure. Nothing is more sad. Dante knew this. And placed people
    accordingly.
How would you like a bunch of wasps in your face all 24/7? How would you
    like to
never have the chance to go up to heaven some day where things are really
    pimped out?

Dante's first passion in life was community service and social responsibility.
He helped others even before he worked on his poems to that lady Beatrice.
    So, we can see
why he wanted to explain to people that the worst thing to be in life is a
    couch potato.

Of course, reading their answers, I realized that
each one was a rendition of something I
had said in class; my tangential ramblings begat

this treasure trove of pontifications I
should have guessed would come back to haunt me. The kids
are sweet, though. With this scene in *V.O.D.* on my

mind as of late, I've taken to stopping mid-
sentence to squawk out: "I know all about run-
of-the-play contracts!"—an especially acrid

denunciation when someone hands in written
homework late. They've come to accept my quirks
but at first I don't think they knew it was in fun.

Last Wednesday, I told the students there are perks
that come with being in my class. Ignoring
the "Oh another movie scene" remarks and smirks,

I put in the DVD and said, "I'm showing
you a snippet from one of the greatest films
ever made in America," as a rolling

wave of fingers made air quotes for "greatest films"
around the classroom (for sure they've mastered *two*
things I've taught them—irony and irreverence). "Films

are a great way to learn about life, too few
of truly great merit are viewed in school," I
offered, though I bet that this half-assed platitude

was less than convincing. The truth is that I
sometimes need to amuse myself in class and
will do whatever I need to do to keep my

bored self from, well, being just that. When Anne
meekly lurks outside the dressing room doorway,
Helen looks up, says with wonderment, annoyance:

"Who in hell are you?" "I'm Jeffery Conway"
(flashback to fall 1989, outside
Allen Ginsberg's office at Brooklyn College).

"You can come in now. Sit down. What made you decide
to wear a motorcycle jacket in this heat?"
"I, I am, I'm from L.A." "So you're going to ride

your way into poetry tutorial to meet
me for the first time, think that jacket will give
you street cred with the greatest living Beat?

Well, think again." "I don't mean to . . . please forgive
me for asking, but that other poet, from
L.A., who studies here, he's very good—I live

for his poems!" Allen pulls his glasses from
his face. "Yes, he is good. David Trinidad
you must mean . . . yes. . . ." This first meeting sounded the drum

which heralded in the next two years of bad
vibes between Allen and me; I who refused
to be starstruck, I who wasn't overly glad

to be a groupie, or to say there was nothing to lose
by reading poets not found in libraries.
In some ways I'm glad I was still drinking booze.

(JC)

It's Father's Day in Andersonville.
I'm sitting at my desk, a/c and ceiling fan
gently humming. 81° here in Chicagoland,

partly sunny. How I longed, this past
winter, for this kind of weather, oven-blast
heat hitting the skin, sinking in, limpening

(I know, it's not a word) muscles. Apollo
permitting, I'll be wearing shorts till
September. And languishing in front of

the TV. Addiction du jour: *Alias.* Late
last night I finished watching season four.
How the seasons fly by: winter, summer,

the disguises of Sydney Bristow. Her many
colorful wigs a large part of the appeal.
I am enthralled with all things Rimbaldi.

Funny, JC, your Helen Lawson-esque tutorial
with Allen. That explains a lot. Once, when
I asked him for a letter of recommendation

he said: "I don't much care for your work,
Trinidad. I'd rather support someone like
Antler. But sure, I'll do it. Put me down."

I didn't. Recently, in an interview for the
Brooklyn Review (which I edited when I was
a grad student), I said this about Ginsberg:

Allen . . . well . . . I've been asked about studying with him before, and I've
always tried to be honest. I don't think he was the best teacher on the planet.
He was narcissistic and misogynistic and at times, I think, even a little mean. He
once goaded a female student until she burst into tears and ran out of the room.
Yet it was great to be in his presence. He was a great poet. It always felt special
to be around him. He of course liked poems that were imitative of his own style.
If you were doing anything else, he either didn't have patience for it or seemed
mystified by it.

Later, when he praised my poems publicly,
I was pleasantly surprised. And I have a
fond memory of running into him in Paris:

he had a driver and gave me and Ira a ride
to a party. It was at that party that I stood
talking to Philip Glass about *Rosemary's Baby*

(the book, not the movie). And Allen wrote
a kind letter to me when my mother died.
So he was a mixed bag. A human monster.

How well I remember my first encounter
with the beast. I stood outside his office;
the door was ajar. He was finishing up

with another student, a mediocre homo eager
to climb. "No good! Shi—lousy!" Contemp-
tuously, Allen tossed his poems onto the floor.

"What kind of a poet are you? Why do they
have to send me some green kid fresh out
of Chicago? Get lost!" Timidly, I knocked

on the door. "Who in hell are you?" "I'm
David Trinidad," I stuttered, "and I—" "Sit
down—you're making me nervous." During

that first tutorial, I professed my love of
Sexton, asked him what he thought of her
work. "What's it like?" he replied, as if he'd

never heard of her. I thought this odd, since
their poetry had appeared in many anthologies
together. Since they'd both reached the summit

of Mount Everest, and our beloved Valley, at
the same time, and in the same way—late 1950s
American poetry. Both such groundbreakers,

and both so tormented, so death-obsessed.
"I'm hung up on it," says Sexton in "The Addict."
Mr. Death who stands, a sane mad brave and

famous monster-poet, with his office door open:
"Look, I'm tired and I'm busy—what do you want?"
"I want to know what happens after I die," Allen

says in "Mescaline": *death death death death death.*
Sexton read and liked Ginsberg, said so in interviews,
that she admired his candor and, I believe, that he

was braver, more honest than she was able to be.
Able to *give a little more.* I sit gingerly on the edge
of the chair as Allen signs—and not with some

lousy ballpoint—the books I've brought. He signed
them quite generously, I see, rereading his inscriptions
almost two decades later. That meeting hazy in my

memory. He was bluntly, invasively inquisitive.
"What are you doing here?" Naive and awkward
and starstruck as Anne, I also asked him to sign my

"autograph book," a notebook (since dismantled)
in which I asked poets to handwrite poems. Most
of them simply transcribed a short poem, but a few,

like Allen, composed poems on the spot. Here's his:

After Class

At Ashbery's bored old desk in Boylan
hear dog barks a block down Hillel to Flatbush
The dopey student's smarter than we punks think
We could give eachother blowjobs in the teachers room
I'm on the honorary degrees committee this Wednesday
in President Hess' office. Next year I get tenure
& retire in 1996 aged 70 just in time to kick the bucket

at half salary. Will I still get hardons 8 years from now?
You'll have your MFA & be teaching in the Arctic Circle
to inspired Eskimo maidens studying white funk.

10/10/88
Allen Ginsberg

Chicago in the winter sure feels like the Arctic Circle.
And I do have a number of talented female students.

Anne meets Helen. David meets Allen. An age-old
rite of passage, the meeting of the mentor-monster.
One who embodies the desire of the young hopeful.

The one on the climb. Caroline Bender (Hope Lange)
looks up at an office building. Up there she'll meet
Amanda Farrow (Joan Crawford), evil queen of book

publishing. Andy Sachs (Anne Hathaway) looks up
at an office building. Up there she'll meet Miranda
Priestly (Meryl Streep), evil queen of the fashion

industry. Cut from *Valley*, a scene, as Anne "beats
a retreat," of Neely and Mel, sitting on the stairs
during a break in rehearsal, heads together, warm-

ing their hands on steaming coffee mugs. Mel
refers to Helen as "that female jack-the-ripper
in the dressing room." Young and innocent Neely

defends: "Mel, don't. Whatever you think of Lawson,
she's a great performer. Gee, if I ever got to be a star,
I'd be so darn grateful I'd go around kissing the world."

All that power that cannot help but burst from the
borders of itself, and shine like a star. A paraphrase
of Rilke's "Archaic Torso of Apollo," which I read

and discussed yesterday, with my friend Van. The
end has always mystified: "for here there is no place /
that does not see you." The light of art, of brilliance,

that makes you reflect upon your own inadequacy,
makes you realize how high you must climb in order
to "sparkle"? The desire of Icarus? Sexton admires

his wings, the fire at his neck. To be up there, center
stage, in that hot spotlight, belting out a showstopper.
There is no one in the audience who does not see you.

It's now 89°. To do: call Dad, watch *Alias*, change my life.

(DT)

Okay, let's start in the middle: I will try to ignore that sinking
feeling of "I can't do it," "I've taken too long already,"

"eventually I'll stop returning their emails," "I'll hear
through the grapevine they replaced me with another
poet (someone more serious—who has actually read

Dante before . . .)"; then imagining the final, future
shame spiral: "If I see either JC or DT on the street
I'll duck into an alleyway." Okay, deep breath, jump

in again, self-assignment: *describe the contents of your
desk* (i.e. coffee table)—a cream-colored jug stuffed
with colored gel pens, a box of Quies earplugs

(drilling next door), my homemade *Valley of the Dolls*
pillbox filled with none of your business, a pair of orange-
handled Fiskars scissors; silver glitter glue; numerous

pictures of my latest fixation, Maddox Jolie-Pitt; a color
copy of a photo of Johnny and Luther Htoo (Burmese
freedom fighting twins, age twelve); jet black archival

ink; liquid paper; pink address book; three remote
controls; my laptop. Outside, drilling; inside, a feeling
that all could all go wrong

at any minute. Sift through miscellaneous notes, one
of which reminds me why I'm here: "Helen Lawson" and
unofficially, Allen Ginsberg? An early experience: The Jack Kerouac

School of Disembodied Poetics, Naropa Institute, Boulder,
Colorado, 1989. I was to take a two-hour workshop with AG
limited to five students; we were told to hand in poems the night

before so AG could read them before class; yet it was the cute
boy who HADN'T handed in any work who received the majority
of the feedback. I was insulted and angry. Even just on a consumer

level I felt gypped ("*I paid good money to come to this place . . .*").
Memory flash—that same week, a student asking AG:
What female poets do you admire? To which he answered

Ma Rainey, and someone he had only recently been turned on
to: Anne Sexton (!) From my actual journal, July 6/89: *Ginsberg*
lecture tonight—well, more question and answer. He said, "Women

feel persecuted, or so I'm told," and admitted he was scared
of women, [then] went on to ignore two women with their hands
up in the front row for over half an hour! Said how all the beats

have survived so well, and conveniently ignored mentioning Corso
and Orlovsky. One neat thing he sad [sic]: "use your neuroses as
your style." Jump to: Helen Lawson's dressing room in Hell's

Kitchen, where she's delivering a tantrum worthy of . . . whatever.
At least Anne has never seen anything . . . *so crass!* (although
Mel and I both have, plenty of times—in 1985 I did a one-month

internship at a Canadian fashion magazine run by none other than
Bonnie Fuller). Stray thoughts: Would my feelings have been so hurt
if I had been snubbed by a poet other than Allen Ginsberg? Say, by

Antler? Would Allen Ginsberg have ever taken the time to read
Anne Sexton's poems if it weren't for David Trinidad? If Frank
O'Hara had been alive, would he have dashed

off a poem about *Valley of the Dolls*? Or about the death
of Sharon Tate? Did Sexton envy Susann's success?
                    Did success spoil Rock Hunter?

Journal entry written exactly eighteen years ago today
July 5, 1989: *Ginsberg said good morning, he is beginning
to seem more human.*

      (GMC)

The first, and *deadliest*, of the Seven Deadly Sins:
Helen Lawsonism. Once, in tutorial,
I asked Allen about Frank. He crossed his shins,

put down his fountain pen. I listened to his ramble:
"Frank O'Hara? His taste in poems unlike
my own. New York art money scene. Some prayerful

poems; almost slept with him once." Allen might
have had a buried resentment, though at the time
he went on to say more nice things before the warlike

relationship between Frank and Allen's longtime
friend Robert Duncan came up. Methinks
our Frank was threatened by Duncan's urge to climb—

when Duncan wrote a letter to Frank, saying he thinks
Frank's work is good, claiming to be the Queen of the West
while pronouncing Frank Queen of the East, "He stinks!"

was Frank's *Helenistic* response. "That's the best
he can do? *Deign* compliments on *ME*? Who does
he think he is? He's a nobody!" *Hell hath*

no fury like an Eastern Queen.
                              "The song goes,
and the kid with it." Susan Hayward spews out
this line with verity, having learned the woes

of Helen Lawsonism in a knockout
fight a few years earlier with Bette Davis
on the set of *Where Love Has Gone*. The blowout

occurred when Hayward offered advice to Davis
about a scene she was acting. Bette tore
off her gray wig and threw it in Hayward's face:

"Bitch!" Not surprisingly, Davis campaigned for
the role of Helen Lawson in *V.O.D.*, which
she lost to Judy Garland—a fact adored,

no doubt, by Joan Crawford, Bette's archrival. Stanwyck
had schooled Davis in Lawsonism way back in
'32 at Warners: "You're a little bitch!

Egotistical, ambitious, and ruthless in
spades!" (This on the set of *So Big!*) Crawford
tried to teach Judy about this deadly sin

early, in '39, at MGM toward
the beginning of Judy's career. Joan shared
with her the ugly way Jeanette MacDonald

demanded that four of Joan's six songs be pared
from the film *The Ice Follies of 1939*—
how she'd cursed like a sailor as she stared

down Mr. Mayer, screaming that this time
she *meant* it: Crawford or herself. Faye Dunaway
laces up a skate (as she plays Joan) and chimes

"Let's go!" in *Mommie Dearest*, depicting the way
Joan had always worked so hard (though Crawford *refused*
to actually skate in the film, which, by the way

was a big flop). And as for Ms. Dunaway,
Bette Davis had *this* to say of her on
The Tonight Show Starring Johnny Carson: "Faye

Dunaway is the biggest bitch of them all, bar none."
The two had co-starred in a TV movie
of the '70s: *The Disappearance of*

Aimee. Davis called Dunaway "blatantly
unprofessional." However, it's a fact
that Davis had always wanted to play Aimee

Semple McPherson herself—and she was racked
with vexation at having to play the secondary
role of *her mother* in the drama! This fact

probably delighted the legendary
Joan Crawford when the movie was aired in
1976. By that time Joan had become very

depressed (after seeing Carol Burnett in
over-the-top garb and makeup do a spoof
of her as Helen-esque Jenny Stewart in

Torch Song as part of her television show [proof
she seemed ridiculous to fans] as well as the fact
that CBS Television gave aloof

Bette Davis the American Film Institute
Award around the same time) and she had taken
to bed. Ultimately, though, the undisputed

truth is that Jacqueline Susann herself said, even
though she based the character of Helen Lawson
on Ethel Merman, if she had known Joan Crawford when

she was writing *Valley of the Dolls*, Helen Lawson
would have been a *real* monster: "Ethel Merman is
a lady and a philanthropist compared to Joan."

Unfortunately, Judy Garland would fizz
out in the role of Helen Lawson after
only six takes on the set. True to Ms.

Susann's characterization of Neely (based, after
all, on Garland), Judy was too far gone on dolls
to make a movie, and would burst into laughter

when the director instructed her (recalls
Barbara Parkins) to play the character
"meaner." In this dressing room scene, Judy stalls,

her emaciated body razor-
thin in the Helen drag. Soon after, she was
fired from the film. "There's only one hit," says Hayward,

"to come out of a Helen Lawson show" (because
there can only be *one* Helen) "and that's me
baby—remember?" *Tie a can to that little broad's*

tail is the message Helen sends to Bellamy.
Miss Welles, shocked and appalled, boards Charon's boat to
cross the river Acheron, to go back to Bellamy

and Bellows, report her failed attempt.
                                        Two
poets on the phone: "Who should be Charon?
An actress or a poet?" "How about you

make it Joan or Bette? Or maybe Sharon
Tate? No, that doesn't make sense." "Stanley Kunitz?
Charon *is* depicted as a skinny old boatman."

"What about John Ashbery? Or Maxine Kumin?"
"But they're not even dead yet." "Does it matter?"
"No, I guess not. But I can't help thinking it's

important to 'name' Charon." About the latter
two poets whose names were "floated" for the role
of Charon in our poem, perhaps their führer

roles aren't finished being played here on earth. The toll
of Helen Lawsonism in Poetry
World is great indeed. Even young poets' souls

are in trouble. Overheard in the poetry
section of Provincetown's used bookstore yesterday:
"That young poet was so livid, so angry

when, busily browsing our shelves, he found a
copy of his book—an uncorrected proof.
He said he was pissed because it meant a

'nobody reviewer' hadn't even read it—proof,
he said, as to why his first book didn't get
the attention it deserved." Then this to aloof

sales girl in corner: "You want this? I'll let
you read it before I price it—it's the new
issue of *Ploughshares*." The young woman flipped

through the magazine: "Geez, I only knew
one name—Jason Shinder. Who *are* all these
nobodies? Look at the bios—who knew

there were so many poetry awards? *Geez*."
As I tenuously board Charon's boat to cross
the river into the next scene of *V.O.D.*,

I see David sitting in the rear, Anne across
from him with her back to me, her arms flailing
with lit cigarettes in each hand, a crisscross

of flame in the dark sky (she's attempting
to offer light for our passage). Trin
gazes at his guide without taking

his eyes off her for a second. Gillian
sits toward the center of the ferry with a blonde
at her side—Sharon Tate! (who could be her twin).

And I, stepping into the vessel like an autumn
leaf detaching itself from the bough of life,
sit down next to my guide Frank (who's not fond

of the way I accused him of being rife
with Helen Lawsonism in the lines above),
and into the night we cut our way like a knife.

(JC)

Canto Four

Navigating their way through the most innocuous of scenes, the three poets descend into the abyss. McCain calls upon her guide, Sharon Tate, for advice. Conway and Trinidad plummet down a series of rabbit holes and time tunnels, where they revisit first meetings and mass murders, and ponder the contents of Anne's purse.

A thunderclap awakens me; lightning streaks
the Provincetown sky beyond the fluttering
sheer white curtain on my bedroom window; shrieks

of seabirds mix with wind, fuse with the spraying
soda water into Lyon Burke's drink as
Miss Anne Welles walks in unannounced, saying

she doesn't want the job. He introduces
himself suavely to the raw recruit, who's just
come from the Vestibule. On the shore across

the street, David, Anne, Gillian, and Sharon are just
coming to in the rickety old boat; Anne
slurs "I am rowing, rowing," lets out a robust

laugh, unfazed by the tempest. Jacqueline Susann
scurries down Cottage Street in a rain slicker,
shielding her wig with a newspaper. Gillian

helps a teetering Tate to dry ground; they wander
off down Commercial Street. Frank pounds at my screen door,
"Hey brother, the rain falls, it drops all over

the place—let me in!" Grateful he's come ashore,
I put on a pot of coffee. It's good to
have a guide in times like these. "Frank, I need more

info about the other side—what can you
tell me about Limbo?" "My dear Jeffery,
we are upon the brink of an abyss, view

the melancholy Valley containing very
loud, thundering, unending wailings. I shall
go first and you will follow me—it's scary,

I know, but just trust me. In this dark locale
we'll find those who lived before the first Hollywood
feature film was made in 1914. Shall

I tell you the title? *The Squaw Man.* You should
try and Netflix it sometime! Anyway, here
we find the souls who lacked baptism, those who would

never have the chance to find salvation, revere
the gods and goddesses of the silver screen."
Great sorrow seized my heart, for this was hard to hear.

(JC)

As is Barbara Parkins's commentary on the Special Edition
DVD of *V.O.D.* "Now look at this guy," she says dismissively,
as her love interest, Lyon Burke, makes his first onscreen

appearance. "When I was in London I'd gone out
with Cat Stevens for a while," she tells E! Entertainment's
Ted Casablanca, "so I'd put the image

of him in my head before I had to do scenes
with Paul—who I thought was just *too old*
to fall in love with. . . ."

    (GMC)

"People can't help who they fall in love with."

    —Edward G. Robinson, *The Stranger*

How *did* Paul Burke end up in this picture?
Was he under contract at 20th Century-Fox
and thus simply convenient? Except for

supporting parts in *Valley*, *The Thomas Crown
Affair*, and a few other movies, he enjoyed forty
years as a solidly competent, if somewhat bland

television actor, most notably in the series
Naked City. Factoid: Burke was born on July 21,
the day after my birthday—twenty-three years

earlier than me, of course. Cancer on the cusp
of Leo. The crab and the lion. Inwardness vs.
the outer. Feelings vs. action. My guess is Burke

was a man of depth. But an Adonis? Lyon,
according to Susann, was toweringly tall, had
Indian black hair, skin that "seemed burned

into a permanent tan," and a disarming English
accent. Anne, when she first meets Lyon, is calm,
her New England iciness an asset; she doesn't melt

like the other secretaries. So whatever happened,
Hollywood, to Lyon being British? Was Dirk
Bogarde already too old—we *know* he was too

highbrow—for the part? (Though he had, the
year before, delivered a camp performance in
Modesty Blaise, a pop-art, comic-book-inspired

romp about a female "secret agent whose hair
color, hairstyle, and mod clothing change at
a snap of her fingers"—sounds right up my *Alias*

alley, actually. . . .) In the mid-nineties, when
Pierce Brosnan emerged as the new James Bond,
I thought he would make a perfect Lyon Burke.

Am I always casting a remake of *Valley* in my
mind? No one at Fox paid attention to Jackie's
wish list: she wanted blond, all-American Robert

Redford to play her black-haired, British Adonis.
I guess you could *smell* superstar on Redford
in those days. She also wanted Mia Farrow to

play Anne, Liza Minnelli to play Neely, Elvis
Presley to play Tony, George C. Scott to play
Henry Bellamy, and Bette Davis to play Helen

Lawson. Hard to imagine what kind of alternate
reality we'd be living in if Jackie had had her
way. Or if Claudette Colbert hadn't injured

her back and been able to play Margo Channing
in *All About Eve*. Or if Natalie Wood hadn't
turned down the part of Bonnie Parker (Faye

yes, but who would want to see Nat riddled
with bullets?). Or if Orson Welles had been able
to cast (as he wanted to) Agnes Moorehead as

the Nazi hunter in *The Stranger* (the part went
to Edward G. Robinson). Or if Joan Crawford's
"wardrobe demands" hadn't kept her from

playing the Deborah Kerr part in *From Here
to Eternity*. Or her feud with Bette Davis hadn't
kept her from playing the Olivia de Havilland

part in *Hush ... Hush, Sweet Charlotte*. Or if
Marilyn's overdose hadn't prevented her from
starring in *What a Way to Go!* (Would Jean

Louis—not Edith Head—have designed her
costumes? What would an entirely pink Marilyn
have looked like?) Or if Jayne Mansfield had

gotten Lee Remick's part in *Anatomy of a Murder*,
a role she desperately vied for. Or if Bette Davis
had been available to play aging playwright Sarah

Goode in *Opening Night* (John Cassavetes had
written the part for her because his wife, Gena
Rowlands, wanted to act with Davis; Joan

Blondell was ultimately cast). Or if Garland
had played Helen Lawson. Or Parkins Neely:
she'd originally sought the "meatier" bad girl

role. And so on and so forth . . . a Yellow Brick
Road of "what ifs" twisting into infinity. Jackie
didn't specify who should play Jennifer. Raquel

Welch had screen-tested but turned down the
film, a decision she later admitted "not awfully
clever." Welch, who didn't wish to be typecast as

a sex symbol, instead starred in *Fathom*, in which
(according to an Amazon.com editorial review)
"a certain lime-green bikini . . . cling[s] as tightly

to Raquel Welch as those phagocytes that attacked
her in *Fantastic Voyage*."
                              Last night on phone: DT
to JC: "I'm at the bottom of a rabbit hole of 'what ifs'

with Raquel Welch." I could talk about measure-
ments: how Raquel's were more appropriate to
the character of Jennifer North than Tate's. Or

about how, though she missed out starring in *this*
camp classic, Raquel would, in a few years' time,
make the oh-so-clever decision to star in *Myra*

Breckinridge. How, like Patty Duke with Neely, she
thought *that* part would bring her credibility as
a serious actress. And I could talk about how, as

I fell down this particular hole, I learned that,
in addition to Natalie Wood (for the role of
Bonnie), Warren Beatty had approached Jane

Fonda, Tuesday Weld, Ann-Margret, *and* Sharon
Tate. And that Candice Bergen and Marlo Thomas
were considered top choices to play Anne Welles.

And that Robert Forster (the object of Marlon
Brando's desire in *Reflections in a Golden Eye*) was
screen-tested to play Tony Polar. And that

Petula Clark and Barbara Harris were seriously
considered to play Neely O'Hara. And that
when Garland was let go, actresses considered

to replace her as Helen Lawson included Joan
Crawford, Broadway star Tammy Grimes, and
Ginger Rogers, who hated (clever girl) the script.

Anne charges into Mr. Bellamy's office, ready to
quit, but is instantly smitten with Lyon Burke.
Might I plummet down another rabbit hole, or

maybe more of a Time Tunnel: a cab pulls out of
an hypnotic black-and-white op-art vortex and
stops in front of The Kitchen on West 19th Street:

it's a September evening, 1989: Dennis Cooper,
Eileen Myles, and I step out of the cab, join the
crowd mingling on the sidewalk. We've come

to hear La Loca, latest and greatest discovery of
Lawrence Ferlinghetti; her book has just been
published by City Lights. Dennis introduces me

to Ira Silverberg, cute as Richard Gere, who I
mistake for La Loca's boyfriend. "Great," I say
to myself, "She has a book from City Lights *and*

a gorgeous boyfriend." I later learn that he's
Dennis's publicist at Grove Press, and curator
of the reading series at The Kitchen. Dennis,

Eileen, and I sit in the front row. Throughout
La Loca's reading, Eileen huffs and puffs. She's
fit to be tied that the cool, avant-garde Pocket

Poets Series, which started with such luminaries
as Allen Ginsberg and Frank O'Hara, should end
with the likes of La Loca and not herself. I agree:

La Loca is sophomoric and high-pitched. But hey,
I'm from New Age L.A. and know that good can
come from more than one source. The next day

Dennis calls and I learn that Ira is not only single
and gay, he's attracted to me. So we begin seeing
each other. Our second or third date he wears

a blue leather jacket and I'm hooked—we end up
living together for ten years. And thanks to La
Loca, my poems wind up being translated into

Czech. So you never know. That first meeting
with Ira was at the beginning of my second year
in New York. It wouldn't take long—the Time

Tunnel begins to swirl—before I, like Anne, began
to weary. "PoBiz is cruel," I'd whine. "People do
despicable things." I land back in the present, eight

years after Ira and I called it quits. I also met Doug,
the last man I dated, at a poetry reading, this time
one of my own. Chicago: March, 2005: Big Star Café

("Yeah, I'm a *big* star," Neely bitterly intones): I go
up to the counter to buy a bottle of water, look to my
right, and there he is: "Did I cut in front of you?" And

there you have it: smitten. The other day, sitting in
my therapist's office, I read a poem by Louise Glück
in *The New Yorker*. A bitter, "love is only for the young"

take on romance. I set the magazine down and said
a prayer: "Please, God, keep me from such hardness,
such bitterness. Let me always remain open to love."

(DT)

"It must be a grand feeling to get everything you want."

—Bette Davis, *Three on a Match*

In Provincetown, gray again, at the end
of August; it has been weeks since I last
wrote, since I've thought about *V.O.D.* and

Limbo, about Frank O., and the rest—
DT, Gillian, et al. That's not
entirely true, as these are recast

(movie, spiritual journey, guides, friends) as subplots
in my daily life as of late. Last week
I spent the night on the Point with friends and caught

a glimpse of the souls in Limbo—a freak
occurrence, maybe, or a dream? I was
half asleep as I got out of my tent to peek

at the moon after midnight. There was
an inlet next to our "camp," so I took
a walk to pee. Frank appeared "mid-stream" in gauze

of night, pointed across the dune, and said, "Look,
there are the poets who died before *The Squaw Man*:
Walt Whitman in his scraggly beard . . . and look,

Emily Dickinson—a crazy woman,
dancing around and howling at the moon!"
By the counterfeit light, I think I can

see what Frank is pointing out! Under that moon
I saw the scene as plainly as a show at
The Hall of Presidents in Disney World. Soon

I could see old Walt take off his hat
as Emily twirled in the sand—perfect
specimens of Audio-Animatronics that

recited poems as they moved. They frolicked
for many moments before the vision
evaporated, and I quickly zipped.

Whenever *Three on a Match* plays on television
(e.g., on Turner Classic Movies), it plays
as a Bette Davis movie. Her role as the driven

secretary is the smallest, and weighs
the least on the plot. The other two female
roles belong to Joan Blondell (who plays

Mary) and Ann Dvorak (as upscale
Vivian Kirkwood). In this eerily
prescient 1932 "three female

roles" movie, we get a kind of kooky
inverted fame pyramid: as we peer
down *this* rabbit hole, we can see that Bette

Davis is the actress who, by the sheer
weight of her fame, is best remembered; Joan
Blondell is next, then the wonderful, but near-

forgotten Ann Dvorak—the lone
star of the film. The story also offers
us a perpetually shifting cyclone

of the archetypes portrayed in each of the roles:
young Mary (Joan Blondell) is a self-destructive,
wild, hopelessly troubled teen who trolls

the streets of the big city and ends up captive
of a reform school. Later, she meets up
with her old grammar school friend (Vivian)

at a beauty salon (shades of *The Women*) as an up-
start actress stuggling to make it. A change
occurs, however, and Mary turns from trollop

into goodie-goodie; Vivian changes
from high society wife and loving
mother into a reckless bitch, deranged

and hell-bent on alcohol, drugs, and sex-seeking.
Ruth (Bette Davis) transforms from bitter
girl, angry at Vivian for getting

everything she wants, into a nobler,
generous friend who, as an adult, helps to
save Vivian's endangered child, Junior.

The gray has just broken here—there is blue
oozing out from the clouds, and pink worthy
of even DT's praise. I think of the two

of you—my collaborators—doing suavely
whatever it is you might be doing.
I'm wondering if the "tropology of threes"

is operating in your unconscious as we
(three) collectively watch this movie over
and over, searching . . . for what? Clues? Do we

seek understanding of our own psyches, or
perhaps windows into our pasts? *The Time
Tunnel begins to swirl*—and I, like Anne, or

maybe more like the reflective DT, am
beginning to weary. "PoBiz is cruel.
People do despicable things." A long time

ago, I'd say late '90s, I did an April
reading at a New York Public Library
for National Poetry Month, a genial

event for Gay and Lesbian poets. Happy
to participate, I arrived and discovered
that there were very few men present—a mostly

Lesbian audience. That evening I read
selections from my long poem "Starstruck"—
a piece that had always gotten lots of good

laughs. The Lesbians, however, weren't awestruck:
when I'd glance up, I saw nothing but barber
cuts and blank faces. There I was, stuck

at the podium with only a few
timid chuckles from the gay guys to my
right, toward the front. The only other

sound in the room came from Eileen Myles:
Throughout Jeffery's reading, Eileen huffs and puffs.
I was so shocked by her behavior, but my

only reaction was laughter: *Jeffery rebuffs
Eileen's huffs and puffs by laughing hysterically,*
which made it seem like I was amused by the stuff

in my own poem—vignettes of funny
encounters I've had with celebrities.
Afterwards, in her dressing room, our surly

Po-Star, angry and annoyed, barked obscenities
at her press agent: *The poem goes, and the Gay poet with it!*
She'd had it, for quite some time, with niceties.

I was the young, bitter Ruth: *How grand it
must be for a poet to get everything she wants.*
Now, an older, nobler Ruth, *I am free in generous spirit.*

(JC)

*"Enough has now been said to show that the bloody sacrifice
has from time immemorial been the most considered part
of Magick. The ethics of the thing appear to have concerned*

no one; nor, to tell the truth, need they do so." Quote
by Aleister Crowley taken from *Anger: The Unauthorized
Biography of Kenneth Anger* by Bill Landis, page 69.

Let me explain. Anxious about writing, I decided to call up
my muse and ask for advice. "I was wondering where the hell
you've been," Sharon teased. "I was beginning to think

you'd decided that I was just another dumb blonde."
I could hear her take a deep drag off of a joint. "So, what's up?"
she asked squeakily. "Stuck," I answered.

"These swells I'm collaborating with, I'm just not up
to their level. They're gonna be on to me in no time."
"Get over yourself," Sharon scoffed (on the exhale).

"How do you think I felt trying to keep up my side
of the conversation with Jerzy fucking Kosinski?"
I laughed. I was seeing a different side of my muse

and I was liking it. "Sorry, I didn't mean to be harsh,"
she apologized, "but have a little faith. Your career
may be in limbo now, but at least you're running

in some *fabulous* circles. Who knows what kind
of impact you could be having in the grand scheme
of things? Take me for instance. Bet you didn't

know that *I* was the one who gave Roman
the copy of *Tess of the d'Urbervilles* that inspired
him to make the movie. By the way,

seen any good ones lately?" I thought for a second.
"Yeah, actually, I did," I replied. "A documentary
called *Anger Me*, about the avant-garde filmmaker—"

"I *know* who Kenneth Anger is," Sharon snapped.
"Roman and I tripped with him in Frisco, on 9/21/67,
the night of his Equinox of the Gods celebration

at the Straight Theater. A band called The Magick
Powerhouse of Oz headlined." She paused.
"I'll tell you about *them* some other time.

Now, here's what I want you to do. Go grab
some biographies—Anger, Susann, whoever;
and a copy of *Hollywood Babylon* while you're at it.

Then you're going to check out all the page 69s,
which just so happens to be the year of my *untimely death*,
and all the 169s, and synopsize. I *would* add the 1069s,

but as you know, we dumb blondes rarely go for *tomes*."
"Except for Thomas Hardy," I corrected her.
"Yes, except for Thomas Hardy," she replied, wistfully.

*According to alchemical legend, if a man
and a woman, both initiates of Aleister Crowley,
perform certain sex rituals, it could result*

*in the birth of a homunculus, much like the spawn
of Mia Farrow and John Cassavetes in the Roman
Polanski film* Rosemary's Baby. *In 1926, starlet*

*Barbara La Marr, once known as "The Girl Who
is Too Beautiful" ODed at the tender age of 26.
Although it was well known that she stored*

*her cocaine in a golden casket (which she kept on top
of her grand piano), the studio cited "vigorous dieting"
as the "official" cause of her untimely death. Her tombstone*

*read: "with God in the joy and beauty of youth."
A topless Peg Entwistle, standing defiantly,
appears on page 169, wearing only a parure*

(possibly diamonds, but probably paste), and
a long black skirt, its waistline cut into a 'V,'
highlighting her taut stomach. The starlet who once

had a bit part in the film Thirteen Women *climbed to the top*
of the thirteenth letter of the famed Hollywood sign
and jumped to her untimely death. "When Flaubert wrote

Madame Bovary, *twenty women in town said they were Emma,"*
Jacqueline Susann once told a reporter. Around the time
of Susann's death, Christian Scientist Doris Day flew to New York

to visit her new best friend in the hospital (they had recently forged
a deep bond over their mutual love for dogs), but soon had to return
to L.A. to testify in court against the business manager "who had allegedly

mismanaged her finances causing her to lose several million dollars."
(Ed. Note: Doris Day is the mother of the late music producer
Terry Melcher, who sublet the Cielo Drive house to Sharon

Tate and Roman Polanski in February of 1969.) After starlet
Sharon Tate wins the part of Jennifer North in the film
adaptation of the best-selling novel Valley of the Dolls, *she tells*

a reporter: "I was just thrilled to get the role. I liked Jennifer
as I read the book. I think she is the most sympathetic girl
in the group. She's sweet, unspoiled, and unselfish.

She doesn't mean anyone any harm, and yet terrible
things keep happening to her." Roman Polanski wanders
through the rooms of his rented home, now stained

with the blood of his wife, unborn child, and three
close friends. Accompanying him
are freelance photographer Julian Wasser, celebrity clairvoyant

Peter Hurkos, and a reporter from Life *magazine. A distraught*
Polanski says in reference to his houseguest, Voytek Frykowski:
"I should have thrown him out when he ran over Sharon's dog!"

*When asked how long the murder victim had been staying
at Cielo Drive—its name meaning both "sky" and "heaven"—
the bereaved film director replied simply, "too long I guess."*

(GMC)

"It's the nature of all tragedies: the hero dies, but the story lives on forever."

—Dustin Hoffman, *Stranger Than Fiction*

How easy it is for me to fall into the Tate-LaBianca
rabbit hole. How all the haunting details swirl around
me as I descend: the beautiful people's last meal at

El Coyote Café; the Christmas lights (strung by previous
tenant Candice Bergen) twinkling along the edge of
10050 Cielo Drive; the fact that, an instant before she was

stabbed, Abigail Folger stopped struggling and said,
"I give up, take me." How easy it is to get lost in the
ghoulish minutiae. The last couple hours spent surfing

the Internet—in particular, the Official Tate-LaBianca
Murders Blog—and researching *House at the End of the
Drive*, a film I hadn't heard about. A horror film in

which a "time vortex" transports four characters back
to 1969, midsummer, the anniversary of a ritualistic slaughter
at a nearby mansion. I myself was unprepared to time

travel this morning, once again, back to the *real* night
the murders occurred. And it does seem a bit premature
(Jennifer hasn't even been introduced, though in

a matter of moments she'll glide down the stairs in her
huge blue six-hundred-dollar headdress—the one no
one will see because they'll be too busy gaping at her tits).

It's still the present of the movie, and Anne's still fumbling
her first encounter with her dream man. In the *real* present,
it's September 1st. August, that death month, has passed.

(DT)

"The blonde bombshell's career was prematurely nipped in the bud by a
suspiciously violent critical reaction to her performance as an on-the-rise
showgirl."

—Noël Burch on Elizabeth Berkley in "Embarrassing Showgirls"

It's September 1st. DT and I on
the phone as I walk up Barrow, cross
West 4th, discussing the difference (yawn)

between "ritual" and "ritualistic," when loss
of concentration is furthered by the
appearance of Elizabeth Berkley, who crosses

my path. Me to DT: "I think the
weirdest thing just occurred, Elizabeth
Berkley just passed me on the street, at the

corner of Barrow and West 4th.
Oh my God she's huge, like a Plasticine
Barbie. She got into a car; her head's mammoth.

She looks pancaked, like she does on film. Is this a dream?
Wow, what a trip." DT: "I'm writing this down."
I proclaim that I've no idea what this means,

but it makes sense, I guess, that, stuck downtown
(in Limbo) this Labor Day weekend, my
guide should put E.B. in front of me, omen

of shocking showgirls to come, quasi-
Jennifer North, evil mutant offspring
of beloved Sharon Tate, whose (soon) entry

into *Valley of the Dolls* is sparkling,
so unlike Miss Berkley's in *Showgirls*, she who sets
the tone for her performance in an early scene

in which she expresses fury by vigorous
shakes of a Heinz bottle, spewing ketchup
all over her French fries, the table, and numerous

nearby diners, splattering it like fake blood from cut up
people in movies. Confession: back in the '80s,
when I lived in L.A., I'd often wind up

at El Coyote Café for double margaritas
on the rocks with salt. You'd have to put your name
on the waiting list for a table, as it was

always packed. In the bar, you'd hear a name
called over the loudspeaker every now
and then. As a joke, I'd always give the name

"Tate," a nod to Sharon and her last meal. I'll allow
that it was rather sick, but back then, being
as drunk and out of it as I was, it somehow

amused me and my death rock coterie
of friends. Meanwhile, Anne, pick up that junk spilled
from your purse and say good-bye, so we can move on.

(JC)

"Barely Pink" is the name of the lipstick
that toppled out of Anne's pocketbook and landed
at the feet of Mr. Lyon Burke (standard Hollywood

technique used to foreshadow a future love affair),
followed by the actor and actress scooping up
the spilled contents (which unlike real life, never includes

a half-wrapped Tampax). Task finished, they look up
from the carpet and into each other's eyes, until finally,
one of them blurts out something banal. "I'm afraid

I haven't made a very good impression,"
Miss Anne Welles says coyly. "Quite the contrary,"
responds Mr. Lyon Burke. "You've made an indelible one."

(GMC)

"You have painted your toenails Car Hop Pink,
A clear choice against the sky's transience."

—Ann Lauterbach

*Curatorial students in the Visual Arts Department at the University
of Western Ontario have produced a multi-sited exhibition which
interrogates the purse as a cultural artifact and gendered icon.*

*Slung over the shoulder or clutched between fingers, the purse is
a container that conceals from view confidential information about
its owner. It is a private space which has been designed specifically*

*as a means for transporting the personal through public space.
The purse . . . contains highly personal items; it is a time capsule
which represents the owner's identity, diverse interests, and activities.*

*Photographs, keys, objects plundered from restaurants, sexual aids,
medication, ticket stubs, makeup, address book, identification, cheque
book, and wallet are all hidden within its interior. The purse is*

*a microcosm of the self which is as unique as a signature or finger-
print. The contents of no two purses would ever be the same. The
purse is the ultimate voyeuristic device, as its mere presence attests*

*to secrets that are held at bay from the viewer's inquisitive gaze.
What does a woman carry in her purse?* Consult DVD: comb,
compact, powder puff, hotel key, perfume, sunglasses

(in the middle of a blizzard?), mascara, check- and address
books, and crumpled silver chewing gum wrapper scatter
on the green carpet between Anne and Lyon's feet. I find

the contents of her pocketbook completely unsatisfying.
Where are the highly personal items, the secrets every voyeur
seeks? She chews Wrigley's? Other than that, nothing new.

So I contacted four women, asking if they wouldn't mind,
for the sake of art, providing me with an honest and detailed
catalog of their purse contents. Here, verbatim, are their lists:

Becca:

In my pink, brown, and orange Timbuk2 bag:

Pocket #1:
Burt's Bees brand chapstick
keychain attached to plastic red heart with the name of my dad's old video store
    on it (Ace Video)
CTA card
old CTA card with no money on it
loose movie ticket stubs

Pocket #2:
100 Terrific Poems edited by David Trinidad
high school student poems for class I'm subbing for
4 poetry collections (Manguso, Harvey, Kocot, Fuhrman) to be used in class
manila file folder full of insurance papers/calendars/SPD catalog
black "shrug" (piece of clothing that is just sleeves connected at the back)
pink wallet
empty pink envelope from a birthday card my grandparents gave me
assorted scraps of paper with scribbles and poem drafts
postcard for a self-published poetry book someone gave me at a reading two
    nights ago
beaded square journal bought for $5 at Urban Outfitters
Blow Pop
walking map of Boston & Cambridge
wristband from comedy show (Zack Galifianakis) I saw last week

Pocket #3:
adapter for headphones
hairbands (2)

Pocket #4:
5 pens (blue, purple, red, green, black), one pencil, one orange highlighter, one
    magenta mini-Sharpie

Pocket #5:
Aleve bottle filled with generic ibuprofen
Eyedrops
Pseudoephedrine tablet
cough drop
computer flash drive

Pocket #6:
Purple comb
pink ipod inside a brown argyle sock that I cut and sewed to make a case
2 types of powder compacts (Cover Girl)
1 tube lipstick (Lancome, "Jezabel")
A couple napkins from fast food restaurants
Plastic knife
Pink business card holder with Switchback Books cards inside
Kid scissors with lime green handle
Tampon
Emergen-C Vitamin C powder packets (2)
Portable plastic wine key with faded Canadian decals
Binder ring from CPR submissions several months ago

*

Brandi:

Well, I carry a ginormous bag more than a purse, so it's gonna be a long list!

Here you go:

Umbrella
Sunglasses/case
Diary
Book
Two poetry magazines
Bag of Switchback buttons
Wallet
Keys
Blackberry

Camera
Business card holder
Makeup bag with makeup
Pencil case with markers, post-it flags, pens, binder clips
Miscellaneous pens
A few emails I printed out
Gum
Deodorant
Checkbook
Packing tape (I don't go anywhere without it, weird!)
Birthday card from my sister
Tampons
Anti-depressants
Allergy medication
Lotion
Preparation H (I just got a new tattoo!)
My mom's house keys
Condom
Excedrin
Band-aids
Spare change
Nail polish topcoat
Extra straps for bag
Empty flask
Comb

*

Cora:

okay, I brought two bags today, one holding just my food and the other (listed
below) is really the everyday, so here it goes, embarrassing and all . . .

keys
Kate Spade pink sunglass case and sunglasses
change purse containing $88.95, debit card, mastercard, school id and driver's
    license
WW journal, monthly pass and membership book (yes, I came home last night
    and stuck it in my bag so I wouldn't forget it again)
loose kleenex
cell phone
nano ipod

lead refills
mechanical pencil
mini journal
three paperclips (two large, one small)
two tampons
one pair of silk panties
Jane Austen's "The Complete Novels" (I picked it up yesterday!)
a green thin sweater

well, that's it . . .

*

Margaret:

My so-called "purse" is actually a mini back-pack. Here goes:

one bunch of car keys attached to a key-chain with a red stuffed mini-bull
one big tube (4.6 ounces) of Aquage transforming paste (hair goop)
one Olay complete all day moisture lotion bottle
one orange highlighter pen
one used white handkerchief
one mini-bottle of Tresemme hair spray
three (unused) Kotex sanitary napkins
Dentyne Ice peppermint gum (5 pieces left)
one silver ballpoint pen
receipts: Jewel, Office Max, K-Mart (all crumpled up)
One brochure: Welcome to the Murphy Guest House Bed and Breakfast, Bristol,
    Indiana — Your hosts: Gary and Ann Andre
One business card: Bristol Canoe and Kayak rental
One ticket stub: Illinois Philharmonic Orchestra, Sat., Dec. 16, 2006, 3 p.m.
    performance / Holiday Pops Concert
Some old Wrigley Extra gum (peppermint) that I have no intention of chewing . . .
    ever.

Almost forgot the piece de resistance: a newspaper clipping from our local paper, re:
"Homewood-Flossmoor music teacher, conductor dies at at (sic) 79." I meant to give
this to a friend of mine who was in the choir under this guy, Emmett Michell Steele.
No date on the clipping.

[and in a subsequent email:]

P.S.
I can't remember if I put down my black makeup bag in my list of purse contents.
(Mascara, lipstick, chapstick, razor are all in the bag.)
xoxo
MoFo

"El Coyote Café on Beverly Boulevard has been serving Mexican entrees since 1931.
On Friday, August 8, 1969, Jay Sebring made an 8 o'clock dinner reservation for
Abigail Folger, Wojciech Frykowski, Sharon Tate, and himself. After waiting 15
minutes in the bar, the four were seated and unknowingly ate their last meals,
leaving at around 9:45pm, heading back to Cielo Drive."

    —from the website *Evidence: The Story of the Manson Family and Their Victims*

That old Time Tunnel keeps aswirlin'. . . . It's 1983 and a group
of us are eating at El Coyote: Eileen (in L.A. to give a reading),
Bob and Sheree, Bob's friend Scott. Prince's "1999" is a hit, it

might even have played in the bar while we waited for a table:
We're gonna party like it's 1999. I'm newly sober, so my partying
days are over. As is my preoccupation with death and dying.

I'm expectant, hopeful, truly excited about the future. We're
seated; I order cheese enchiladas. Because of the Prince song,
the end of the century is on our minds. The five of us make a

pact to meet, perhaps on an island somewhere, on New Year's
Eve, 1999. By the time that date rolls around, Scott will have
drunk himself to death. (His full name was James Scott; he

was called both Scott and Jim. Nice guy, and supportive pres-
ence in the Beyond Baroque poetry scene.) Bob will be dead,
too (from cystic fibrosis). I will not be on speaking terms with

either Sheree or Eileen. I will spend a quiet evening with Byron
in New York City, Ira and I having broken up earlier that year.
[Gillian: just got goosebumps when I looked at the bottom of

this Word file and saw that I'm on page 69.] Time Tunnel swirl:

I'm still in Los Angeles, but now it's about ten years later, the
early nineties. I'm in town to give a poetry reading at Beyond
Baroque. Afterwards, a large group of us (Dennis, Amy and

Benjamin, Bob and Sheree, Ira, etc.) sit at an outside table at
a restaurant in a strip mall in Santa Monica. During the meal,
my eyes fix on a sign in one of the shops: Jay Sebring Hair

Care Products. I didn't know that his business had lived on.
(Sebring, I just learned this morning, once told a fellow hair-
stylist, "When I go, the whole world's going to know about it.")

Dramatic music announces another time shift: I end up
in the mid-sixties, in the Thrifty Drug Store in Chatsworth,
California. I walk past the makeup counter, as slowly as

possible, in order to glimpse the Yardley of London products:
lip gloss, eye shadow, mascara . . . the colorful Mod curlicues
and stripes designed to entice teenage girls. As well as teen-

age homosexuals: at school, I watch the girls take their
pink-and-orange-striped Slicker tubes out of their purses:
they look like little toys, little curios. Soon I'll start

Chatsworth High, be a student there when the Tate
murders occur, and find out—after the fact—that the killers
had lived nearby, at Spahn's Movie Ranch, and that members

of the Manson Family had sold drugs to kids at my high school.
What a trauma that will be for me: the death of the blonde
Doll. In the meantime I'm in love with makeup, lost in a litany

of shades: Flutter Pink, Fainting Pink, Spellbinding Pink. . . .

(DT)

Canto Five

The rehearsal hall where Sharon Tate, as Jennifer North, is offered up as a sacrificial bunny. The three poets reveal their fascination with the gruesome. Trinidad, in an attempt to see everything, is swept up into a netherworld of eBay murder memorabilia; and utilizing Google, McCain works to break the code of her guide's demise.

Top-Heavy Showgirl descending a staircase
    Dumb Blonde Joke descending a staircase
        Sacrificial Lamb descending a staircase

           Promising Newcomer descending a staircase
           One of the Beautiful People descending a staircase
            Random Murder Victim descending a staircase

                Mrs. Roman Polanski descending a staircase
                  Sixties Sex Symbol descending a staircase
                    Celebrity Ghost descending a staircase

"While we all have our opinions on the matter, and yes, there are a lot of locations that TAPS visits where murders have taken place (like the Lizzie Borden house for one!), the use of the 'blinky thing' in an effort to prove that the ghost of Sharon Tate still haunts the location was absolutely ridiculous."

      —comment from chat room of The Atlantic Paranormal Society (TAPS)

we must all eat sacrifices.
We must all eat beautiful women.

      —Anne Sexton

Woke up this morning with the murders on my mind:
heart shuddering at the thought of knives entering the
victims' bodies—frightening and appalling imaginings.

Eight-and-a-half-months-pregnant Tate begging for
her unborn child's life. Utterly vulnerable, defenseless.
My psychic Helen once told me she'd seen, prior to the

murders, a photograph of Tate and Polanski and thought:
"Ut Oh." And that it was difficult for Tate, once in spirit,
to accept not being able to bring her baby to term. Does

her translucent form wander, in the midnight hour, the
twisting streets of Benedict Canyon pleading, "All I want
to do is have my baby"? She did, finally, said Helen, move

on. Then why haven't I, I ask myself, this overcast morning
in September. I do not wish to romanticize. Only to re-
visit, yet again, to bless and release? The teakettle whistles

and I start. I tremble, nervous at my own kitchen knives.

(DT)

A purple & silver headdress with long blue
Dr. Seuss-esque feather boa tentacles—
"and not a soul will see it." Its debut

in the rehearsal hall quickly fizzles;
Miss Jennifer North, in showgirl drag, oozes
to-be-looked-at-ness. The director gazes

lustily at her body and breasts, places
his hand in front of his own body
to effectively block out her face, and erases

any chance of her ever being truly
actualized as a whole person. We viewers
become like infants whose ego boundaries

are yet to be formed, and just then the film lures
us back to the moment at which our ego
came into being. We identify with the specters

of glamour and beauty on the screen—*ego
ideals* who act out a complex process
of likeness and difference in an echo

of our infant self's misrecognition of itself
as the Other in the mirror, one who is more perfect,
complete, and in control. In this scene,

Jennifer is the one who stands erect,
facing her own image in the mirror;
she too sees an "other": the subject

of the male gaze, a woman in the mirror
playing a traditional exhibitionistic role; she's
basically a showgirl playing a dumber

showgirl—a figure American culture has
both celebrated and despised as the
quintessential commodification of "today's"

womanhood. Her roots go back to vaudeville, to the
Ziegfeld girls, and early sound movie musicals
immortalized by Busby Berkeley. Our era

saw the "updating" of the showgirl's trials
with *Showgirls* (1995), a vulgar
post-feminist, post-Stonewall ditty that dabbles

in lesbianism, drug addiction, "private dancer"
lap dances, gratuitous nudity, rape,
and projectile vomiting into a gutter.

In other words, this trashy update
is perfectly in keeping with the vulgarity
of the tradition it updates. Sharon Tate,

as Jennifer North, however, is a casualty
of this shady realm of *showgirldom*,
a modern day Francesca da Rimini,

trapped in this Second Circle—a chasm
where the Lustful are forever buffeted
by violent storm, a hellish hurricane: a gruesome

rehearsal hall where every light is muted,
and wannabes are battered by opposing winds
as they clamor for lines and songs desperately wanted.

(JC)

Looks like the wind is just beginning
to die down. Through the weeds I can see
a blonde child lying comatose

on the beach towel. Is she dead?
Is she sleeping?
Has she been dosed?

My guess would be the latter.
Her expression is wistful. The tide is out,
the "beach" is actually the bottom of the sea.

Pull forward and there is her older sister,
tweenie-aged, also naked, gazing east,
her honey-colored hair teased and matted

like a teen on roller skates. Gripping her wrist
is a bunny half her size, his body contorted,
yet even in letterbox I can sense that

his limp is exaggerated. In her other hand
the girl holds a rattle like it's a police baton.
Is someone calling her name? A light breeze

agitates the stuffing dotting the shoreline.
Through the fog I can see the dirty green
drumlin on the horizon, and the water

in between, a murky Wedgwood cocktail
reeking of nail polish remover and Scrubbing
Bubbles. I know what you are thinking, but

it's not easy to escape one's measly little
world when your limbs only rotate in circles.
Perhaps it is finally time for me to hang them,

put them out of their misery once and for all.
P.S. From my experience, anyone who doesn't
dig this painting is seriously lacking

in depth

(GMC)

"Okay, so you're planning to marry the love of your life, and you want to get her an
engagement ring that'll provide happy omens for the rest of your lives together. So
you'll clearly be interested in spending $25,000 to buy the engagement ring that
film director Roman Polanski gave to his wife-to-be Sharon Tate in 1968, right?
After all, it's not as if there's any bad omens there, such as, ooh, his wife getting
brutally murdered a few years later by a bunch of mad cultists. Oh . . ."

—www.bayrider.tv ("You flog it. We blog it.")

"Upon her death in August of 1969, a turning point in American history, her
husband instructed his business manager that her personal possessions be given
away to friends. Judy Gutowski (wife of Gene Gutowski, friend and partner of
Polanski's) inherited Sharon's engagement ring, a beautiful fire opal surrounded by
garnets. The circle of friends in London included Suzanna Leigh who was an
English actress who co-starred with Elvis, Tony Curtis, and Jerry Lewis, and
appeared in many of the famous Hammer horror films of that era. She remained
friends with Judy into the 1980s, which is when she was given the ring by (then)
Judy Evens. A letter written and signed by Miss Leigh accompanies the ring stating
when she became owner of the ring, as well as an appraisal letter from Montague
Jewelers in Memphis, Tennessee stating the condition and makeup of the ring.
Pictures of Sharon wearing this ring are on different websites that can be viewed by
any potential buyer. You can email me privately and be directed to these sites. Miss
Leigh has the deepest respect for Sharon and her memory and asks that all
responses be respectful and courteous and that all inquiries be serious as well.
According to the appraisal, the ring is an opal and garnet ring measuring 29
millimeters in length and 22 millimeters in width. Opal measures 22 millimeters in
length and 11 millimeters in width and is surrounded by 20 garnets weighing
approximately .04 points each. Approximate carat weight of the opal is 4 carats
with 3/4 carats of garnets. 4 garnets are missing and have not been replaced as not

to compromise the originality and integrity of the ring. Total gem weight of the ring
is 8.6. This is the one and only time the ring has ever been for sale. Miss Leigh will
personally mail the ring to you with all correspondence, appraisal, and the
authentication letter."

—eBay description

Online: a painting by Dexter Dalwood entitled *Sharon Tate's House*
(1998, oil on canvas, 183 x 235 cm). Except for an American flag thrown
over a white (rather than gold) couch, Dalwood's images bear, on purpose,

little resemblance to reality, for *Dexter Dalwood paints famous places he's
never seen: Camp David, Che Guevara's Mountain Hideaway, Kurt Cobain's
Greenhouse—unseen landmarks of a collective conscious. Dexter Dalwood*

represents Sharon Tate's House *not as the gory aftermath of the infamous
Manson murders, but rather as the 'close-up and impersonal' interior of a* Hello!
magazine spread. Creating the perfect ambience, Dexter Dalwood gets into the

*mind of subjects by recreating their environment in every detail: the swank late
60s furniture, basked in the warm comfort of a Southern Californian sun. It's
only the feminine dressing table in the background that suggests this is the home*

*of a budding star, and the American flag draped as a subversive sofa cover that
signifies this is the site of legendary helter skelter.* An innocuous exercise.
Not so of another painting (also online): Luigino Valentin's *Sharon Tate*

and Friends the Moment Before (2000, acrylic on canvas). Here we have
all the correct components of the chilling mise en scène: couch and flag,
armchair, zebra rug, fireplace, piano, loft ladder, ceiling beam over which

the rope will be looped, window through which the lights of Los Angeles
glitter, and the characters poised, as the title of the painting indicates, the
instant before it "all comes down": Folger in white nightgown, knife at

her back; Sebring in striped pants, protective of Tate; Frykowski on couch,
leaning away from the Longhorn revolver; Tate in panties and bra, arms
around her pregnant stomach; and the three darkly clad creepy-crawlers.

Oh my collaborators, I have fallen down an old rabbit hole: for nearly a
month now, doing research in fear: reread *Helter Skelter*, watched both
TV-movie versions, trolled YouTube for parole hearings of the murderers

and archival raw footage: reporters outside 10050 Cielo Drive the morning
after and at Jay Sebring's funeral: the mod-attired mourners silently (there's
no sound) entering and exiting the church, the frenzied movement of

photographers as a grief-stricken Polanski (obviously drugged) is led out,
supported on either side. Have also been engaged in my own private
Roman Polanski film festival. More on that later; for now I'll say it's hard

not to believe in cosmic predesignation when, during *The Fearless Vampire
Killers*, the film that brought Polanski and Tate together, blood drips on
and off Sharon Tate's name during the credits; Tate is presented, a passive

sacrificial lamb, to a roomful of ravenous blood-suckers; and Polanski
says (we know the odds are against him) to his future wife: "I'm going to
save you." What have I learned? That "the most bizarre mass murder

case in the recorded annals of crime" still terrifies me as much—if I let
it—as it did when I was a teenager. That I can still check, compulsively,
the locks on doors and windows. That this particular chasm is deep, endless

really—more Manson bottomless pit than rabbit hole. That it all makes me
feel dirty, ultimately, a feeling I associate with looking at certain kinds of
pornography—the gagged mouth and bound wrists, the fist up the ass—and

that I must pull back. But not before looking at, online, the actual crime
scene photos: there's the same lamp from Valentin's painting, and the red
cushions to the left of the fireplace, but this is the *real* living room twelve

hours after. The overturned coffee table, matchbooks strewn everywhere,
the lurid, blood-drenched sofa cushions and carpet. And the bodies. Two
there, and two outside, on the lawn. In my early twenties, when I saw the

whited-out bodies in photographs in my copy of *Helter Skelter*, I had a
strong desire to *see* everything, a desire that disturbed and mystified me
until, years later, I came across a photograph of a lynching in Asia: as the

crowd tortures its victim, a boy attempts to push through, strains to *see*.
It correlated. Now that I *have* seen: *I am incapable of more knowledge.*
(Not entirely true.) And by the way: not one brave soul bid on her ring.

(DT)

Aboard a bus from Philly to New York; I just
started reading an introduction to an
anthology of essays—a book that

Walls borrowed from the library at UPenn,
titled *Literature and Visual*
Technologies ("A prophesy from 19-

08: 'you will see that this little
clicking contraption with the revolving
handle will make a revolution in our global

life—in the life of writers. It is a humbling,
direct attack on old methods of literary
art.'")—when the bus's mini video screens

popped on suddenly and music started blaring,
announcing the beginning of *Casino*
Royale. The written word paled to this glittering,

"grosser power," and I wanted to know
what was happening in the movie, so I
tried to do both (read *and* watch the show).

But now I've got New Order playing low on my
iPod shuffle—it's helping drown out the noise
so I can write these lines in my travel-size

notebook. And although the movie annoys
me immensely, I can't help but look up
at the screen every few minutes to see the poise

of Daniel Craig through one explosive mishap
to another. Gee, he *is* really hot.
Every time I glance up, his face is in close-up;

it's like watching a silent film. It's not
unlike Darwin's *The Expression of the Emotions in
Man and Animals* (the first scientific work

to rely on photography) in
that the enlargement by close-up on the screen
brings an emotional action to Craig's face, and

I can clearly detect: anger, lustful cravings,
bemusement, deep thoughts. Way to go, Mr. Star.
Be gone. Don't forget to collect your earnings.

If I close my eyes, I can see all of our
beloved dolls in the Second Circle of the
rehearsal hall: Jen exits; her hour-

glass figure disappears (*vaboom, vaboom*) up the
stairs. The "connoisseur of sin," Henry Bellamy,
(along with Lyon and Anne) enters the

balcony, and casts his eyes down on Neely
as she takes her chair in an Oxford shirt and elf-
like leotard, starts to belt out one of her lovely

songs for the show: "try my friend, to face yourself
with all that you have in store, but if you can't,
hold it [interjects director] then brace yourself

HOLD IT! and try. . . ." The director doesn't recant:
cut the song. Neely is aghast—that's the best
piece of music in the show—and she rants

about Miss Lawson's abundance of songs. Her protest
is met with cold, hard fact: Miss Lawson presides
as star. Mel, Neely's faithful lover, suggests

that Bellamy is protecting "Old Ironsides"
(a reference to the USS *Constitution*—
the first naval warship built in 1794, which resides

in Boston Harbor today). But Neely won't cheapen
her reputation, takes Bellamy's advice
and intends to leave the malignant, stinkin'

show, with dignity. I open my eyes, this slice
of film engrained in my memory like some awful
trauma, ends; and I am still stuck in the vice

of these two plastic bus seat armrests, hands full
of pen, notebook; head full of movies, music;
of more knowledge, today, I am incapable.

(JC)

Guys, check this out. David's magnet theory
is inescapable. Uncanny—the same artist
who did the doll painting I described earlier

also did a still life called *Candice Bergen's
Home*, which, as you know, was once 10050
Cielo Drive. The painting (oil on board,

12 x 10) features a chair, a coffee table,
the infamous ceiling beams, and a white fire-
place, with the puzzling "Ernie's ankle" scrawled

graffiti-like across the mantel (but *not*
in blood). At first I thought that Ernie was
a reference to either Bergen's father,

or his ventriloquist dummy, but no, they are
Edgar and Charlie, respectively. Googling
Candice Bergen + Ernie resulted in references

to Ernie Hudson, a co-star of Ms. Bergen's
from 2000's *Miss Congeniality*. Doing a
search of *Ernie's ankle* led me to a badly written

synopsis of Ken Russell's *Lair of the White Worm*,
and a blog mention of some teenager's unfortunate
soccer injury. Exasperated, I Google *Candice Bergen's*

home which drops me off in "Recursive Science Fiction Drama,"
where I locate the following:

"*Starting on the Wrong Foot* [Teleplay]. Cybill [Shepherd] is playing in a science
fiction series opposite Jonathan Frakes (who was Commander Riker on *Star Trek:
The Next Generation*). He invites her to attend a *Star Trek* convention with him in
Anaheim. She refuses. During the course of the episode he calls her at places
where he ought not to know she is. Finally, he shows up at her home. When no one
answers the door, he pulls out his communicator and is beamed to **Candice
Bergen's home.**"

Don't ask, I have no idea (yet), but a much more
interesting magnet than what *Ernie's ankle*
drew in. Now for a description of the Cielo

Drive residence by Bergen herself, as written
in her best-selling autobiography *Knock Wood*:
"a gingerbread hide-out that hung high above

the city. There were stone fireplaces, beamed
ceilings, paned windows, a hayloft, an attic
and four-poster beds. It was a fairy-tale place,

that house on the hill, a Never-Never land far
from the real world where nothing could go wrong."
Backtrack to Jennifer, balancing a "headdress" as she carefully

descends the staircase that leads into the rehearsal
studio. "Six hundred bucks and not a soul will
see it," says the rogue director, his hand momentarily

blocking her head to make his point. "I feel a little
top-heavy," announces Jennifer as she tries to adjust
one of the massive blue boas growing out of her head.

"Honey, you *are* a little top-heavy," Director quips.
Everyone laughs; she has been simultaneously
ogled and dismissed. She reminds me of photos

I have seen of the so-called "Giraffe Women of Myanmar,"
their necks seemingly "stretched" swan-like, set rigid
by brass coils, when in truth it's their collarbones that

have been pushed down by the weight of the rings,
the result being "eerily graceful, the head floating
above the shoulders like the crown of a dandelion,

the chin projected forward as if in perpetual curiosity"
(*New York Times* Travel section, May 20, 2001).
Many of these women, having fled the war in Burma,

live in camps along the Thai border, where
they are considered tourist attractions, supporting
their entire families on the small monthly stipends

that the "authorities" grant to them. "Okay, Gillian.
Enough of this *National Geographic* shit. Our lives are *all*
a balancing act. Let's go back to where we came from. ME."

"Sharon, what timing. I was just about to pull an old
quote of yours to add more weight to my 'point.'"
From *LOOK* magazine, September 5, 1967,
                    "The Dames in the Dolls" by Betty Rollin:

"'When I was put under contract, I thought, *Oh, how nice, but*—' she stops, as if
holding back a sob—'I was just a piece of *merchandise*. No one cared about *me*,
Sharon.'
        'People expect so much of an attractive person. I mean people are very
critical on me. [sic] It makes me tense. Even when I lay down I'm tense. I've got an
enormous imagination. I imagine all kinds of things. Like that I'm washed up, I'm
finished. I think sometimes that people don't want me around. I don't like to be
alone though. When I'm alone my imagination gets all creepy.'
        'If you just take it down to bare facts, the reason for living is the reason you
make it. I mean the brain was made to create. I'm trying to develop myself as a
person. Well, like sometimes on weekends I don't wear makeup.'"

"First you cry *this*, bitch." Not only did I hardly
recognize Sharon's voice, but I was a bit shocked by
her lewd gesture. She was *fuming*. "That witch

took what I said totally out of context. She made me sound
like I was Dorothy fucking Stratten or something. I mean,
The Last Picture Show **was** a genius character study, but it had

none of the exhaustive, labyrinthine narrative
that Roman incorporated into *Chinatown*, literally
turning film noir into Greek tragedy."

"Your point is?"
"My widowed husband did not go so far as to marry my sister for god sakes."
"Point taken."

Sharon sighs, her shoulders suddenly sloped. "Poor Peter
Bogdanovich." She looks at me. "But I hear he's doing quite well now,
is that true?" I nod. "That's nice. I always liked him."

(GMC)

"I've found that when you're making a movie and relying on – either on purpose or
for other reasons – more and more on your unconscious – I guess what you'd have
to call instinct – and that if a movie is going pretty well – that it becomes a magnet
for certain things – that certain things happen that wouldn't have happened
otherwise. In my case it was that my brother sent me – and it was an LP in those
days – of Simon & Garfunkel – and I would play them every morning as I was
showering and getting ready to go to the studio – and after about three weeks of this
I thought, 'Schmuck! You're listening to the score to your movie . . .' The magnet of
whatever it was about *The Graduate* began to pull this stuff towards it. Haven't you
found that, that when something is very alive it just pulls everything in?"

—Mike Nichols to Steven Soderbergh, DVD commentary for *The Graduate*

August, die she must

—Simon & Garfunkel

Magnet Theory: on Nov 15 JC emails me: "this is the painting
that Gillian was writing about in that one patch. She owns it;
it's called 'Riverbank Scene' by Lepus Articus." A blonde doll

holding a stuffed rabbit. My first thought is of one of the photos
in *Helter Skelter* (which I lingered on when I recently reread it):
the guest bedroom at 10050 Cielo Drive, where white-nightgown-

clad Abigail Folger was reading when Susan Atkins came down
the hall: "Sitting atop the headboard of the bed, his legs hanging
down, was a toy rabbit, ears cocked as if quizzically surveying

the scene." A creepy detail, this rabbit. I'm curious, so I do what
I often do: Google. And find, on a blog called Tarnished Lady, a
photograph of Sharon wearing a blue Alice in Wonderland dress:

sitting in a director's chair that says "Happy Easter," she smiles
and holds the selfsame rabbit. A souvenir from a photo shoot,
this rabbit. Says Sylvia as Sharon as Alice: *I have fallen a long way.*

Magnet Theory: I'm watching *Death and the Maiden* (part of my
Roman Polanski film festival) and am struck, in the scene where
Sigourney Weaver cudgels and restrains Ben Kingsley, by similar-

ities (that Polanski must have intended) to what happened in *that
house on the hill*: Weaver slips off her shoes (barefoot Manson chick),
equips herself with gun and electrical cord (Tex Watson with Long-

horn revolver, rope), enters living room (beamed ceiling, fireplace)
where Kingsley is asleep (Frykowski) on couch, the drone of crickets
(hot Los Angeles August) the only sound. Then it "all comes down."

Magnet Theory: Sept 19 (three months ago) I have this dream: Charles
Manson tries to follow me into the side door of Comanche Ave. (my
childhood home), but I hold out my right arm, point at him, and zap

him—twice—with a super psychic power, keeping him at bay. I'm
able to get inside and lock the door. A few weeks ago, sorting through
Tim Dlugos's poems, I come across this, in his "April Dream Series":

10 Apr 75

In park beneath some bushes I discover Charles Manson sitting cross-legged,
eating something awful out of wooden bowl. It looks like an overboiled turnip
served on dirty rice. I have been hooked up with his family for some time, and
people keep calling me Tex. But I know I'm not Tex Watson, the hit man in the
famous murders. This is a continuation of the previous dream, and my relatives
keep making guest appearances. Connie's little son appears, looking like a
miniature Polanski. Joe O'Hare has disappeared. Manson's gang is living in a

bungalow which makes me think that this is California. I go through the same
scene several times, in which I pack my canvas suitcase and tell Manson I am
leaving for good. He is totally crushed.

Magnet Theory: it's Monday night, I'm bored, so I put in the DVD
of *Julius Caesar* (1953 version), which I've owned for over a year
(it came with the five-film Marlon Brando Collection; had to buy

the set to get *Reflections in a Golden Eye*) but haven't felt enthused
enough to watch. Think I'll only be able to tolerate about ten
minutes (Flashback to high school: my first exposure to the Bard:

The Tragedy of Julius Caesar: English class is right after lunch and
I find the play excruciating, can barely stay awake) but am riveted,
watch it straight through. Conspiracy and assassination, hands

bathed in "costly blood." Caesar's wounds "like dumb mouths,"
"ruby lips." The Roman dictator was stabbed twenty-three times.
According to Suetonius, a physician later established that only one

wound, the second to his chest, had been lethal. Sharon Tate was
stabbed sixteen times, five of which wounds were in and of them-
selves fatal. Folger was stabbed twenty-eight times, Frykowski

fifty-one. O ghastly tally! When Antony uncovers Caesar's corpse
and the camera pans the faces in the crowd, it correlates. They form
a tight circle around the piteous spectacle. They *see* the bloody sight.

Magnet Theory: I'm on the phone with JC, telling him how miffed
I am because, about a year ago, a woman I'd met at an artists' colony
in the early nineties contacts me and asks me to write a blurb for

her daughter, who's written her first novel, and when I say I'm
not a novelist, she butters me up by saying she wants someone
famous to write a blurb, so what can I do. I read the manuscript,

write a blurb, and the daughter, via email, expresses her gratitude.
She later emails to say her publisher thinks my blurb is too long
can they cut part of it and I say sure no problem. Then, a few months

ago, I start getting emails and phone messages from the mother
inviting me to a "dinner party" for her daughter—the book is out—
at her apartment, which happens to be in Water Tower Place, where

Oprah lives—or lived, apparently she sold her condo. I'm busy
yet think I might go and plan to respond one way or another but
then when I receive another invitation, this time in the mail, it feels

like the mother is being a little too pushy, a little too proprietary,
like she wants to make sure she has enough *famous* people at her
party, so . . . I let it go. In other words (this is an old joke between me

and JC), *D. didn't respond.* I next receive an email from the daughter
saying how sorry she is that she didn't get to meet me at her "book
signing" but she wants me to have a copy of the novel where should

she send it? So I email her my address and say good luck with your
book and a few days later her package arrives. I open it, pull out the
book, and look at the back cover. There are two blurbs, but neither of

them is mine. I read her note, which says her publisher was "very
stingy" and did not, despite her pleas, allow my blurb on the finished
book. I notice that the two blurbs that her publisher *did* allow on the

finished book are by writers more *famous* than myself—this one
a Pulitzer Prize winner, that one a National Book Award winner.
What a thud her finished book makes when it lands in the trash!

"Cut the <u>blurb</u>!?" says JC, mock-shocked. It doesn't register. He
has to say it several more times. Finally its relevance dawns on me:
Cut the <u>blurb</u>!? The poet goes and the blurb with him. JC, trustworthy

magnet, pulling me back to the scene at hand. I'm delinquent with
my lines, though for weeks I've been chanting the following litany,
inspired by Neely's head-held-high departure from *this stinkin' show*:

 Broke up with Ira—with dignity
 Left NYC—with dignity
 Helped Byron move from this plane to the next—with dignity

When Jennifer sticks her head in Neely's dressing room and says
That old witch ought to be boiled in oil, her words produce a magnetic
field that pulls, like iron filings, all sorts of objects and associations

toward them ← A.S., my guide, "possessed witch" inhaling a Salem
"then sitting here / holding a basket of fire" ← My fascination with
the monster model kits manufactured by Aurora Plastics Corporation

in the mid-sixties: Frankenstein and his Bride, Dr. Jekyll as Mr. Hyde,
Dracula, The Mummy, The Hunchback of Notre Dame, The Creature
from the Black Lagoon, Guillotine, and (my favorite) The Witch: a

wart-nosed hag dropping bats and rats into a bubbling cauldron ←
The three witches in Polanski's *Macbeth* ← How one Halloween I
dressed as a witch: bought a mask and pointy hat at Thrifty Drug,

but the real thrill was wearing the waist-length wig I made out of
black yarn ← Sharon Tate's supposed cameo in *Rosemary's Baby*,
"girl at the party" according to the Internet Movie Database; I've

tried finding her many times: it's possible she's the blonde sitting
on the couch at the beginning of the scene ← Tate's pre-*V.O.D.* role
as a witch in *Eye of the Devil* ← Barbara Parkins's post-*V.O.D.* role

as a bourgeois Satanist in *The Mephisto Waltz* ← *Bewitched* (the TV
show, of course, but also the book [a 45¢ Dell paperback] based on
the series, which I stole, in 1965 [I was eleven], from Thrifty Drug,

then felt so guilty and fearful I'd be found out, I threw it away before
reading it; years later I came across it at a used bookstore, bought
it for $12.00, have it still [it's here in front of me: the cover drawing

shows blonde Samantha airborne on her broom, wearing a witchy
black cocktail dress, long black gloves, and pointed hat (adorned with
a red flower); behind her Darrin hangs onto the broomstick for dear

life], but have never been able to read it; having it, possessing it, is
the point, I guess, like the Barbie dolls I own: too late to play with
them, at least the way I wanted to then, inventing situations and

dialogue, losing myself in that highly fashionable imaginary world)
← Marion Lorne's brilliance as dotty Aunt Clara in that series ←
Veronica Lake (whose autobiography arrived in the mail, Magnet

Theory-style, just a few days ago) as the prototype of Samantha
Stephens in the 1942 movie *I Married a Witch* ← How one Halloween
Jeanne Marie Beaumont dressed a blonde Skipper doll as a witch—

perfect to the last detail: black dress, pointy hat, broom—and I gave
her a vintage party favor (miniature plastic jack-o-lantern with handle)
for the doll's trick-or-treat candy ← Wendy the Good Little Witch, who

on the cover of one of her comics, flies across a full moon on a vacuum
cleaner instead of a broom, her friend Casper the Friendly Ghost gliding
beside her; did you know that Wendy's three aunts, the witches with

whom she shares a cottage in the haunted forest, are named Thelma,
Velma, and Zelma? God bless Wikipedia ← Speaking of comic books:
writing this, I remembered that in the sixties there was a Lois Lane as

witch story, but I wasn't sure whether I owned it (I still have 60-odd LL
comics from my childhood), so I Googled "Lois Lane witch", which led
me to a website that has a Lois Lane Chronology, where I did a search for

"witch" and learned that "The Witch of Metropolis" appeared in the
premiere issue of *Lois Lane* in April of 1958 and was reprinted in October
of 1967 in an 80-page Giant *Lois Lane* (#77) featuring "a Collection of Lois'

Greatest **Shockers!**", so I went to eBay and searched for "Lois Lane 77" and
found a copy (on the cover Lois flies her broom across an orange full moon
wearing a patched witch outfit and pointy Pilgrim hat; Superman glides

beside her) in G-VG condition and used the Buy It Now option to purchase
it for $9.91 (plus $5.00 s/h) ← Sylvia Plath's poem "Witch Burning" ← How
as I child I saw, in an encyclopedia, a drawing of an accused witch, tied to a

dunking stool, being lowered into a pond; how that image made me feel:
a sense of queasiness bordering on vertigo; naturally it didn't help to read
that after some time the woman was taken out of the water and given the

ability to confess; if she confessed, she was killed; if not, she was submerged
again; a process that was repeated until she drowned or gave up and let
herself be executed another way (hanging or burning) ← How when I read

at St. Mark's Church this past Halloween, Elaine Equi handed me a gift
bag with several items she'd bought at Crow Haven Corner, "Salem's
First Witch Shop": a pad of *Bewitched* fold & mail stationery, a bar of pink

attraction soap, and some dried Statice flowers (and pink magic bag to
carry them in) to bring good luck and love; I'm using the soap and carry
the pink bag with me, and expect, any minute, to meet the man of my dreams.

―――

I would like to say, by way of a footnote, that last year when I wrote the
blurb for that woman's daughter, Byron lay on the couch with me while
I read the manuscript. Some of the last sweet hours we spent together,

as he died about a month and a half later. So expanding M.T. to include
occurrences in daily life, that blurb was precisely the right thing to have
happened, to have attracted, at that exact moment, and for that I am grateful.

(DT)

I have listened to these injured souls: DT,
Roman's horror story, Gillian's telling
of the Giraffe Women's plight, and Sharon T's

struggle to become a "whole person" (not wearing
makeup on weekends as transformational
act). And now Neely at the end of this scene,

held in her lover's arms, trying to deal
with getting canned from a Helen Lawson show,
being consoled: "It's a rotten business." She'll

wipe her tears and sheepishly admit, "I know.
But I love it." We wonder which is her true
love—the biz or Mel? I bend my head, hold it low

until the poet asks of me: "What are you
thinking?" "Gee Frank," I begin, "so many sweet
people with kind thoughts, such longings, and strong hearts through

all of it, reeling in, like magnets, from the deeps
the darkest memories and associations."
So now I address my speech to them: "Dearest peeps,

have courage and strength. DT, your ruminations
intrigue me. But don't linger too much on the pain
of the past—you've still got great destinations

ahead (after all, you've acquired more fame
and praise with your recent *New York Times* review);
Roman, I'm sorry about Sharon. Don't blame

yourself, though. But please, just try not to renew
sexual relations with any thirteen-year-
olds—we miss you here in the U.S.! Why don't you

buy back Sharon's old engagement ring? It might cheer
you up; Gillian, don't be hard on yourself—
your fascination with all things bizarre, my dear,

is what makes you so, well, dear. Thank you, odd elf,
for the little striped "DOLLS" jars—DT and I
love them; Sharon, Gill's faithful guide, love yourself—

I know it's work—to develop ourselves takes time—
as DT's guide will tell you: "Once I was beautiful,
now I am myself." You're safe in heaven, and I'd

like to think you got the chance to be grateful
for becoming a whole person (God can do
things with time, right? Let you "relive" a whole, full

life in a separate dimension before restoring you
to the day-to-day of clouds and white feathers?);
and finally, Neely—what can I say? You

won't settle for crumbs like other singers."
A slow clapping of hands brings me back. "Bravo!"
says Frank, "now can we get moving?" He lingers

near the door of this rehearsal hall. Although,
before we depart, I must speak to good-hearted
and lustful Jen, who twirls around in the turbo

wind holding onto Tony Polar's fated
hand: "Happy New Year, Jen! It's 2008.
That leotard still looks great on you—these blasted,

never-ending winds must keep you in good shape."
The sadness of these two lovers is too much
to bear, and as if meeting my own death, I faint.

P.S. On Jan. 1, JC and DT clutch
phones to ears, and poetize this Happy B-
day wish to Gillian, as personal touch.

(JC)

As I read over DT and JC's last two
patches I encounter these "memos" scrawled
in the margins: Sadness I felt when my nephew

asked me: "What if it turns out I *don't* have super-
natural powers?"; Theresa Duncan (gang-stalked
by Scientologists at St. Mark's Church?); Diane Von

Furstenberg's new lipstick, a "sumptuous fuchsia"
that mimics the stain left on her lips following
a week-long beet juice fast; Vampira (*not* Elvira);

*The Satanic Screen: An Illustrated Guide to the Devil
in Cinema* (great cover photo of Rosemary/Mia
holding a bloody carving knife); Mom nicknaming

me "Veronica Lake" after I grew out my bangs,
age eleven; my obsession with comic books
(*especially* Betty & Veronica), ages seven to ten;

"EBAY AS RESEARCH TOOL—YES!"; scariest movie
scene number one: afternoon TV "matinee"
with Mom—a young woman lying in a shallow

grave, her head and feet protruding, watches
as a group of Mennonite-looking elders methodically
stack bricks along her torso until her neck breaks;

scariest movie scene number two: after getting
her head shaved by a female prison warden,
a pretty girl, formerly blonde, thrashes against

the wall of her bunk (*was her scalp cold?*) as my sister's
boyfriend (snug denim shirt, shaggy blond hair, hunk)
encases my nose in Silly Putty in an attempt

to distract me; the plot to destroy Roman Polanski
re: underage-girl-quasi-setup; and re: Neely, a verse
from Leonard Cohen's "Bird on a Wire": *I saw*

a beggar leaning on his wooden crutch. / He said
to me, you must not ask for so much. / And a pretty
woman leaning in her darkened door, / She cried to me,

Hey, why not ask for more?

(GMC)

Canto Six

After guest star Wayne Koestenbaum introduces Joey Bishop, Emcee of the Telethon of the Damned, the poets find it's impossible to fathom "that special bead moment"—Patty Duke flailed by an uncontrollable necklace. Conway speaks with Joan Crawford, a "charitable" lush, who demands that he reestablish her reputation.

Introducing Joey Bishop

Joey Bishop, the cystic fibrosis telethon's emcee, introduces Patty Duke
(Neely O'Hara) in her first rebound appearance after being dumped
by Susan Hayward (Helen Lawson). Joey Bishop's initial words, intro-

ducing Duke, are "Ladies and Gentleman." Bishop ("Miss Bishop," let's
call him, as poets of a certain generation referred to Elizabeth Bishop)
has a lateral lisp, so he pronounces "Ladies" "*Lay-Deej.*" His outfit

is black tux, black bowtie, red pocket-hankie. His hair: shoepolish black.
Dyed? Though the "last surviving member" of Frank Sinatra's Rat Pack,
and though Italian-looking, Joey was a Jew, born Joseph Abraham Gottlieb,

3 February 1918, a mere seven years after Elizabeth Bishop (born 8
February 1911 in Worcester, Mass., the town where Frank O'Hara attended
St. Paul's School and then St. John's High). Readers of this epic might wish

to know that Joey Bishop "served as master of ceremonies" at JFK's
inaugural gala: Jackie Kennedy was one of the "lay-deej" (ladies)
whom Joey Bishop "interpellated" (hailed) with his lateral-lisping intro.

"Ladies and gentlemen, one of the nice things about doing this telethon—I mean,
in addition to raising money"—says Joey Bishop, arms hammily stretched wide
open, as if he were Ethel Merman belting "Everything's Coming Up Roses"—

"is helping to discover new talent": his outslung arms, cantor-esque,
bespeak a "false-self" life of trying to please, a personality trained to cajole
and convince. "I think you're going to love our next performer." His mode

is mortuary. "Let's have a nice cordial reception if you will": he pronounces
"cordial" like "co-ja," "coe-ja." Joey Bishop, like Susan Hayward, has done time
in diction's back alleys, and so he slurs, ruins, bends, crams syllables, mangling

simple words, as Hayward, in the powder room scene, will torque "Broadway"
into "Broad-WAY." Last night I dreamt I bought an orange and yellow
portable typewriter, the same bright sleeping-pill colors as my "Fabulous Four"
    Nike

Air sneakers: the typewriter's keys tipped upward at an abrupt angle,
a cliff-face impossible to climb: I could admire the keys but not master them.
"Lovely Neely O'Hara: everybody, let's hear it out there": aggressively Bishop

claps his hands, one loud smack, demanding our applause: thus he wedges Neely
into fame, his pinkie ring, left hand, a quick glint only visible when I freeze
the image for this scrupulous accounting. ("I flunked sand pile," said Joey Bishop,

about his academic unsuccess. His wife, Sylvia Ruzga, no Sylvia Plath, died
in 1999 from lung cancer.) Why does Joey Bishop (like Tony Scotti as Tony
Polar) seem a "retard" or "cripple" (to use the offensive parlance of *V.O.D.*'s era),

and doubly sexy as a result? Why does Joey Bishop's funeral-parlor sleazy allure
symbolically match the "gimp" and "crip" enterprise of a cystic fibrosis telethon?
More germane: Patty Duke's *Miracle-Worker* "disability studies" street cred

queerly mirrors Joey Bishop's mentally-disabled-seeming sex appeal,
his "wah-wah" (Helen-Keller-speak for "water") lush-lipped oral delivery.
Said simply: you could pile into one corner all the people in this movie

who seem "retarded" (or mentally dented): Sharon Tate, Barbara Parkins, Tony
Scotti, Paul Burke, Martin Milner. In the other corner you could pile the people
who seem alert, bright, avaricious: Patty Duke, Susan Hayward, Lee Grant, Naomi

Stevens, Jacqueline Susann. Joey Bishop is emcee of the "retard" pile, or, to put it
less nastily, the "lobotomized" pile. *Co-ja la-deej*: cordial ladies. Miss
Bishop, there's something pornographic about your undertaker sexiness, your

bit-part status, your tux, your pronunciation of "performer" ("per-form-ah"), my
knowledge that Sylvia Ruzga has dibs on your naked body, tuxless, at home
(faced with a dolled-up tanned Jewish/Italian man, instinctively I imagine

his wife or mother undressing him): crucial to *V.O.D.* is *the magnetism of the miscast,
the ignored; the fuckability of the unclassifiable, the rejected.* The extras, minding
phones at the cystic fibrosis telethon, are women. Each is a Sharon Tate or Barbara

Parkins understudy. Each types, takes dictation. They are Joey Bishop's minions.
They are the silent (Helen Keller) back-up chorus for Patty Duke's number,
"It's Impossible": dumb chorines. Joey Bishop's other films include *Johnny Cool,*

*A Guide for the Married Man, Betsy's Wedding, Mad Dog Time, Pepe, Onionhead,
The Naked and the Dead, The Deep Six.* He was a frequent panelist on *What's My
Line?, Password, The Hollywood Squares, Celebrity Sweepstakes, Liar's Club,*

Break the Bank. The Joey Bishop Show ran on ABC from '67 to '69. Nothing more
bottomed-out than being an emcee, a guest star, a cameo, a bit player,
speechlessly taking dictation while Patty Duke lipsynchs "It's Impossible." As
    Elizabeth Bishop

put it in "The End of March": "A light to read by—perfect! But—impossible."
(A poem she published in 1976, the year I graduated from Prospect High.)
Joey Bishop reminds me of school speech-and-debate failures: my mincing,

inauthentic mouth: our coach's Marlo Thomas hair, mirroring Jackie Susann's:
I gave a speech called "Man's Inhumanity to Man," with Holocaust
excerpts, tearjerking. To emcee—to be extracurricular—is to be damned.

                                                                    (WK)

                                   *   *   *

It's a rotten business, I know, but I love it! We are watching a girl perform
on a telethon, a slim but curvy girl-next-door singing her heart out; a girl
belting it out and not yet belting it back, a girl whose lover is watching her

from the sidelines, God, he loves this girl, this little milk-drinking carny veteran
pre-Hollywood embrace, this adorable stray dressed in a red turtleneck, grey
A-line skirt and sensible shoes, those delicious tits encased in a power point bra,

the double-strand chain he bought her at Ohrbach's executing a perfect figure
eight across her white lace cross-your-heart. He is in love with a girl who
is just starting out yet well on her way, a girl who is going to have tongues

wagging, a girl just about to burst. A girl on the brink. An explosion waiting to
happen. A girl just brimming with talent and energy; a girl who is going to make
him a very happy man someday, a girl who is *his*. Cut to: a man, leaning against

a mahogany desk, a scotch in one hand, a phone cradled against his shoulder,
trying to light a cigarette without taking his eyes off the TV; a man who has just
stood up and taken notice. Deep drag, face suddenly lights up, sets down drink,

transfers receiver to free hand, manic soliloquy ensues. "Rod, I'm looking at a girl
who is gonna knock L.B.'s socks off. She's extraordinary. A spitfire. A pitbull.
Not quite a long cool drink but knock off twenty and she'll look six inches taller.

Send her a plane ticket, book her a bungalow at the Beverly, and then get Lotte
Berk on the phone, it's time to slenderize, goodbye profiteroles, hello Obetrals.
We're gonna go heavy on the contour and highlights, bring out her bones, slim

those hips, bang out a heavy fall, footwear c/o Frederick's, put the emphasis
on OOOOMMPH. And Rodney? If she brings some suitcase pimp boyfriend
with her—KEEP HIM THE FUCK OUT OF MY FACE."

(GMC)

Easter Sunday, 2008. I sit here surrounded by my Patty Duke collectibles
(dug out, upon rising, from various closets). Patty Duke Paper Dolls (1964);
"inspired by *The Patty Duke Show*," this Whitman set features two

dolls (Cathy with pageboy, Patty with flip) and "31 outfits with accessories":
"Clothes ready to punch out – no scissors necessary". Two books: *Patty
Duke and Mystery Mansion* (also from Whitman, 1964: "Authorized Edition

featuring the characters created by Sidney Sheldon for the well-known
television series THE PATTY DUKE SHOW") and *Patty Goes to Washington*
(Ace Books, 1964: "It's Panicsville on the Potomac when those two terrific

teen-agers of TV's PATTY DUKE SHOW invade the Capital!"). On both
covers: shots of beaming beflipped Duke from the same photo session, her
exuberance as hyperbolic as the copy on the inside page of the latter:

"Television's PATTY DUKE SHOW has captivated audiences and
critics alike with its freshness, warmth and humor, and with the radiant
performances of its talented young star. Playing the demanding dual

roles of Patty Lane and her look-alike cousin, Cathy, the Academy Award-winning actress makes the weekly series that bears her name a double delight for the whole family." Various issues of *16 Magazine* from the

mid-sixties, one with a Patty Duke "Super-Giant Autographed Signed Pin-Up" centerfold, another with the article "Patty Duke: How Love Changed Her Life!" Two copies of her 45 (with picture sleeves):

"HER VERY FIRST RECORD!!! PATTY DUKE SINGS DON'T JUST STAND THERE. B/W EVERYTHING BUT LOVE." Patty recorded both songs on April 2, 1965. United Artists Records released the single on April 27.

"Don't Just Stand There" reached #8 on the Billboard charts on July 17, three days before my twelfth birthday. I listened to it over and over. A dramatic and mournful little number, "Don't Just Stand There"

depicts Patty's confrontation with her boyfriend. If it's over let's end it; don't make me suffer like this. *How can you be so unkind? Tell me what, what, what, what's on your mind.* The song on the flip side,

"Everything But Love," is a rich girl's sugary, oddly jaunty lament: *Oh I have everything most girls dream of, everything, yes I have everything but love.* Her singing voice, though not particularly strong, isn't half

bad. She sounds a bit like Lesley Gore: adept at putting across catchy pop show tunes. Neither of my 45s is the one I owned as an adolescent; I picked them up in the nineties, at flea markets in New York. One

picture sleeve is pristine. The other is creased and worn. Underneath "HER VERY FIRST RECORD!!!" the disgruntled original owner printed, with a black pen, "**AND HER VERY LAST!!!**" He or she also took the pen

to the color photograph of snappy, upbeat Patty (wearing a pale blue blouse and matching headband), adding dark mascara and eyelashes, a mole on her cheek, and dangling earring. I'm equally attached to

both: the perfect and the defaced. When "Don't Just Stand There" began to slip down the charts, United Artists put out Patty's second (and yes, very last) single, another distraught breakup ballad called

"Say Something Funny." It made it (in October '65) to #22, and appears
on her LP *Don't Just Stand There*, one of five albums spread out on
my floor. The others: *"TV's Teen Star" Patty Duke*, the original motion

picture scores of *Billie* and *Valley of the Dolls*, and *Patty Duke Sings
Songs from* Valley of the Dolls *and other Selections*. I wish you could
see the photograph on the cover of the last: Patty's all drama-hair

and heavy mascara (this time for real), and looks, bizarrely, like
Jorie Graham's long-lost identical cousin. I wish I had a turntable
so I could listen to her sing all five songs from the film (in the movie

and on the *V.O.D.* soundtrack, Duke's voice is dubbed), but this is
really—according to Gene Kelly, who wrote the liner notes—"the
excited voice of Patty Duke." He says: "This is the personality of

'Neely O'Hara' in 'Valley Of The Dolls', the destroying and self-
destructive, self-centered and eruptive singer which Patty Duke
portrays with such power and versimilitude [sic]." Confession:

I've been listening, the whole time I've been writing this "patch,"
to Patty sing (yep, I own the CD *Just Patty: The Best of Patty Duke*)
"Don't Just Stand There" and "Everything But Love" and "Say

Something Funny"—over and over, just like I did when I was
eleven/twelve. What better way to celebrate the most important
religious feast in the Christian liturgical year. What have I brought

back to life? My pre-teen idolization of Patty Duke's short-
lived singing career? Is that all this amounts to? While Patty,
hair bouncing like a Breck Girl, lip-syncs, beads a-swinging.

(DT)

I can't bear to look at Neely's beads a-swinging
today; I've been home for three days—since Tuesday
when I woke up dizzy, stood up, started barfing.

I had to go to the ER on Wednesday—
dehydrated, head spinning, stomach sore from
all the *vomitage* (French for vomiting?). Anyway,

suffice it to say, I'm exhuasticated from
all the interior drama, too—I thought
I was a real goner. Turns out, a dumb

viral infection of the inner ear brought
it on, caused the severe vertigo. Maybe
my "magnet" (of aforementioned Theory) caught

some negative vibes. Let me explain. Wally
and I were watching *Gigi* on Saturday
night—neither of us had ever seen it. We

struggled through the boring songs that went on way
too long; I think we even fast-forwarded
through some toward the end. Determined, though, we lay

on the bed staring at the screen and waited
for the end credits to roll. The reasons I
suggested we watch it were because I wanted

to see why Little Edie Beale decried
Leslie Caron as the most sublime actress
(I had watched *The Beales of Grey Gardens* after my

[what seems to be] monthly viewing of *Grey Gardens*
the weekend before last), and I also thought it might
be fun to watch a Vincente Minnelli (Miss

Garland's, a.k.a. Helen Lawson #1, loafer-light
husband) directed film. I was wrong on both
scores. When I whined to DT on Sunday night

about how bad *Gigi* was, he said that both
Auntie Mame and *Cat on a Hot Tin Roof* were
nominated for Best Picture—and that *both*

lost to *Gigi*—in 1958. Better
yet, said DT, that was the same year as
Vertigo—which wasn't even a bearer

of the Oscar nomination! What madness.
And in the middle of my Tuesday vertigo spell,
here in my Polly Pocket apartment, as

I was moving toward the toilet to hurl, I fell,
head a-swinging, looked up to see the orange cover
of the book DT gave me when he said farewell

and moved to Chicago in what must be over
five years ago: *VERTIGO: THE MAKING OF
A HITCHCOCK CLASSIC*. Can't say for sure whether

said "magnet" brought the vertigo on (though I love
musing about such things). Perhaps this all sounds
"dizzy." (Maybe the Meclizine I'm on?) Above

my desk is a black-and-white picture (that foregrounds
all the other Post-it notes) I downloaded
and printed from the Internet. It resounds

with significance for this scene of beaded
Neely on her go-go podium. It's a
photo of Joan Crawford (who would've celebrated

her 100th [gasp!] birthday last Sunday)
and her daughter Christina answering
telephones and laughing like best friends at a

1968 telethon—attempting
to raise money for muscular dystrophy.
A perfect image to take us into the stinking

Third Circle, where the Gluttonous supine in filthy
Aqua Netted rain; telethonettes howl
for fame, hoping the eye of the camera stealthily

crosses their path as they answer calls, prowl
behind the scenes hoping to be discovered,
as a newcomer sings, as phones ring and befoul

the stormy, studio-lighted air. I've uncovered
the backstory to the Joan and Christina
photo: while her soap star daughter recovered

from emergency surgery, Joan stood in for Christina
on *The Secret Storm* (1968-1969)—taking
over her role as a twenty-eight-year-old diva!

The picture shows aging Joan in mid-guffaw, laughing
heartily as a secretly bitter Tina
looks on, attempting to act amused, fake smiling.

(Think diabolically resentful Christina
manqué Carol Harbin in *Strait-Jacket* biding
her time for revenge and concocting a

frame job of her formerly axe-murdering
mother Lucy [Joan Crawford].) No doubt, a shit
storm ensued when the cameras clicked off, ending

the money drive *and* their relationship. It
was the last time Christina ever saw her
mother alive. An enormous wiglet

tops Joan's spiraling hairdo; her daughter
wears no wig, but the locks are full, bouffanted.
They each resemble their counterparts who answer

the phone lines during Joey Bishop's tormented
telethon, *The state of the damned after the Resurrection*,
filled with cold, and dizzily swinging beads, rancid

hailstones around Neely's neck. An audition
presided over by Cerberus, the last of
the Rat Pack, his fame-hungry mouths wide open.

(JC)

Patty Duke is sitting in a New York hotel room, surrounded
by windows, in what I'm imagining to be a downpour—colossal
(of course), interspersed with sleet, a hailstone in place of the mandatory

exclamation mark; wet, damp, grey (Patty on the making of *Valley
of the Dolls*: "We were flying blind, in a fog"); she is smoking and eating
scrambled eggs at the same time, one naked toe curled around the other,

occasionally fingering her first *good* piece of jewelry—a gold turtle
from Tiffany's that Walter Pidgeon bought for her when she was nine—
or twirling her bouncy ponytail around her index finger; age twenty-one

("going on twenty-two"), she wants to be treated as an adult, and since
there is no time for small talk (her mother is in the next room, packing
for Patty's trip back to L.A., terrible weather to fly in, yes, but fly in

she must, *so let's get started shall we?* and so begins her "conversation"
with Rex Reed, who describes her as a "candy-box bow-ribbon mouth
of a girl" whose "eyes are red from crying" and who is "summoning all

the strength in her mini frame" to not let any strain show; still simmering
over the journalist who dubbed her "Little Miss Sewer Mouth," she is trying
not to come off like a "pint-sized Jimmy Cagney," or a "midget [on] vitamins"

as she makes a little frown that "turns her nose up like a half-nibbled
gingersnap," before diving into the subject of "Mistake #990,000-B,"
which was allowing her husband, director Harry Falk, to convince her that

seeing herself in *Valley of the Dolls* would cheer her up (after all,
everyone had told her that she was *magnificent* in it), but what she ended
up seeing was an "unmitigated disaster," that required an "air-sickbag

to sit through"; a film that made her look like "Tugboat Annie"
and had her "eat[ing] pills that were filled with powdered sugar
and had to be washed down with booze that was really Coke

and watered-down tea [and] were so fattening that [she] gained
twenty pounds." (Ed. Note: in her autobiography, *Call Me Anna*, Duke said
that she got back at the director "in sneaky ways," like camping out next to

the donut box and gaining thirty pounds during the filming—
"Thirty pounds!" she exclaimed. "And I don't even *like* donuts!")

(GMC)

"Our eyes locked and we shared the amazement and joy of standing on top of the world. We'd climbed Mt. Everest together and it was wonderful to breathe the rarefied air."

—Sonny Bono, about himself and Cher, after their first hit

"Candy was so excited, she bleached her hair at a salon called Valley of the Dolls on Tenth Street and was never the same again!"

—Holly Woodlawn on Candy Darling

"Long, slow process:
climbing Mt. Everest.

Short, fast process:
getting a Citibank
personal loan."

—Citibank advertisement

Well, it's been about three and a half months since I sat in the driver's seat and this is the best I can come up with? Three measly *V.O.D.* sightings diligently recorded in my purple Staples notebook. A *long, slow process*

to be sure, this climb of ours. It's amazing, waiting for (or stalling) my turn at the wheel, how reality seems to teem with such referents. Take *Mannix*, for instance. Do either of you remember this popular hour-long crime show?

Both too young probably, not born yet. The series aired on CBS from 1967 to 1975, and starred Mike Connors as Joe Mannix, a Los Angeles private eye. From an Amazon.com customer review (written by E. Hornaday, who lives,

appropriately enough, in *Lawrenceville*, New Jersey): "In its eight-year run, *Mannix* quickly became a TV staple airing on Saturdays at 10 p.m. Not only was it noted for its great writing, acting, unusual camera angles, hot cars and

visuals, but also its violence. Mannix was, by one count, shot 17 times and knocked unconscious another 55 during the show's run." I used to watch it when I was in high school, baby-sitting for a couple who lived on Labrador,

a cul-de-sac one street over from us. Was I watching *Mannix* the night of
August 9, 1969? Summer, it would have been a rerun. Consulting *Helter
Skelter*, I learn that Leno and Rosemary LaBianca would have been on the

road when *Mannix* was on: they left Lake Isabella, a resort area 150 miles
from L.A., at 9:00 p.m., and arrived in their neighborhood, the Los Feliz
district (where I'd later live, in the mid-eighties), at about 1:00 a.m. Had

the couple I sat for arrived as well? It was only a block, but the husband
always insisted on giving me a ride home. I would have preferred to walk:
a chance to sneak a cigarette in the dark cul-de-sac. Or maybe his wife

insisted he drive me? Most likely I didn't baby-sit. With the Tate murders
all over the news, my mother would have wanted me home that night.
Confession: in recent weeks I've been watching the first season of *Mannix*,

new to DVD. I won't wax poetic about the fabulousity of early color TV
shows or the fabulousity of skinny ties. But unmistakably, in several episodes,
D.O.D. beckoned. (I don't think we ever announced this, but on 5/23/07—

one year into it, one year ago—the title of this collaborative climb became
Descent of the Dolls. Is that an oxymoron?) In one, Mannix investigates a
strange hippie cult. Hard not to think of Manson (two years before the fact)

when drugged-out, barefoot youngsters stagger around in the underbrush.
They will come wearing headbands, with "murder in their hearts." In another
episode, "Falling Star," Marian Seldes plays the (villainous, it turns out)

secretary of a fading actress. The original airdate of "Falling Star" was
1/6/68. Later the following year, Seldes would play Anne Sexton's alter
ego, Daisy, in the off-Broadway production of Sexton's *Mercy Street*. A

whiff of cigarette smoke: I knew it was not from a neighbor in the hall, but
from my own true guide. However it was a third episode, "License to
Kill," that gave me a jolt. It opens with a darkly clad figure hopping a wall

and prowling about an estate. Inside, a couple sits on a couch, drinking,
making out. We learn, before the darkly clad figure creeps up to the window,
that this episode will center around a character whose last name is Tate.

Then, the figure shoots the couple, first the woman, then the man. Then:
Mannix theme, dynamic split-screen opening credits. A few days later,
browsing the Internet, I happen upon this news story: Susan Atkins, who has

spent 37 years in prison for her role in the horrific murders of Sharon Tate
and six others, is seeking a compassionate release; she is dying of brain
cancer and has had a leg amputated. Doctors say she has six months to live.

The first to die. We do have her to thank for squealing, for bringing the truth
about the killings to light. August-December, 1969: the cases still unsolved,
each bush, after baby-sitting, full of murderers, that short walk home in the dark.

(DT)

As DT recently reminded me,
I'm the only one paying attention to
Inferno's Cantos & Circles. It's *so* JC—

to obsess on peripherals. But a few
things occurred to me rewatching this scene: first,
doesn't it make sense that Joey Bishop, true

to his status as the less-than-slick, straight-laced
member of Hollywood's Rat Pack, is Cerberus?
He's really the only one of the five accursed

(albeit cool) stars who wasn't *so* gluttonous:
he eventually butted heads with party-
hearty Sinatra and split from the voracious

group; he also remained married, chastely,
to the same wife for fifty-eight years. Second,
the jug-eared jokester guest-hosted, successfully,

The Tonight Show Starring Johnny Carson
a record 177 times,
so it's clear he has the *mouth* to be stationed

at the entrance to this Third Circle. His crimes,
incidentally (this is my last point), also
include a big hunger for fame: he ofttimes

begged Sinatra to let him open his show,
and became known as "Sinatra's comic." Only
Bishop could play emcee for Neely's solo

debut, her first public performance. Joey
emits sound, his *throat barking*, then falls quiet
as he gnaws the song and rapt applause for Neely.

But let's continue on with our journey; poet/
guide Frank, you ready? We descend further, into
this movie—circling down an enormous wiglet

submerged in a toilet, filthy, covered with goo.

(JC)

Listen Jeffery, I kinda resent being accused
of not paying attention to the cantos and circles
it's not easy to throw in a casual mention of

"Two Headed Dog," the great Roky Erickson
song, nor can I come up with a clever anecdote about
the stuffed one that Legs bought at a dollar store

and gave to his editor for his birthday: and just a couple
of pages ago I *did* mention Patty Duke and her venge-binge
on donuts. What do you want me to do: confess to you

that my pants are all too tight? Well, my pants
are all too tight, and which, like DT's blind trust
in Wikipedia (under gluttony they had written:

See Bulemia [sic]), is just another one of my current worries
like the pancake size bruise on the top of my right foot
having been stomped on at the Stooges show, even though

I was only on the *periphery* of the mosh pit, now, could
we please get back to what I know and maybe you don't?
Such as the fact that Tex Watson once owned a wig shop

called Love Locks? And that Rosemary LaBianca carried
wiglets at her store, Boutique Carriage, as did Jay Sebring
at his salon? Perhaps these are just peripheral facts, or perhaps

they are some kind of clue, or maybe they'll just lead
us on an interesting path—like my photos of the Beales
done by the Maysles who also brought you Altamont, that other

tragedy that helped end the sixties,
and who also shot some amazing footage of Sharon
Tate in London, dancing with her co-star David Hemmings,

both looking loaded and beautiful and a wee bit hot for each other
as they took time out from filming *Eye of the Devil* "I am
the devil and I am here to do the devil's work" is what

Tex Watson supposedly said to Voytek Frykowski
after having so rudely awakened him from his nap.
In L.A., at dinner, Jason had blurted: "Just a thought—

devil's work—do you think he was referring to the Straight
Satans?" referring to the motorcycle gang who occasionally hung out
at Spahn Ranch, but only on the periphery, just as John Aes-Nihil

was on the periphery of the crowd that surrounded Meredith Hunter
that night at Altamont, and who recently sent me the following email:
Gillian: Yes certainly. As for Healter Skelter [sic] the Last Super [sic]

was on 8-8-08 at 8 with 8 at El Coyote. We almost got the table but then
they gave us the one next to it and dumped these other people into
the right one and one of them looked like Abagail [sic]. After about

15 minutes Dukey announced to them where they were at
and so forth. The entire Super [sic] was video-taped this time
and we took stills at the talbe [sic] and in front of El Coyote.

Then went to Falcon Lair and got this great shot of the Monstrisity
[sic] house with downtown behind it. Went to the gate at midnite [sic]
and ran into several guys who drove there from Salt Lake City

and some guy who had bought stuff from me in the past. The Graveline tour
guy had been there earlier and apparnelty [sic] there was another séance
at the 3rd house which was on that TV show. Then went to the Ranch

and got there at 1:30 am. Music was being played at the church and this dog
was barking manically [sic]. We drove to the gate and right when we got there
this guy called the Art Bell show and claimed he was at that moment flying a private
    plane over

Area 51 which was incrediable [sic] in that the last time I was on
that bridge Legs was talking to the church woman about Area 51
since she claimed her husband was a test pilot there. As we drove

down Topanga I kept the cam on for the entire call
getting all the car-lights out the window. I found more phtos [sic]
such as a shot from above of Red, Blue and Sue and another

of Red and Blue and several interior shots of the house and
more exterior ones and Red by the camp fire and so on.

All for now, John

(GMC)

"When Anne meets dreamy Lyon Burke (Paul Burke) over a tube of lipstick, it's love
at first sight. Lyon becomes even dreamier in Anne's eyes when he lands Neely a
spot on Joey Bishop's Cystic Fibrosis Telethon. Neely belts out 'It's Impossible,' the
first of the movie's gonzo showbiz ditties. Duke's interpretation of a stage
performance is a sight to behold. With vocals by Gail Heideman, Duke tries
desperately to 'sell' the song, but it's no use. Even her jewelry is working against
her. At one point, her beaded necklace amusingly outlines her breasts."

—www.coolcinematrash.com

"As Neely will do, she storms out of Helen Lawson's musical and surfaces upon the
stage at the annually televised Cystic Fibrosis telethon (there's a metaphor in there
somewhere). She storms through her next song, appropriately called 'It's
Impossible,' and because the rendition is so relentless her double strand of beads
takes over. We're first curious and then transfixed by this swinging necklace. As if
rewarding our patience, near the song's climax, as Duke continues shrugging and
mugging, the beads separate and then magically loop themselves around both of

her breasts. The song is a bummer, but in the world of *Valley of the Dolls*, with those beads (and the film editor) working overtime, *Variety* (and then seemingly every other newspaper in the continental United States) can report YOUNG SINGER WOWS AUDIENCE, and a star is born."

—www.lamemovies.net

"None of the film seemed corny and indeed I did find it shocking and brutal, full of mean people doing awful things to these pretty girls. If anything struck me as 'dirty' and unsuitable for kids, I have to say that my mind did flips when in this musical scene this necklace of Patty Duke's takes on a life of its own, eventually framing each boob in glittering beads. I don't think I heard a word she sang! Boobs were new to me then (let's be honest, they still are) and I couldn't take my eyes off of that offending necklace. I thought it was done on purpose, like some dirty special effects joke that only adults understood."

> —Kenneth Anderson, on seeing *V.O.D.* in 1967 at age ten (user comment on the Internet Movie Database)

A few nights ago, before an AA meeting, Brooke told me and Steve a funny story: in high school, she judged a playwriting contest. Every entry, she said, contained a scene in which one of the characters threw

him- or herself down on the ground and cried, "God!" or "Dear God!" or "God in Heaven!" There was even an Hispanic character who, once he'd hurled himself to the floor, howled "¡Ay Dios mío!" The three of

us howled, and I naturally thought of Neely in the alley at the end of the film, a heap of existential blubbering. All that runny mascara. A nudging reminder: my turn to write. The night before that, another

nudge: at the end of another film, Anjelica Huston descending (via elevator) into the Inferno, one of her own making. Aren't they all? *Character is fate.* Profound, I thought, when I first read that; still think

it says it all. Most people victims—many hopeless, malignant—of their own unexamined stuff. Translate "stuff": thoughts, feelings, words, deeds. I ♥ (a Jefferyism) *The Grifters*. Not many can match

Huston's brilliance in that role. Jane Fonda in *Klute*. Gena Rowlands
in *Gloria*. Davis in several: *All About Eve* always, though today (casting
her mannerisms to the wind) I'm leaning toward *Now, Voyager*. Ellen

Burstyn also in several; today's pick: *Resurrection*. Annette Bening in
Being Julia. Carmen Maura in *Law of Desire*. No, *Women on the Verge
of a Nervous Breakdown*. "¡Ay Dios mío!" I cry, as I throw myself into

another rabbit hole, one of my own making. Anne, patient and saintly
guide, sits in a plastic frame on my desk, smoking, smiling knowingly
(© Rollie McKenna, from the same shoot that produced the photo on the

back of *Transformations*), reminding me that this scene, first and foremost,
is about beads. In her suburban sunroom, posing in a white wicker chair
and surrounded by striped pillows and potted plants, white statue (Grecian

lady pouring water from a jug) in the background, Sexton wears a white
blouse and skirt, and a single strand of black plastic beads. A point of
honor, these plastic beads. The first time my teaching was observed, I

happened to be discussing, in a college-level Introduction to Poetry class,
Confessional poetry, Sexton in particular. When I played a tape of Anne
reading a few poems, I passed around a copy of *Transformations* so students

could see what she looked like. The colleague observing the class later
wrote (he meant to do me harm): "There were hints that some of the
students didn't care for Sexton. It occurred to me that their judgment

may have had a basis in social class. The photo of Sexton seemed to
heighten the social difference between our students and Sexton. She was
posed in white dress and pearls as she sat at the window of her upper-

middle-class home." Pearls! They're clearly plastic beads. This inaccuracy
bothered me more than the fact that my colleague was plunging the proverbial
dagger in the back. (He also pointed out that I used words like "Zeitgeist"

without explaining to my students what those words meant: "In my experience,
such terms need to be explained to undergraduates.") His ploy backfired on
him: he was removed from my tenure committee, and his deleterious letter

stricken from my file. The quotes give me away: I saved his letter, tucked it in
my immortality box (*So it has come to this*) for posterity to read and be appalled
by. St. Anne of the Black Beads nods approvingly. Observation: in the photo

on my desk, the beads fall naturally between her breasts. But in the one on
the back of *Transformations*, the beads slide to the right, and loop around
her right breast. All she needs is another strand, to loop to the left, and the

beads would crisscross in the style in which we (demented *Valley* fans) have
grown accustomed. Last night, in preparation for today's patch, I rewatched
the beginning of *Thoroughly Modern Millie*. Doug Powell (months ago now)

suggested I take a look at it when I told him we were on the current scene
(he'd asked about our progress). Beads, it's all about them: Julie Andrews
bobs her hair, raises her skirt, and dons a strand of green beads. Of course

her boobs get in the way of the desired flapper drape: *Gee, I wish my fronts
weren't so full . . . they sure ruin the line of your beads.* So she fashionably flattens
her chest. (Incidentally, *Thoroughly* came out in 1967, same year as *Valley*—

year of beads, year of breasts.) Anne's attire (blouse, beads, skirt) reminds
me of Neely's, who's still singing. And Patty Duke and Joey Bishop remind me
of two anecdotes that have been hovering about since this canto began. The

first: Bob Flanagan, who suffered from cystic fibrosis, once showed me an old
newspaper clipping, an article about a cystic fibrosis fundraiser he'd attended
as a child. He knew, from my poems, that I was a Patty Duke fan. There she

was, or rather, there she and *he* were—Patty Duke (Oscar-winning TV teen
helping those less fortunate) and Bob Flanagan (future Supermasochist, who
would publicly hammer a nail through his penis), arm in arm, mugging for

the camera. The second: in the late seventies, my college friend Rachel
Sherwood heard about a casting call for poets, and dragged me to one of
the major studios for an audition. We were given passes and shepherded

into a conference room with a dozen or so other hopefuls, and each asked
to recite a poem for none other than Joey Bishop. A new variety show was
supposedly in the works, and he (or someone) was interested in having poets

appear on it. Rachel and I were the only authentic poets in the room; the rest
read their amateur rhymes with over-the-top gestures and inflections,
desperate to impress Mr. Bishop, desperate for a few precious television

minutes. I dourly read my poem "Dream Creatures," and remember feeling
humiliated—humiliated to be lumped with such desperate characters, humiliated
to be auditioning my poem (pearls before swine), while Joey Bishop, who that

afternoon could be seen on *Match Game 77*, sat there stone-faced. Rachel, though,
was great; Mr. Bishop should have recognized that, and discovered her like he
does Neely, crisscrossed beads and all. This canto ends with Neely still singing.

(DT)

A few summers ago, I went to see
a staged reading of *Valley of the Dolls* in
Provincetown. The cast was composed mainly

of local drag queens (though Michael Cunningham
played the role of Lyon Burke). It was a lot
of fun, save one major disappointment: the damn

beads never looped around Neely's boobs, not
even once. I was appalled. (To be honest,
the drag queen who played the coveted part

of Neely sucked.) One scene did stand out as best:
Jen's French movie was turned into an amusing
lesbian porn film—Jen being chased and seduced

by Miriam, Tony's sister! There's something
oddly sexual about two men in wigs,
dressed in panties and amply stuffed bras, making

out in a bed to Frenchy music. And bigwig
drag queen Varla Jean Merman ("the illegitimate
love child of Ethel Merman and Ernest Borgnine")

played the role of Jen. A few months ago, late
June maybe, someone posted the video
footage of the cystic fibrosis—wait,

muscular dystrophy—telethon that Joan
Crawford appeared on in 1968
(aforementioned a while ago in this canto).

She's introduced by Jerry Lewis (the great
humanitarian and comic); Joan stumbles
out in her over-the-top shiny gown, ornate

bib necklace, and tremendous wiglet. She dazzles
the crowd and TV audience with a reading
of a poem, "The Clumsy, Falling Down Child." She hurls

melodramatic sentiment and irritating,
predictable rhymes at the camera. The
highlight: Joan screams out unexpectedly

(in an angry tone) right in the middle of the
recitation: "Muscular dystrophy.
POND'ROUS, POND'ROUS NAME! For a clumsy, fallen

down, helpless lame! For trying, but dying
all the same." Then she bows her head, sheds a tear.
After slurring through her banter with Jerry,

she introduces Christina, "My *daw*ter" (sheer
genius highfalutin pronunciation).
Christina walks out, greets Jerry, while austere

Joan looks on. But Christina's conversation
with Jerry is cut short: Mommie Dearest
grabs Tina's arm, pulls her away, uses diction

more truck driver than star as she addresses
her, "Come on—we got work to do!" They sit
at the phone bank and prepare to pose for their last

photograph together. Re-YouTubing the clip
just now made me think of Frank, my indifferent
guide. I typed his name into the search box, hit

"enter." Up came a post of him reading the brilliant
"Having a Coke with You." I watch. I watch again.
And again. My obsessive rewatching is fervent,

mechanical, like the body of Charlie Chaplin
in *Modern Times*: spasmodic, repetitive,
dislocated—an automaton. Amen

for YouTube, that other world where so many live,
are *still singing*. Wait! During my present viewing
of Frank's clip, he pauses, looks back at me, rather pensive.

"Conway," he says, "ready to move on? Living
your life in here isn't really, well, kosher.
Things can get pretty irritating and boring

and dispensable. Shall we move on?" "Great author,"
I begin ("Oh brother!" Frank replies), "I just
want to watch the Joan clip once more, watch her

drunkenly slur her words—it's the choicest
posting since that one last year (which was removed!)
of Joan in pink cowgirl hat at LAX,

riding on an electric cart, being interviewed
completely sauced, just before a trip to England
to film what must've been *Trog*—her last film. I was glued

to it for weeks before it was yanked." "I'm maddened,"
says Frank. "But do what you have to do, and I'll meet
you in the next Circle." I re-click Joan, fund-

raising for dystrophy: "POND'ROUS, POND'ROUS—oh, we meet
at *laast*," she says, looking straight out at me! I freeze,
total shock. "Me?" I say sheepishly. "Yes, it is you I greet.

Bless you, gay New York poet. You'll never be
O'Hara, but still, you *are* gay, and you *are* a
New Yorker. I've been wanting to speak to you, geez

for *years* now. You and that Trinidad! Two gays
who seem to be *obsessed* with me!" I stumble
for words: "Gee, Joan, I mean Miss Crawford, what can I say?

I . . . I—" "Never mind that. I want you to humble
yourself before me—a star of the first magnitude:
sign off and go back into the world to bumble

about as you always do, but from now on allude
to my generosity and kindness—my work
for charities, for example, like this one. You'd

be beginning the necessary groundwork
for paying back the karmic debt you owe me—
all these years of mocking me, being a jerk,

laughing at me, imitating me derisively!"
"Gee Joan, I really don't know if I'll be able
to change my ways so decidedly, so swiftly."

"You must!" she screams. "Don't make any more trouble,
Conway. Go back into the world, restore my good name!"
"Sorry," I whisper to Joan. *"It's Impossible."*

Her straight gaze grows twisted and awry. "POND'ROUS NAME,"
she continues, easily slipping back into
her poem, "for a clumsy, fallen down, helpless lame."

(JC)

Keep watching those beads—you won't be sorry.

Canto Seven

*In the Fourth Circle, where all cats are gray, all are held hostage by Tony Polar, a jabbering
headliner if there ever was one. Conway and Trinidad, escorted by their glamorous guides,
settle into ringside seats, while McCain reflects on avaricious Blue Light stampedes and
billion-dollar corporate bailouts.*

Saturday, October 18. 46° here in Chicagoland,
partly cloudy. It's supposed to be a full-on sunny
day (according to gauge on computer Dashboard).

I spend this a.m. in the dark: a "crowded, smoky
and jumping" (according to the script of *V.O.D.*)
boîte de nuit. Don't know why I'm waxing fancy

on y'all—by deflecting I subtly resist? Slip DVD
into the side of my Mac: Main Menu: click Scene
Selection: click 5: The Night Life: position movie

(*avec* wireless mouse) beside Word file (a dream,
a glorious dream, of Anne's "business of words"):
"live" dolls on my desktop. Note color scheme

of Fourth Circle: red and black beats the third's
orange and blue-gray for hellish. Bulbs pop as
couples hop. Neely gets champagne. Boss heard

(via Lyon) of telethon. Jiggling her body to jazz,
Neely's surprised by his formal hello—first taste
of bubbly *and* fame. Tony Polar's big biz, he says,

then moves on. Lyon, tailing him, doesn't waste
a second, hustles his newcomer a stint at the club.
Neely swoons at news; she'll build her act post-haste.

Moments before, Jen, poised amidst the hubbub,
entered with a wealthy beau. In script, her escort
has a name: Arnold Prince. This actor's more sub-

ject than sovereign. Was the maitre d', sporting
the exact same tuxedo and the same barrel chest,
only moustached and better looking, an aborted

choice for the role? Was the extra cast the best
friend or golf buddy of director Mark Robson?
All eyes, I realize, are expected to ogle breasts

in this scene, but I find Jennifer's far-from-stun-
ning date more noteworthy. Did it come down
to a mere toss of a coin? Why was the sexier one

given the menial task to seat them? Jennifer's gown
is commented upon by Neely (she still has beads
on the brain), prompting prudish Anne to frown.

At the same time I'm online seeing if I can weed
out the identity of Jen's "distinguished-looking
gray-haired man." Ralph Montgomery? No leads

in his 35-year career: Man in Bar here, On-look-
er at Accident (1949's *Gatsby*) there; Hotel Clerk
or Fingerprint Cop on this TV show, Fry Cook

or Ticket Taker on that. Bright as Paul Burke's
credits. Hold on. The Internet Movie Database
yields some Montgomery minutiae that perks

up goosebumps: Ralph played (Gillian, brace
yourself) the Grand Jury Foreman in the first
Helter Skelter. I could crack the clamshell case

and slip *that* DVD into my Mac if I'd a thirst
tonight (yes, day—its sun, clouds—has flown:
terza rima eats time) for veracity. At worst,

Montgomery ain't our man. He's unknown
even if he is: an endless list of walk-ons on
IMDb does not an immortal make. His clone

(maitre d') gets to hold the chair for Sharon
for DVD eternity. And he's cuter! *Valley* is
rife with quotidian "Man in Bar"s—spawn

of a prosaic casting director. Poor Ralph. His
fate: Tony shamelessly woos his date. Stan-
zas and lights dim. Such is Show- and PoBiz.

(DT)

Enter Jennifer, walking like she's balancing a book
on her head. "I look like Malibu Barbie on Thorazine!"
screams Sharon, and I have to agree—she's the sacrificial

airhead about to be devoured by a grotesque
love interest. As I watch her watching Tony Polar
watching her—I feel sickened. *Their eyes meet . . .*

As my late shrink once said, "If you see someone
across the room and your heart starts beating
really fast—run in the opposite direction."

Little does she know that she would have been better
off sticking with her lecherous escort, at least then she might
have had a chance of someday becoming a primary cardholder.

(GMC)

Lyon informs Neely she'll be playing the club,
though she'll need to work fast and get herself an act:
the boss, swollen-faced Frank, has agreed (though he'll snub

those who don't want it bad enough). Neely reacts
with glee, promises to work hard. Tony Polar,
squanderer of protocol & sound choices, makes

his move on Jen—despite the other Polar's
(Miriam: hoarder of money, emotions) wishes—
and sings his heart out for the buxom blonde. Polar

opposites, Miriam and Tony are sad wretches
who spend their lives pushing against each other,
acting out their respective roles in lounges

coast to coast. "Why do you hoard my earnings?" the younger
brother asks of sis again and again. "Why
do you squander your time and talent on bimbos?" the elder

sister yells out. And so it goes, the constant cry,
their chant of scorn, on and on. *Come live with me,
and be my love, if only for a day.* Jen dies

for this song, for this hot dark man. His bawdy
stares and shiny red silk suit fluster her core.
She squirms in her seat, unsure of her own beauty.

I see myself at a cocktail table, waiting for
my "date" (Frank O. in drag tonight, donning
a brownette wig) to walk out the door

of the powder room and return to our "ring-
side" spot. I'm feelin' this big goon who swoons
over Jennifer North—I think I see a growing

"chubby" in his pants! I pause the DVD. No. Resume.
Frank emerges in a slinky sixties shift
(borrowed from *Ms. Dog* for the night). As Tony croons,

I'm thinking, *how did I get into this movie?* "A gift,"
says Frank slyly, "from me and DT's poetess
guide." Too many impressions and sights to sift

through, I relax and let it happen. Frank's queerness
intrigues (and also his wig is a bit askew).
Still, I watch and soak up the song's gorgeous badness.

(JC)

So it's Saturday morning (November 22) and I'm sitting
at my desk, *D.O.D.* Word file open, DVD of *V.O.D.*
paused on a long shot of the infernal nightclub

just before Tony makes his entrance. I've lit
my yellow candle (for mental stimulation), said my
prayers (a few Sappho fragments about

inspiration and this new quote, from Gertrude Stein's
Paris France: "One of the pleasantest things those
of us who write or paint do is to have the daily miracle.

It does come."), set Sexton's *Complete Poems* to my left
for easy reference (without thinking, I opened it
and touched the leaf, taken from her gravesite, pressed

between the first two pages of "Suicide Note").
I'm almost ready to go and . . . the phone rings. It's JC.
"I'm just about to write," I say, "I'm rereading what

we've written so far of Canto Seven. My last patch,
the terza rima, is better than I thought." "Yeah,"
he agrees, "it's great." Since gabbing is easier than working,

we scrutinize the scene together. I comment on the cuteness
of the waiter (the one pouring champagne), then notice,
when he sits back down after talking to the club owner,

the size of Paul Burke's basket. "It makes me like
him more," I say. Then: "I've been noticing
lately, in old movies, that you can see a lot in the

men's pants. Especially if they're wearing boxers."
We concur that the best cinematic ass shot is of
William Holden when he's pulled dead and wet

from Gloria Swanson's swimming pool. JC tells me
that someone recently told him that in *Batman*
(the sixties TV series) the size of Robin's

box was digitally reduced. An urban myth?
Must read Burt Ward's *Boy Wonder: My Life in Tights*. Or maybe
not: I've never seen so many one-star customer reviews.

Says one: "Sleazy, trashy, and VERY over-
exaggerated nonsense." Says another:
"The Quest to Control His Huge Crotch Bulge!"

JC shows me where he and his gussied-up guide
are sitting, at a table in the second row
in the center of the club, under the starburst chandelier.

He realizes that Frank's wig is not a bouffant; neither
is it black: it's brunette. "Why don't you say 'brownette'?
That's a Barbie word." I show him where I plan to have

the handsomer-than-Jen's-date maitre d' seat me and
my guide: "See the empty table up on the platform?"
"No." "To the left of the post." "No." "It's the post

in the middle." "I still . . ." "*The middle post.*"
"I see a waiter seating a woman in an orange dress."
"I hope he's not seating her at my table!" "Oh

yes, I see it. Above the woman with mile-high
gray hair." "Yes." Now that I'm telling JC
about it, I don't know if I can suspend disbelief

(I don't tell him this), present the scene I imagined
"in the moment" of the film. This is what I was going
to depict: Anne and I enter the nightclub. Unlike Neely,

who's still wearing her skirt and blouse and
mind-of-their-own beads from the telethon,
Anne's had a costume change. She's discarded

her *Transformations* author photo outfit (white skirt
and blouse, black plastic beads) and donned one of her
famous halter dresses, blood red; a pair of T-strapped

thong sandals, red patent Italian leather with jewel
ornamentation; and her gold "Don't Let the Bastards
Get You Down" choker. The maitre d' leads

us to that empty table. All the eyes that ogled Jen
a few moments earlier are riveted on Anne.
"This is how a Pulitzer Prize-winning poetess enters

an Inferno," she announces proudly; then in a whisper:
"Though I actually haven't won it yet." New York
School poet Kenneth Koch (the man wearing thick

black glasses, sitting at the bar behind Neely, Mel,
Lyon, and Anne) makes his way through the crowd.
"Miss Sexton," he says, "we haven't officially met,

but next year (November 1968) we'll be reading
together in Chicago at a black-tie gala in honor of
Poetry magazine. We'll be photographed (both

smiling, my arm around your shoulder, you holding
a cocktail and cigarette); it will run in a write-up in
the *Tribune*. Almost forty years later, Rich Rice will

clip the article (brown with age) and send it to
David Trinidad here . . . Hello, I don't believe we've met."
He shakes my hand. "Hello, Mr. Koch. I regret

not meeting you when you were alive. I like your
work a lot, especially *New Addresses*, which I'm teaching
next spring in one of my classes at Columbia College.

I was a friend of Jimmy Schuyler's." "Thank you," he says.
"In the springtime the Sentences and the Nouns lay silently on the grass."
He wanders back to the bar reciting one of his most anthologized

poems. Anne orders a Stinger (2¼ ounces brandy, ¾ ounce
white crème de menthe), I order Perrier with lime.
She asks about my recent trip to Northampton (to do Plath

research). I tell her that I stayed at the Autumn Inn
on Elm, just down the street from the house Sylvia and Ted
lived in, the year Plath taught at Smith.

"That was right before I met her," Anne says, lighting a Salem
with her red Bic. "She followed me into Lowell's workshop,
you know." "There's actually some question about—"

Before I can say more, she asks me to tell her about Aunt Bee.
As if hypnotized, I dumbly comply: "Channel surfing one night in my room
at the Autumn Inn, I came across an episode of *The Andy Griffith Show*

on TV Land. Episode 194 to be exact, 'Aunt Bee's Crowning Glory,'
originally aired on October 10, 1966. Aunt Bee is the talk of Mayberry
when she buys a blonde wig and becomes the sudden object of the new

minister's attentions. Bee is then faced with the dilemma of letting
the minister know that she is not as she appears. She removes
the wig permanently when she realizes that everyone loves her

for herself, not her hair. I don't know, I loved that the whole
episode was centered around Aunt Bee's wig. Should she wear it,
shouldn't she wear it? Of course the women of Mayberry, in their

jealousy of Bee, became quite nasty. They acted like they wanted
to rip that blonde wig off the head of their fluttering bovine friend."
The lights go down, Tony Polar bursts into the room;

spotlit, he begins to sing his schlocky song. Anne,
noticing that Tony is crooning directly to Jen,
exhales smoke and sadly exclaims: "O blonde thing!"

(DT)

Sharon begs me to draw attention away from her embarrassing performance, and
focus on something innocuous—the interiors for example. Not much to say on
the subject: cheap tablecloths the color of discontinued tomato paste; a couple

of modern chandeliers, which (after doing some research on eBay) I can now
categorize as mid-century Eames-era space-age sputnik chandelier lamps.
Red walls a shade darker than the waiters' polyester jackets. For the first time

I notice that Lyon has ordered a bottle of Dom Perignon (spell-check delivers
paragon, *porn* and/or *pregnancy*) circa 1959, served, regrettably, in a coupe,
the "bride and groom" variety of champagne glass, which is also commonly

used to serve sherbet, and unlike the elegant flute, does not *capture* the bubbles, but instead releases them—onto your face. Perhaps Jen had her make-up in mind when she ordered a vodka tonic. On Black Friday, I consumed leftover

Veuve Cliquot as I sat glued to news footage of Mumbai, which was periodically interrupted to report that although "sales at Wal-Mart stores exceeded expectations, the company's sales figures were overshadowed by the death

of Jdimytai Damour, who was trampled at a store in Valley Stream, N.Y., when an estimated 2,000 shoppers burst through the doors at 5 a.m. on Friday morning. The six-foot-five, 270-pound Damour, who had been hired as a temporary security

worker, died of asphyxiation. 'We consider Mr. Jdimytai Damour part of the extended Wal-Mart family and are saddened by his death,' announced vice-chairman Mr. Castro-Wright." And in Palm Desert, California, two men

shot each other to death over a dispute at a Toys "R" Us, but the company released a statement saying the deaths were not related to Black Friday shopping. According to the *L.A. Times*, "mayhem erupted in the electronics

department about 11:30 a.m. . . . Joan Barrick, 40, of Desert Hot Springs said she was buying a Barbie Jeep for her daughter when two women started brawling. As the women swung at each other, the men they were with also

started arguing. The younger of the two lifted up his shirt and flashed his handgun, pulling the grip from his baggy pants pocket. The other man yanked out his own handgun and started chasing him down the aisle and firing.

Barrick hid behind a stack of DVDs and recited the Lord's Prayer. 'If I'm going to die, I need to make peace,' she said. As the two men ran shooting through the aisles, shoppers dumped their purchases. LaToya Jenkins, 20, had already

bought a remote-control bike. She dropped it and ran. Others left behind shopping carts full of the bargain-priced toys they had come in search of. Dozens of shoppers poured out a back emergency exit and fled to the nearest

havens: a Jiffy Lube and a World Gym. Outside Pizza Hut, where witnesses were being interviewed, 3-year-old Landon Stitt sat on the grass munching on his pizza. He spoke matter-of-factly, almost as if he was describing a video

game. 'I saw it,' he said. 'They were fighting. They were shooting.' He shaped his
fingers into a gun, then fired into the air. As night fell, the coroner's office had
still not removed the bodies from the store. But authorities said they expected. . . ."

(GMC)

"Oh JC," a horrified Frank whispers,
"what a dreadful time you live in." "Yeah, I know.
Why do you think I'm in *here*, with these B actors?—

sitting with *you*, my poet-guide, watchin' this show?
Not to mention the fact you're in drag—what's that
about?" "What can I say? I like nurturing my alter ego.

There's a tradition amongst poets to don wigs and hats,
full drag, if you will. My biographer, from your time—
Brad Gooch—he's been known to dress up like a big fat

tranny mess, go out to the bars. You'd look fine
in a tight top or a nice dress, a little mascara
to pump up those already lush lashes." "Yes, mine

are rather . . . fluttery. I want to pass a
note to DT. He's sitting up there near
the middle post. I want to tell him that he made a

mistake quoting me, or maybe I was a little unclear—
it wasn't the Batman TV series with the
digitally reduced box; it was, I fear

from a much later time *and* superhero: the
controversy (and reduction) was to *Superman
Returns* actor Brandon Routh. Is it really worth the

money to reduce, frame by frame, a man's
protuberance? These are odd times indeed.
I much prefer these fabulous sixties. Look at Susann's

world—so cool. Though, the book is set in the forties,
not the sixties. Maybe that's why this film suffers
from that weird syndrome, that 'it feels

like it's translated from another language' thing. Neely offers
that odd line about only ever seeing a bottle
of champagne cracked on a ship—in newsreels!

It's like she's been transported from a long ago
place and time." "You know, don't you have shopping
to do—for Christmas? I hate to say it, but you'll

have to go back to '08 at some point." "I'm avoiding
all sorts of reality as of late, Frank. When
I'm not in *here*, with you, I'm living

in the movie *Showgirls*." "Really? Then
is it safe to say you're off your Joan and Bette
kick?" "Well. . . ." "Oh brother, *them*—again?!"

(JC)

Me to JC, as we read over
his last patch: "'Whispers' is
capitalized." "What?" "In

the first line: the word 'whispers'
shouldn't be capitalized." "Oh,
right. Just lower-cased it."

We joke about a character
named Frank Whispers, and
I think of the Dory Previn song

"Mister Whisper," from her
album *On My Way to Where*,
about being confined to a

psychiatric ward. Mister Whisper
is the harbinger of insanity ("when
I am going / 'round the bend /

I got a wild / imaginary friend")
and can be directly linked (if this were
an undergraduate thesis) to the

"Mister" in my guide's poem
"Music Swims Back to Me," also
about mental breakdown. All

this will come into play later,
in the insane asylum scene,
when Neely sings the song we're

listening to right now, to flush
Tony out from the crowd of
nutcrackers (though all she has

to do is take a look around the
rec room, as Tony's right in view
in the corner, in his wheelchair;

maybe his head's hanging down,
so Neely doesn't recognize him?).
Remind me to mention, when we get

there (where?), that not long after
V.O.D., Barbara Parkins played
an incurably insane inmate in the

movie *Asylum*. I sense a rabbit hole
opening, a portal to an alternate
dimension in which everything has

at least two or three meanings
and twice as many associations to
useless Wikipedia-cribbed factoids

from popular culture. Tony Polar
is Mister Music, serenading doe-eyed
Jen with this Dory-penned ditty.

Her lyrics ("Come live with me
and be my love"), stolen from
Christopher Marlowe's poem

(learned just now via Google search),
bring to mind the song Debbie Reynolds
sings (one too many times, if you

ask me) in *How the West Was Won*:
"Away, away, / Come away with
me . . . And I'll build you a home in

the meadow." Cloying . . . but as
a child, that song made me woozy
with romantic fantasies. Just as

Dory's, as an adolescent, filled me
with, well, the same. Virile Tony
Scotti added more than a little anxious,

young-homo lust to the mix. (This
hunk doesn't appear—keep an eye
out, you freeze-framers, as the movie

progresses—to wear much under-
wear.) After an extremely brief
acting career (other than *V.O.D.*,

just one TV movie), Scotti went on
to become a successful music,
television and film producer, and

seems to have found personal
happiness with French singer
Sylvie Vartan, whom he married

in 1984. Thank you, Goddesses
of Destiny and Fate, for providing
one of the participants in this

"trash fest" with a happy ending.
It's Saturday, January 3 (Happy
New Year, Jeffery and Gillian,

may 2009 bring forth canto after
completed canto). I'm listening
(thanks to Pandora.com) to Debbie

Harry sing "Maria" ("Walkin' on
imported air"), but thinking of Dory's
"Come Saturday Morning," written for

the film *The Sterile Cuckoo*. Dory
received her third Oscar nomination
and a hit version was recorded by

The Sandpipers. It reached its peak
chart position (#17) in 1970. I was
still in high school, still traumatized

by the Tate murders, but the song
filled me with romantic dreaminess:

Come Saturday morning
I'm goin' away with my friend . . .

La la la, Oh music swims back to me

Mister Whisper's here again
Mister Whisper's here again

(DT)

As we near the end, I would like to introduce
a few words that I feel are essential to this canto:
AVARICE stands for Bernie Madoff (pronounced

MADE-OFF—as in *made off with your money*)
who my accountant Steve compared to "an arsonist
on vacation in a wooden village";

EXTRAVAGANCE stands for each auto CEO
who *took his own jet* to Washington to request
a bailout from congress (and didn't get it);

PRODIGAL stands for the banks who asked for more
money AFTER the 70 billion bailout, and the government
that gave it to them. "This disparate treatment, unappealing as it is,

appears unavoidable," said Mr. Ben S. Bernanke, the chairman
of the Federal Reserve, in a speech to the London School of Economics.
"Our economic system is critically dependent on the free flow of credit."

SPENDTHRIFT stands for all those heroes maxing out their credit
cards in order to better stimulate the economy (and take advantage
of the once-in-lifetime sales); and PRUDENCE refers to all those

carpe diem-opposing whistle-blowing commie
risk-assessing motherfuckers who get hard-ons
over new legislation requiring more regulation;

and PRUDENCE also stands for the name of Sharon
Tate's dog, named after Mia Farrow's sister, who was
immortalized in a song by the Beatles, and whose namesake

was run over by Sharon's sister, Debra, in their parents'
driveway, ten years after her murder; and FORTUNE
in this section stands for easy-come-easy-go

(GMC)

I am riding a train (again). On my
way to NYC from Philly, day before
Obama's inauguration (which I might

be feeling more excited about, more
included in, if he hadn't've asked that homo-
phobic California preacher to open the show, pour

his "blessings" all over our country). I say no
to you sir. Last week intense, sitting in my
classroom after school, hearing a very low-

flying plane (shades of 9/11); on-the-fly
news cameras, streaming live shots of the mighty
Hudson and the downed jet. All this while I

kept on, kept on, making the gym each and every
morning of the week at 5:30. Madness.
Showgirls, 84 Commercial Street, and *D.O.D.*

my anchors, my reasons to *be* as of late. (Yes,
I'm being a little melodramatic.) Outside
my window, lovely white, and tree skeletons, sleet (less

water and more flake). There are only five people inside
this car. . . . "Ah, there you are!" (It's Frank O.) "It is me,"
I whisper. "You heart haunting trains, don't you?" "I ride

for clarity. Whatcha doing?" "Typing." "Jackie
typed. You write!" "Bad Anne?" "Bad Frank." "Anyway,"
I say, "I need to finish off this canto, end the scene."

"What's left?" "Not much. Just the 'At night all cats are gray'
line." "What does that mean in layperson terms?" "I've no
idea. Look, there's a cemetery. 'In day

all tombstones are gray.'" "Bad Anne?" "Bad Jeff." "I know
you're in mid-January introspection
and all, but hadn't you better get back to the main show—

Dante led by Virgil, Tony picking up Jen,
me leading you through mid-life?" "Ouch. It's true,
isn't it? I'm *there*." "*Here,* my dear friend. And then,

you die. And when you do, I'll guide you
through this Fourth Circle into the Fifth where the Wrathful
and the Sullen wade in the muddy Styx." Frank, now through,

moves toward the front of the car, and with a dull
wave of his hand, motions me to come. "'*La nuit
tous les chats sont gris*'—I think I found a full

definition online, Frank." He stands, staring. "We
have to *go*." "But wait, my WiFi connection is strong . . .
well, one site says it's a proverb . . . but, gee,

there's no explanation of its meaning. What's wrong
with this—oh, here the phrase is a lyric in some
song from 2000. There's a play, same year as *King Kong*—

1933—titled, 'At Night All Cats Are Gray, A Comedy in One
Act.' Oy. But look at *this*. DT will love this,
a website that lists Portuguese idioms.

I wonder if he ever heard it from his
parents? It says here: 'At night, you can't distinguish
objects and people too well. It's easy to make mistakes.'

I'll have to ask him next time we talk." "I *wish*
you'd shut that thing down and come along with me!"
Frank glares—he looks serious and rushed.

The train is heading for the tunnel to New York City.
Out the window I see a polluted marsh. A waste-
land. A swamp. I click off the paused DVD of *Valley*,

join Frank at the door of the train. His face
is reflected in the glass. Soon we're on the other side,
Manhattan, Penn Station, at last upon a tower's base.

(JC)

Canto Eight

The three poets float on murky waters: Conway faces childhood demons; McCain sixty-nines her way through six degrees of Abigail Folger; Trinidad meditates on his preoccupation with fallen angels Plath and Sexton. Denise Duhamel makes her first appearance as the disembodied voice of Jennifer North's mother, and embraces all things pink.

Yesterday I got saved driving from Tempe
to Indio on my knees stop at IHOP jiffy
lube clasping hands "before, when I was on meth-

amphet . . ." holy grapefruits drained, *today I am* speaking
in tongues strawberry syrup conversion is a process
Free Indeed Needles, California search results Neeli

+ Milk Can you smell it Dykesploitation Flick
That Tender Touch/Beyond the Valley of the Dolls
Pipettes Pull Shapes Geri Halliwell *look at me* . . . Neeli

che guevara cached – similar pages And when you do
pay attention to the necklace worn by Patti Duke (Neeli
O'Hara) when she is . . . Got Milk? To Wong Foo, thanks

for bringing that tear to my eye . . . Cherkovski, Neeli, Elegy
for Bob Kaufman (First Edition) . . . De Vries, Peter. Valley
of the Dolls (one-sheet film poster) . . . Cat's Pajamas

and Witch's Milk . . . royal books/cached = please teacher
dark trap slip knot milk rose MIXed WRESTLING . . . bible
black beyond the valley of the dolls "Broken Bottles, Brass . . .

(Patty Duke in VALLEY OF THE DOLLS anyone?) Neeli
two out of five stars this movie is far less than it should have been . . .
if I had never read Bret Easton Ellis's . . ."

(GMC)

The way to the Valley is dark and dangerous;
we three must make our way across the ~~Styx~~ Hudson,
and into ~~Dis~~ Manhattan, our guides with us.

We three continue toward a tall ~~tower~~ tome,
with two small ~~flames~~ screens flickering there,
while another ~~flame~~ screen returns their signal, though

far off it is scarcely visible. On one screen up there
we can see *Valley of the Dolls* playing (an endless
loop); on the other is displayed a Google search page, where

the words *Neely + Milk* are typed, and feckless
"researchers" are poised to click. In the distance,
the third screen features a Word document where ~~depressed~~

(O.K., too strong) moody and introspective poets
type sporadically, taking turns, taking breaks. Gillian
in L.A., DT in Chicago, and JC immersed in the West

Village, where he, too, dreams of "two rooms and
a kitchenette." (First clue of impending bourgeois climb:
my apartment is too small and a dump.) Our boatman?

Check out the satanic bunny on a pole—you can find
it propped up in the corner of Neely's room: "Now you
are caught foul souls!" I turn to Frank O. "Would you mind

explaining what's up with the bunny?" Frank turns: "You
there, Hefner reject, we're just passing through this scene,
so step aside—I've got JC at my side, as I am his guide true."

"He's a truculent little thing, ain't he Frank." The bunny
hops to block my path: "Sorry, dude. No live peeps here."
"Good goddess," I lament, "Dante's rules are so funny!"

Frank: "Hilarious. Just let me do the talkin', bro. Don't fear."
I wait while the two negotiate. This stage set
feels like home—though without the fourth wall it's clear

that it's much larger than my Polly Pocket on Jones Street.
Look at this wild magazine picture pinned next to Neely's
mirror, above her dresser: tear sheet of Neely modeling streaked

wig—an enormous, intricate wiglet, with a plethora of really
generous curls, some dyed brown, some bleached lighter
(Note: I just added "wiglet" to my Word dictionary),

creating the look of a hunting trip gone wrong. This wig is mightier
than a double triple. It is all encompassing, omnipotent.
It is the *Fall* of the American Empire.

(JC)

Neely's got milk, filched (well, she does throw down
a few bills) from a neighbor, and a boyfriend-on-a-string
and an upcoming gig at the Fourth Circle, hotspot of

the chic elite and springboard for mega-fame. But it's not
enough. She looks around her suddenly-too-small single
(utilities included) apartment. It was big enough this

morning when she left for rehearsal, when she belted out
her sure-hit number in *a Helen Lawson musical*. Who knew
her hopeful little world would fall apart, a great flood

of tears cascading down her milk-white cheeks. Who
knew that cataclysm masked all her dreams-come-true:
give a little more? are you kidding me? from now on I'm gonna

take take take. Now nothing but disgust for such cheap digs:
bare light bulb, loaf of white bread (empty calories) on
fridge, bottles of five-and-ten cologne on thrift store chest

of drawers, panties hanging on knob, nylons hanging on
strand of packing string below wrinkled window-shades,
garage sale painting of reclining nude (with whip?), and yes

creepy bunny-head-on-a-stick (souvenir from a photo shoot,
no doubt) leaning against dismal wallpaper. The dark,
flopping wings of Neely's ambition bird can be heard offscreen.

The bird wants a multitude of spare rooms and a kitchen
out of *Good Housekeeping*, full of pink appliances and sparkling
linoleum. She wants a maid to follow her about with a Dirt

Devil sucking up her candy bar wrappers, her cigarette butts,
her nose-pickings and dandruff. She wants to drive up to
Grauman's Chinese in a limousine and come out wearing a fur

coat. She wants the audience's love to rise up and wash over
her like a tsunami. *She wants, I want.* My guide says this
listlessly, having little energy after hovering about the AWP

conference that took place here in Chicago last week. "There's
no good reason," she says, "for that many poets to be together
at the same time." She lights a cig and sips her cocoa, *that warm*

brown mama. "Wouldn't it be good enough to just . . . No, I suppose
not. I wanted fame, to be the one poet at the top of the steeple,
and for a while I was. In Boston, in the mid-seventies, I packed

them in. When I read at Harvard, Sanders Theatre *was filled to*
the rafters: every seat, every aisle was crammed; some people were sitting
in the windowframes, and others were stationed on the fire escapes.

Elizabeth Bishop, at that time, could barely fill a waiting room.
Now the tables have turned; they always do. Now a million poets
are dancing on the head of that proverbial steeple." I ask her

what she thinks, if anything, of flarf. "You mean the avant-garde
poetry movement of the late 20th and the early 21st centuries, whose
first practitioners espoused an aesthetic dedicated to the exploration

of 'the inappropriate' in all its guises, and who mined the Internet
with odd search terms then distilled the results into often hilarious
and sometimes disturbing poems, plays, and other texts?" "I see

you have access to Wikipedia where you are." "Obviously another
postmodern evasive tactic, an intellectual smokescreen, a way to avoid
confessing anything personal, or putting one's life on the line, or just

stating something simply, clearly, and directly. . . ." Anne slowly pulls
down Neely's wrinkled window-shades, fades out like an old movie.
She is gone, but belongs to me like memorabilia from that movie—

a poster and a few lobby cards. I click on the Safari icon, check
both my email accounts (Yahoo and Columbia College), then go
to Google and type in *got milk + patty duke + anne sexton*. And get:

The Post-Depressionist Almanac

Anne Sexton. John Keats. Kitty Dukakis. Kristy McNichols.
Lary Flynt . . . How he walked to party, **got** drunk, and told
everybody he wanted to walk to work with . . . **Milk** was once

the Queen of happy foods but is now a dangerous drug . . . Jr.,
Kitty Dukakis, **Patty Duke**, Thomas Eagleton, Margot Early,
Robert Evans, . . . Silver teapot, silver tongs for cubes of sugar,

milk in a silver jug . . . Some tiny shards **got** into takkies. Thought
we'd picked up every millionth piece . . . **Anne Sexton** Time is but
the stream I go a-fishing in . . . I think my real depressions started

when I was about 16 and doing The **Patty Duke** Show . . . It's **got**
terrific visual style and it's fun communicating with her, even if
I barely understand a single . . . Don't drink **milk**, avoid rain, and

wait for news updates . . . Rhoda Penmark (played brilliantly by
Patty McCormack, . . . Sent us out with **milk** cans, pea tins, jam-
pots. Where briars scratched and wet grass . . . (g) I look at you

and instantly know our friendship has **got** to stop . . . Is it because
I hurt **Patty**? Who cares? Oh no, I did something, The belt! No!
Not the belt! . . . Anne Sexton (The Complete Poems) Henry David

Thoreau . . . Alec Baldwin, Meg Ryan, Kathy Bates, Ned Beatty,
Patty Duke, Sydney Walker . . . PRICE OF **MILK**, THE, 3419,
2000, DRAMA, A New Zealand couple living on a small dairy

farm . . . they also forgot edgar allen poe's death and also I think
patty hearst was . . . EVery tongue **got** to confess . . . I'm either
hearing tones of Linda Ronstadt or **Anne** Murray, I can't tell which . . .

A phone rings, saving me from this exercise in futility. Saving Jennifer,
too, from her apparently-as-pointless nightly breast-flexing. She strides
across the room. "Hello . . . Yes, I'll accept the call . . . Hello, Mother . . ."

(DT)

Denise Speaks:

You can't even hear my voice, can you? Besides,
my "daughter" didn't hold the pause long enough
for you to believe I'm on the other end, chiding

her for her top-heaviness. OK, I'm gruff,
but what if I really do need that oil burner fixed?
I'm just another bitter hag against the fluff

of Hollywood Cinderellas.
Transfixed,
I watch my mother and aunts trade their "dolls"
at the kitchen table. My cousin mixes

ginger ale and whiskey, making highballs.
I'm six, singing *When did I get, where did I,*
why am I lost as a lamb? Pall Malls

languish in the beanbag ashtray. Why
does the fractured syntax of this song
obsess me so? *What's in the back of the sky?*

My mother was addicted right along
to Valium.
I'll wire you first thing
in the morning, Jennifer says, her lifelong

ambition to be free from her clinging
family. I open the special edition
DVD, in all its plastic glory, an evening

not even a week after my transition
from wife to divorcée. The psychic
told me to embrace everything pink, permission

to amuse myself. The first of two disks
is secured on a nub that reminds me of
a 45 RPM "record insert" that clicked

into the middle of a single. "Love
and labels," said another Jennifer
when asked about why she came to New York. Above

her loomed sage Sarah Jessica Parker,
trying to right the wrongs of all the catty
older heroines before her. Caring mentor,

self-aware. The kind poor Patty
Duke could have used. But *Sex and the City*
(the movie) was unbearable—a ratty

plot promoting consumerism. Glitzy,
shallow problems against the backdrop of a real
Fannie Mae collapse, useless finance committees.

Remember when Charlotte gave Carrie
her engagement ring (HBO, season four)
to pawn so she could close the deal

and buy her apartment? Now that's hardcore
friendship. The hag here, Bunny MacDougal
(Charlotte's mother-in-law), has flaws galore:

she's judgmental, racist, wealthy but frugal
when it comes to compliments. Jennifer's
mother may be demanding, a numbskull,

but why didn't she get more time to suffer
on screen? Didn't anyone but me
want to see where those big tits came from? I defer

now to the stars of this poem: David, Jeffery,
Gillian and their three otherworldly guides.
Mother will call again, though she never made the marquee.

(DD)

* * *

Denise, as a cinematic tool I think that—as in Polanski's
Rosemary's Baby—it's more powerful NOT to show the true
face of the monster . . . And, in all probability, doesn't one project

the image of Doris Tate as the woman on the other end
of the phone anyhow? The unfortunate-looking matron
who appears to be happy for her daughter to sacrifice her

parental-instilled Christian values as long as it means brushing
up against the stars? Sharon, I apologize. I just think there's
a lot more to your relationship with Doris than meets the eye.

(Sharon disagrees vehemently, but we all know
that there is no such thing as a geographical
cure when it comes to denial . . .)

David, I did not know that one of the techniques we've been using periodically
in *Descent* has a name, let alone is a literary movement . . . but then again FLARF—
to me—sounds like the name of a paramilitary organization

just as one could easily assume that OULIPO is a classified
intelligence program . . . all I know is that once, when I Googled
"language of evasion," the top search result was for an essay

by Jordan Davis, and since Jordan is the first person I ever heard
use the word 'blog' then it all seems to me, well, magnetic, that I
thought *I* was the inventor of the page 69 exercise when in fact

it was fellow Canadian Marshall McLuhan who first suggested
that instead of judging a book by its cover, judge it by the content
of its page 69 instead, which is somewhat different than my experiment

which is more like a literary I-Ching, or a DIY version of Brian
Eno's "oblique strategy" cards which brings me to the Florence
Feathers blogspot, who after having read about the McLuhan

experiment, even though "it seemed pointless, picked up
Please Kill Me by Legs McNeil and Gillian McCain, turned
to page 69, and this is what I read . . .

*Iggy Pop: When we started recording, Nico and John Cale used to sit in the booth looking
like they were in the Addams family—Cale was wearing a Dracula cape with a great big
collar on it. He looked like Z-Man in* Beyond the Valley of the Dolls *and he had this
funny haircut. And Nico was knitting. Throughout that whole album, she sat there
knitting something, maybe a sweater.*

My father was in *Beyond the Valley of the Dolls*. What a random
coincidence." I tend to disagree, Ms. Feathers. Google *beyond
the valley of the dolls + mcluhan + feathers* and you get . . .

Rushdie Fury part one 8 his earliest dolls, the little characters
he had made, when younger, . . . but the chemical assistance
makes you think it's a feather. no, . . . to beat their demons

without entering the valley of the dolls. so when she felt low,
. . . to prove beyond all doubt that their love was stronger than
fury by . . . **valley of capsules** tvc 13 - a fear of feathers.

This is the full 7th episode of which the four main parts
. . . luna dogosto – from mario bava's five dolls for an august
moon; . . . never poem for the other; marshall mcluhan – the medium

is the message (pt. . . . **MOVING** rocks & feathers because you're going
where it's empty listen the black earth . . . the communist manifesto,
marshal mcluhan, hemingway's stories & a . . . to the movies beyond

the valley of the dolls. ed gets up, goes back . . . **Comparative
Literature and Culture** Bond and Beyond: The Political Career
of a Popular Hero. . . . Dressing in Feathers: The Construction

of the Indian in American Popular . . . McLuhan, Marshall.
The Gutenberg Galaxy: The Making of Typographical Man . . .
Who and What's What, From Aerobics and Bubble Gum

to Valley of the Dolls and Moon Unit Zappa. . . . **The Sixties:
Videotapes in the Media Resources Center, UC Berkeley**
McLuhan On McLuhanism: discusses his theories of mass . . . War

Protests in the San Francisco Bay Area & Beyond . . . ugliness of Iggy
Pop and the campy amateurism of the New York Dolls. . . . **Silicon
Valley Watcher—reporting on the business and culture of** . . . With SOA,

corporations can move beyond real-time processing of business data . . .
CSS makes visible Marshall McLuhan's famous and confusing insight:
"The . . . Did you catch the Dresden Dolls at Bimbo's? If not . . . they're

performing . . . and costumes - this is a party not to be missed
(Unless you fear feathers . . . **Sergio Leone and the Infield Fly Rule:
MR. SHOOP'S SURFIN' SUMMER** . . . Beyond the Valley of the Dolls

13) Salo: The 120 Days of Sodom-- yes or no? . . . Horse Feathers,
Monkey Business, and Animal Crackers. . . . I think I've used this
before, but Marshall McLuhan in *Annie Hall* is pretty much as good as . . .

List of notable brain tumor patients: Facts, Discussion Forum and . . .
Herbert Marshall McLuhan CC was a Canadian educator, philosopher
and scholar . . . victims' rights movement, mother of murder victim Sharon Tate . . .

(GMC)

It is the Fall of the American Empire.
Sharon's mother on the other end
of the line, desperate to keep the fire

on Susan Atkins's feet. An amends,
she, will never accept from this murderer:
"Sharon never got a chance to defend

herself in court. And I've been forever
serving a sentence in prison with no
chance of parole." Ms. Atkins can remember

back to her late teens, in San Francisco,
working as a topless dancer, hired to be a
blood-sucking vampire for a stage show—

that's when she met Church of Satan founder, a
crazy named Anton Szandor LaVey. (Frank O.,
still waiting for a "pass," for the demons to say

it's O.K. for me to enter Lower Hell, to go
to a place where the living aren't allowed,
whispers: "JC, didn't DT tell us a while ago

that sacrificial Sharon Tate played
in *The Fearless Vampire Killers*? Weird.") Running
in such circles, in no time Susan Atkins was led

to Manson, and soon they were embarking
on a summer road trip in a converted school bus
painted completely black (with the rest of his growing

"family.") Later, they settled at the infamous
Spahn Ranch, where Atkins gave birth to a son
on October 7, 1968. Conviction for the senseless

murders terminated her parental rights: her son
(then 1½), was adopted and renamed
"Paul." (Somewhere, this unknowing Atkins son

lives without a clue—just like the adopted
Christopher Crawford [I]—the first male baby Joan
obtained, who had to be returned after she'd cared

for him for over a year; he was taken
away by his biological mother, who wanted
him back. Joan and Phillip Terry [her then-

husband] were both utterly devastated.
The birth mother ended up selling Christopher
sometime later to another couple for $250. Undeterred,

Joan adopted Christopher Crawford [II] a year
later.) My guide hails a metaphorical cab;
we ride a few blocks away, arrive at Jennifer

North's apartment. We stand *sans* blab,
watching Sharon Tate speak into the prop
phone. At last Frank whispers, "Who would stab

a girl like that? Never mind one about to drop
a baby. Sick, sick, sick. Incidentally," he
continues, "isn't it telling that one of the top

assholes to head the U.S. Securities
and Exchange Commission under Bush
is named Paul Atkins. I believe in such foundries

of coincidence." Director Mark Robson turns: "Shush!
We're rolling!" Frank and I move back a few feet to
whisper in peace. "There must've been an ambush

of America's psyche after the Manson case," I offer. "You
were already dead, Frank. But when I was in first
grade, an evil gang of kids took over (this was '72

I guess) my class. Our teacher, Miss Borden, was the *worst*
human being, totally allowed these psychos to hold us kids
hostages for weeks. The leader of the 'family' (Mike) had a thirst

for terrorizing. He attracted this scary girl (Mary) with red eyelids
who became his 'wife.' They 'lived' in the coatroom and coerced
some of the boys to be their followers. They made barricades

in front of the coatroom entrance—no one traversed
the divide, except their followers. Mary drew frightful
pictures on the wall with paint, sang songs and conversed

in a made-up language that supposedly only Mike full-
well understood. Their reign of terror climaxed in an hour-
long rebellion that was nothing short of a full-

on trashing of the room: they threw paint, over-
turned desks, ripped up books, screamed and howled
like, well, Manson maniacs! They had complete power

over Miss Borden, who just stood there watching, held
the rest of us back from the insanity with her thin arms—we
all huddled in one corner, helpless. The thing that's dwelled

in my mind all these years is the word that Mary
scrawled with red paint across the cabinets, that word,
a zeitgeist, she'd somehow gleaned—the misspelled: 'pigy.'"

I turn and look at Frank; he stares at me visibly altered.
"JC, how come you've never mentioned this before? It's
horrifying!" "I don't know. Funny, but I've never uttered

a word of this story before." "Not even to your shrink? It's
worth mentioning." Jennifer, I mean Sharon, delivers her
line, "Let 'em droop." The director yells, "That's

a wrap." Frank and I, emotionally drained, return to our
awaiting cab. Frank barks at the driver, "Jones Street."
"I'm tired," I say. "It'd be nice to nap for about an hour."

(JC)

Exercises for Shapely Breasts

Exercise 1:

a. Lie on your tummy with the elbows bent, and fingertips facing inwards. Rest your forehead on the floor.
b. Slowly raise your head and body, pushing down with hands, arching your spine and bending the neck backwards.
c. Pull in your stomach muscles and lift your stomach off the floor.
d. Slowly lower upper back and shoulders to floor to the original position. Relax.
e. Repeat.

Exercise 2:

a. Hold your arms straight in front of you, at shoulder level.
b. Bring your hands slowly towards your shoulders, clenching your hands as though you are pulling something strenuously.
c. Repeat 5 times.

What Can Exercise Do for Your Breasts?

Breasts contain no muscle, only fat cells, milk-ducts, and glands, held together in a web of soft connective tissue. So by exercising you cannot increase your bust size. Neither will exercising directly reduce a heavy bust. This is especially true if your breasts are large but your body weight is what it should be. If, however, you are overweight, a weight-reducing diet combined with regular exercises will help you to reduce your weight as well as your bust size.

Exercising has several other advantages. It tones up the muscles on which the breast tissue lies. So, if your bust-line measures less than what you would like, exercising will give you a firmer and a more prominent line, making your bust appear larger. Conversely, if a heavy bust is your problem, you would lose some of the droop (which can spoil your shape) and gain a firmer contour, though there would be no loss of inches.

Apart from the exercises which we have already mentioned, swimming is a superb exercise for bust shape. It exercises the "breast muscles" considerably via resistance to the water. This really can do wonders to your shape.

The décor of Jennifer's room is meant to convey the shabbiness
of boardinghouse transience—easy to put up with when you're
a shapely chorus girl on the go—a temporary, almost comforting

air of squalor. A room replete with thrift (Gran's beloved, much-
used sewing machine, clearly ready to stitch its last seam) and
with secondhandedness: mauve-skirted stool at makeshift vanity,

Gauguin-esque tropical scenes (palm-dotted island, native girl
bearing fruit) in cheap frames, stainless steel percolator, ceramic
Siamese cat, portable TV set on wobbly wheels, squat black tele-

phone ringing with shrill insistence, frequently pawned mink
draped on headless dressmaker's dummy. (Mention of Uncle Ira,
a sweetie no doubt, brings to mind Rod Steiger's performance,

three years earlier than Sharon's, as Sol Nazerman, tormented
Holocaust survivor, in *The Pawnbroker*: which is worse, the in-
humanity of concentration camps or the brutality of New York

City ghetto streets?) The room is also another example of the
"it feels like it's translated from another language" art direction
mentioned earlier: a sixties version of a forties showgirl's shoddy

lodgings. The script called for a "small, modern apartment"
(which this is not) and for Jennifer, at the beginning of the scene,
to be "creaming her face" (not firming her breasts) and listening

to Tony singing ("Come Live with Me," presumably, on an off-
screen phonograph). After she says good-bye to her mother and
hangs up ("defeated"), the script has her sigh, dutifully start her

breast exercises, but then rebel: "To hell with it—let 'em droop."
In the movie she flicks off the overhead light, crosses the room—
past the drab green Naugahyde armchair with pink sweater tossed

on it—and slips into her twin bed. End of scene. Per the script:
"She . . . stares wide-eyed at the ceiling. She tosses, sits up again.
She reaches over to the night table, swallows a sleeping pill. She

pulls the covers up to her chin, takes a deep breath, closes her eyes.
Tony's voice starts over scene again. She smiles softly." In the film
we can see the bottle of pills, next to a tray with a drinking glass and

a blue Fiestaware pitcher. I, for one, would like to have seen her
pop that pill. This is, after all, a story about addiction. Time these
dolls downed some dolls. Next to the pitcher: a red hardcover book.

What could Jen be reading? *Sonnets from the Portuguese* is my guess.

(DT)

"Hey, Sharon? What book was Abigail Folger reading that night
she waved at Susan Atkins from her bed?" Sharon looked pensive.

"Hmmm . . . probably something political," she replied. "Or sociological.
Abigail volunteered in Watts, and campaigned for Tom Bradley, an African-
American councilman running for Mayor of Los Angeles. But who knows,

Gibby read voraciously. In fact, if it hadn't been for literature she probably
never would have made an entrée into our sad story. . . . Bet you can't guess
how. . . ." I knew, but pretended I didn't. Feigned ignorance. A trick I learned

in the oral history trade. I wanted to hear it coming from Sharon's voice, not
Bugliosi's brain. "Well, after she graduated from Harvard, with a Master's
in Art History, she worked briefly at the university art museum in Berkeley

before returning back East, where she was hired by Andreas Brown to work
at the Gotham Book Mart, a New York literary institution with mimeo crowd
street cred whose well-heeled clientele included such luminaries as Truman

Capote and Tennessee Williams. It was there that Abigail ran into her old
acquaintance Mary Emma Weir, the widow of steel magnate Ernest T. Weir,
who was then amicably divorced from Polish novelist Jerzy Kosinski, and it was

he who later introduced her to his friend Voytek Frykowski, a Polish expatriate,
who, having helped Roman (financially) with some of his early films, was eager
to move to the City of Angels to become a screenwriter—and from the day they

met until both of their deaths Abigail was Voytek's gravy train so to speak.
It's not that he didn't love her—it's just that Voytek was a *boy*—a boy
with an ex-wife and a son back in Poland—a boy who thought he could conquer

Hollywood without being fluent in English, a boy who believed smuggling
MDMA in from Canada was a no-brainer. Not dumb, just *naive*. And here's
Gibby, who could have spent her days shopping at Jax and lunching at the Daisy,

but who chose instead to devote all of her energy—and most of her money—to
helping the downtrodden and fighting for political change, but is known almost
exclusively as the 'heiress to the Folger Coffee Fortune'—though no one

mentions that by that time Folgers had already been sold to Procter &
Gamble, and that whereas Abigail died leaving an estate of 200,000 dollars,
fellow murder victim Rosemary LaBianca left one worth two million, an

impressive sum for a former-waitress-turned-small-business-owner whose
clothing boutique was located in a strip mall owned by her husband, which
brings us to another oddity in this odd case—Leno LaBianca owed 30,000

dollars—possibly to the mob—for gambling debts. Now I know that some
couples choose to keep their finances separate, but my god, if it came down to
Roman getting his goddamn finger chopped off—perhaps I'd reevaluate . . ."

In front of Anne's face there is a display
and it's not exhibitionist it is shiny it is
part of an interchange & stalemate

i.e. he is not a cheapskate & when she reverts
to littlegirldom like any Judith or Meredith
who may have considered becoming a stewardess

youthful aspirations that sometimes included a prosecutor
and a translator but never a process server or an exterminator;
now window-shopping on Madison Avenue with her "beau"

who is never driverless or umbrellaless & even though
the future of pork looks somewhat bleak
here he is dashing his new "girl" off to the Village Gate

after a steak and salad on Beekman Place, there are no
trivial considerations when it comes to this "eligible"
who is sending his driver home as we speak

this is a man without a negligible bone
in his constitutional makeup, a face
that Anne looks up to/into/projects onto

it is perhaps an era that lends itself
to propositions veiled by innuendo
consideration paid to the variety of clasps

observed with poise & attention
to detail and is this why the price tags
always face down? I do mean to insinuate

that Anne is lavish *au contraire*, she brown-bags
it to work, though she would not be caught
dead ring shopping on 47th Street *if you'd been brought*

up by nitwits hung up on frugality, she is merely
lingering in front of a window "when there
is so much downright forgery" oh what difference

does it make that this is only their second date
it takes a great deal of worldly wisdom to castrate
your past & become a suitable catch "a lot is buried

under that smile" it's nearly universal that most men
consider prudishness despicable & yet our Anne manages
to convey that it only makes the future that much more magical

when a man can change directions
as long as it doesn't end them up
in Lawrenceville please take into

consideration Anne's pride, her need
to create diversion in order to get attention,
in laymen's terms, plain old pigheadedness

                    (GMC)

I remember watching *Valley of the Dolls*
in Toronto, in 1995, on
VHS, dazzled by all the wonderful falls,

pancakes, fake lashes. DT and I had gone
up there for a *Plush* reading—a book
of our selected poems edited by our friend Lynn

Crosbie and her bf Michael Holmes. The trip took
a lot out of us, as I recall, but the home
viewing of *V.O.D.* at a friend of Lynn's place took

us out of ourselves for a couple of hours. Some
of us sat on the floor in the darkened living room
(I did, anyway). I remember this scene as a fun

moment—Lynn pointed out that as soon
as Anne and Lyon are shot walking down
the sidewalk, Anne's head looks like a giant bloom,

a disembodied pod of sorts that "floats" down
the street in tandem with Barbara Parkins's body.
(In retrospect, and by no means in an attempt to frown

upon Lynn's acumen, I think the distortion was mostly
caused by the age of the video tape,
and a less-than-modern TV, which probably

couldn't crank out the kind of contrast for shapes
to appear sharply.) It's funny the things you
remember and the things you don't about a

film. (Or a friendship.) Anne to Lyon: "You
like women, don't you." She is concerned his desire
for her is not as pure as the strand of pearls. "Are you woo-

ing me?" she asks without irony. Lyon (hoping to raise her ire,
or maybe just wanting to go all Socratic
on her ass): "If you *wish* to be wooed." The fire

rises to her cheeks (fourteen years has been good for critics
[voyeurs?]—the DVD and my backlit Mac screen reveal all).
Methinks Miss Welles *will* be wooed ("Dybbuk! Dybbuk!"):

    Anne's "wooery" (a partial list):
    Frette pillows, bed sheets and towels;
    Bulgari watch; Louis Vuitton duffle bag;

    Prada suitcase; Rolex watch; Nakamichi
    home sound system; laptop computer (2);
    digital camera; PalmPilot; iTouch; iPod (2);

    cell phone; Prada shearling coat; Prada belt (2);
    Prada wallet; Louis Vuitton wallet; Gucci watch (2);
    La Prairie skin care products; cash (acres and acres of it)

                                 (JC)

JC and GMcC, I've been keeping notes
during this canto, as each of you have
taken your turns, thinking I would write

a dazzling patch, a grand finale of sorts,
in which I would answer, or at least address
your various images and statements.

But all I have is this paltry list:

    p. 69
    Doris Tate
    Wait Until Dark
    Kosinski quote
    Folger book
    trip to Toronto
    literary terrorism

                    Thought
I'd do a run-through, touch on each, but
now think I'll let it stand, maybe return

to it later, in another canto or cantos.
Instead I slide my *Valley* DVD into my
computer and rewatch the third and final

scene (they've all been somewhat paltry,
don't you think?) of Canto Eight: Anne
and Lyon's rain-slick romantic walk. They

window-shop and talk, of goosebumps
and mink, pink pearls and white lilacs,
wooing and wishes of being wooed.

Miss Everything and Mr. Nothing—
perfect match for the Dance of Death,
minuet of advances and retreats, the

ache of what she can't have and what
he can't give keeping them perpetually
in step. Goose-step, I think, as they

view the mannequins in bikinis, replacing
them, in my imagination, with Plath's
Munich effigies: *Naked and bald in their furs,*

Orange lollies on silver sticks. A woman,
nude under her mink coat, slipping into
a hotel lobby in the middle of the night,

to fuck her Nazi lover. That image supplied
by my guide who, not to be upstaged by her
dead friend, reminds me she is no stranger to

department store dummies: *Am I approximately
an I. Magnin transplant?* Anne S. interchangeable
with Anne W.: *I have hair, black angel, / black-angel-*

*stuffing to comb, / nylon legs, luminous arms /
and some advertised clothes.* Impervious to
the cold, our ice princess admires diamonds

in a store window. "Oh no," instructs Lyon,
"jewelry's not for you. But maybe . . . one
single strand of pearls, but not creamy, pink,

to match your skin." His pronouncement
reminds me of Holly Golightly's speech
about Tiffany's: "Not that I give a hoot about

jewelry. Diamonds, yes. But it's tacky to
wear diamonds before you're forty; and
even that's risky. They only look right on

the really old girls. Maria Ouspenskaya.
Wrinkles and bones, white hair and
diamonds: I can't wait." *Valley of the Dolls*

and *Breakfast at Tiffany's*: my primal texts.
Anne Sexton and Sylvia Plath: my primal
poetesses. (I'm not anti-feminist, I just like

all those s's.) Will I ever outgrow their
influence? They loom and inform, color
my perceptions. And when I can connect

the dots, as in this passage from Sylvia's
journal,

"Truman Capote this weekend: a baby-boy, must be in his middle thirties. Big head, as of a prematurely delivered baby, an embryo, big white forehead, little drawstring mouth, shock of blond hair, mincy skippy fairy body in black jacket, velvet or corduroy, couldn't tell from where we sat. Ted & men hated the homosexual part of him with more than usual fury. Something else: jealousy at his success? If he weren't successful there would be nothing to anger at. I was very amused, very moved, only Holiday Golightly left me more chilly than when I read her."

       I get excited. Think it's interesting
to imagine Plath and Capote in the same room.

And that she wrote about Capote on a Tuesday
morning, December 16, 1958, a few days after
hearing him read; she doesn't specify where

the reading was held. I assumed at Harvard
(Plath and Hughes lived in Boston at this time)
the previous Friday or Saturday night. Online

I just learned that Capote read at Harvard's
Sanders Theatre (where nearly twenty years
later Anne Sexton would pack them in) on

Sunday, December 14. The week before,
a piece called "Cocktails With Truman Capote"
ran in *The Harvard Crimson* (on December 9);

the reporter, John D. Leonard, interviewed him
in the Ritz-Carlton Bar, which he described as
"a sprawling, antiseptic, and canapéd cocktail

lounge, staffed by *maître d's* and cluttered with
bowls of peanuts." I think it's interesting that
only two months later, February 1959, Plath

would start auditing Robert Lowell's workshop
at Boston University, after which she'd go,
famously, with Anne Sexton and George

Starbuck to the Ritz-Carlton Bar and drink
martinis and talk about suicide. I think
it's interesting that in Sexton's memoir of

her friendship with Plath, "The Bar Fly
Ought to Sing," she says they ate free
potato chips with their drinks, not peanuts.

I think it's interesting to ponder whether Anne
is misremembering this detail (I'm inclined
to believe Leonard on this point, since he wrote

his article immediately after the experience) or if
the Ritz offered both peanuts and potato chips
to their boozy clientele. At any rate, I think it's

interesting that one can place Capote, Sexton,
and Plath in such close proximity. Interesting
that on December 17, bitching in her journal

about an argument with Ted, Sylvia says she'd
wanted to change seats at the Capote reading:
"It would have been better looking-at Capote

to change seats." Plath was such a keen observer
of details, I can understand her feeling thwarted.
It's why she was unable to say, in her description

of Capote, whether his jacket was velvet or
corduroy. She wanted to know. Just as I want
to know whether the Ritz served free peanuts or

potato chips. Welcome to my rabbit hole. "Deke,"
says Barbara Parkins, of her fraternity pin, and
the laughable word and her even more laughable

enunciation of it snaps me back, in time for
the dissolve to Anne's hotel room. To dreamy
theme song, she dreamily raises the window

and in diaphanous curtain billow, contemplates
her lack of self-knowledge, her oozy desire to be
fucked by a Nazi lover—one who looks, preferably,

like Liam Neeson in *Shining Through*. (Why, I've
always thought, would Melanie Griffith choose
Michael Douglas over *him*.) It's what, Sylvia tells

us, every woman adores. Anne's sheer nightie ripples
her breasts in the wintry breeze as, all goosebumply,
she breathes in the whole of her future before her.

(DT)

Canto Nine

*A New Haven theater. Gorgon's big number under huge, revolving, Calder-esque "tree."
Bloody sacrifice of aspiring versifiers. A malladroit [sic] Manson messenger. The flight of
Anne's blue towel. Conway and the Queen of Gay Poetry supply McCain with prompts to
help her overcome that "feeling of dread" and finish this year-long (yawn) canto.*

"HELEN LAWSON OPENING NEW HAVEN
IN 'HIT THE SKY'" is the *Variety*
headline. Frank O. and I sit next to the blonde-bun

woman, a few rows behind Anne and Lyon. We
are here to witness this out-of-town opening
of Miss Lawson's newest. What could be

more thrilling? I'm a little worried—the thing
is, Frank's been squirmy since we entered the theater,
has been surveying the hall, mumbling

something about three Furies. The orchestra
starts with a riveting number, lights pop—
an enormous Alexander Calder

mobile dangles onstage, and we sit in shock
as Helen Lawson belts out, in Merman-esque
style, a razzle-dazzle anthem of schlock,

a song of personal autonomy, best
performed in the psychedelic shadows
of the whirling Calderian mobile. Lighting effects

give the whole ensemble a wild "wow-
factor," the aesthetic charge of disco
illumination *avant la lettre*. Lawson is now

the tree trunk, and the Calder thing is *so*
the leaves and branches. "I'll plant my own tree,
and I'll make it grow." Consider "Poem

to Alexander Calder and Louisa" by Henri
Pichette (1954): "My ancestor, the mobile
said, is the Tree Moved by the Wind." We

are witnessing the transition from Calder's artful
aesthetic movement (under the influence of
Jean Arp, Joan Miró, Yves Tanguy, etc.) to the fitful

threshold of '60s psychedelia, the drama of
Helen Lawson's Broadway ancestry butting
heads with the *au courant* world of

our soon-to-be Gillian "It Girl," unknowing
Anne Welles. Lyon comments about Helen:
"Offstage I hate her, but onstage," he says whispering,

"I'm madly in love with her." Seemingly perplexed, Anne
puts her eyes back on the star, studies her,
tries to piece together Lyon's admiration.

She recalls meeting Lyon for the first time; they concurred
that Helen Lawson was despicable. "For every Helen Lawson
there's always a Helen Hayes or a Mary Martin," he'd said to her

in Mr. Bellamy's office. "Frank," I say, getting his attention
(he's still *very* distracted), "Lyon's remark
reminds me of that line in *Showgirls* when

the powers-that-be at the Stardust Hotel embark
on trying to replace Cristal Connors in the show *Goddess*
and mention Janet Jackson and Paula Abdul." "This stark

comparison will probably undo me, but I'll ask
anyway," says Frank, "so give it to me: *why*
does Lyon's comment remind you of *Showgirls*?" "It unmasks

the narrative of the film, rendering it fictional. We rely
on things being as they are in both films, but suddenly,
when Lyon mentions Helen Hayes and Mary Martin (high-

profile stage stars), and the *Goddess* producers seriously
float the names of pop stars Jackson and Abdul, we, the viewers,
are jarred: these references upset the film, imposing mighty

extradiegetics signified, which, as I mentioned, forces
each of these film narratives to surrender their heretofore
'realities.'" "I think," says Frank after a restless

pause, "you are still suffering jet-laggage from your
return trip from Madrid." "Maybe," I concede, "but
I'm well enough to report that I couldn't find my most adored

films on DVD in Spain (I wanted to get
real Spanish versions of *V.O.D.* and *Showgirls*). In one store,
when Wally asked for me, the guy said, 'No. And what

a pity,' in perfect English!" "Shsss!" a sore
theatergoer hisses at Frank and me. In deference
to Saint Helen (who's about to blow), we end our rancor,

turn our eyes back to the stage, to the semblance
of star and molecule-looking danglies (think
Monsanto's Adventure Thru Inner Space

ride at Disneyland: humans shrink
to a size smaller than an atom; water crystals
become giant, and hydrogen atoms slink

about, hanging from the ceiling, panels
as large as the red and blue ones swirling
around Helen's head onstage). And we, mere mortals,

are in turn seduced by the magic of Miss Lawson, swooning,
madly in love,
watch the old battle-axe confidently crooning.

(JC)

There's a monster singing onstage right now.
And I think, once again, of A.C.R. (Plath journal code
for Adrienne Rich), or more specifically, what she says

in one of her later books: *this life of continuing is for
the sane mad / and the bravest monsters.* The fire-breathing
virago axing talented comers from her show. The new

faces of 2009, fresh from graduate school (M.F.A. =

My Future Assured
Many Furtive Ambitions
Mean Ferocious Angry),

waiting for an in. Or rushing the stage door, asking her
to sign her latest book of poems, feeble though it is,

secretly thinking: Admit it, you Broadway beldame,
your time, your relevance, has long passed. My name
is Neely and I can sing roses around your pathetic mobile

of a tree—*constructed of broken traffic-lights!* "That's what
you think!" roars Helen. The severed head of the upstart
rolls across the stage, eyes and mouth wide open, leaving

a smear of bright red blood, which Helen straddles as she
continues to belt out her number. (In the early nineties,
when I was poetry editor of *OutWeek* magazine, I kept

getting submissions from someone I'd met in graduate
school, the "mediocre homo" mentioned in Canto Three.
And kept rejecting him. At one point he wrote a letter

of protest, in which he referred to me as "the queen of gay
poetry." The editors pressured me to respond, in print,
and I've always regretted what I wrote. My comeback,

as I remember it, was defensive; I also took a cheap shot
at "the poor quality of his work." Since he'd dubbed me
the Queen, all I should have said was *Off with her head!*)

"This is my tree," warbles Helen. "I planted it in hard soil
and watered it, day in and day out, with blood from the backs
I stabbed on my own climb to the top." *Whack!* Another lopped

noggin rolls toward Lyon and Anne. *Valley of the Dolls* meets
Mel Gibson's *Apocalypto:* Once in the theater, some of the M.F.A.s
are designated for sacrifice. Slathered in blue body paint,

they are led down the side aisle, where, along the wall, they
see murals depicting blue-painted figures with their chests
cut open. They become part of a long line of captives that

files up the proscenium steps and ends center stage. One
by one, the mobile revolving above them like an enormous
color wheel, they are splayed (by gay chorus boys) across an

altar, and their hearts ripped out by Helen Lawson. They
are then decapitated and their headless bodies flung into
the orchestra pit to the cheers of well-dressed theatergoers.

I love her poems on the page, but in person she's a monster.

(DT)

My father used to come here
when he was at Yale
I'm an Oxford man myself

Sherry, please, warming hands
in front of fire
It seems the two of us are

like Henry Higgins/Eliza
Doolittle, we are
alone in the world, *you know*

that, I've known it for a long
time, Anne Welles looks out
into the distance, dreaming

wrapped in cobalt terrycloth
Lights off (!) thick towel
dribbles to feet, silhouette of

actress Barbara Parkins
to *Movie World*:
"Men make me sick, the way

they make such a to-do
about sex. I spend
hours getting ready

for a date, combing my hair,
and then all he wants
to do is muss me up!"

As for make-up, Ms. Parkins
approves, as long as
it's done "tastefully."

"But if a man I'm going
with doesn't like it
then you can be sure I take

it off—or at least make him
think I have," she adds
with a maddening smile.

        (GMC)

Helen's out-of-town New Haven opening,
as well as Anne and Lyon's cozy
fireside snuggle, recall the *Footsteps on the Ceiling*

out-of-town debut in *All About Eve*,
and also the insalubrious tête-à-tête
in a semi-seedy hotel room—Eve

hoisted on her own petard, her bet
that she can pull the wool over her peers'
eyes (that she can trick Addison DeWitt!)

utterly lost. Both *A.A.E.* and *V.O.D.* veer
toward New Haven and the Ivy League to
weave a thread (albeit a sheer

one) connecting the post-war march of the arts to-
ward academia. Hear me out: constant self-
assessment is a basic, ru-

dimentary aspect of M.F.A. programs; a stringent self-
reflection ("reflexive modernity")
in artists' workshops mirrors the health

of this practice in our larger culture. The key
requirement of the Title II G.I. Bill of 1944
(which provided forty-

eight months of tuition for
veterans who enrolled in colleges and universities)
was that tuition be used only for

study in certificate or degree
programs, which is why creative
writing courses grew into degree-

granting programs. (We live
in a country today that has 153 creative writing
programs—in 1975, there were fifteen.)

"Jeffery, what in hell are you going
on about? Makes no sense, and your terza
rima is a mess." "Frank, I'm trying

to show how the institutionalization of
the arts blossomed in the latter
half of the last century, and to make a

point about how Jackie had her
finger on the pulse of America.
She touches on this matter

ever so subtly with this little visit of
Anne and Lyon's to Yale's ivy-clad
club." "Methinks, you're kinda

losin' it, bud." "Well, I'm not mad
with you. Hey, do you know what's up with sherry—
was it in vogue in the '60s? Some kind of fad?"

"How in hell should I know about sherry?
I drank the hard stuff. Meanwhile, even if I grant you
the Jackie/Yale connection, it doesn't seem very

related to *All About Eve*, the preview
of *Footsteps on the Ceiling*." "Frank, do I
have to spell *everything* out?" "Yes, you do."

"O.K., remember Margo Channing's line, 'I wish I
could have gone to Radcliffe, too, but father
wouldn't hear of it: he needed help behind

the notions counter'?" "Jeffery, you're
completely whacked. Besides, *I* went to Harvard
on the G.I. Bill, and *you* have an M.F.A., so we're

by-products of the same, whatever you'd
said before—institutionalization of the
arts." "Yeah Frank, I wish *I* could have gone to

Harvard, but father wouldn't hear of it: he needed help in the
plastics factory." "You're obtuse and impossible today!
Let's get back to the scene, to Anne and her fellah."

(JC)

But before we do . . . can I just say I never noticed, until
I rewatched Helen's number yesterday on my computer,
what's happening in the wings: the director (played by

Robert Viharo; did you know that after *Valley* he had
a long and illustrious [it's still going on, actually] career
in television, appearing in such shows as *The High Chaparral*,

The Mod Squad, Gunsmoke, Ironside, Kojak, S.W.A.T., Quincy M.E.,
Starsky and Hutch, Baretta, CHiPs, etc., and that from 1972 to 1980
he was married to actress/model Anne Helm, who also had

a long and illustrious [until 1986] career in television, appearing
in such shows as *Sea Hunt, Hawaiian Eye, Gunslinger, Perry Mason,
Rawhide, Alfred Hitchcock Presents, Route 66, Dr. Kildare, Wagon Train,*

Burke's [and I don't mean Lyon or Paul] *Law, The Fugitive, Gunsmoke*
[seven years before Robert], *Daniel Boone, The Big Valley, Bonanza,
Adam-12* [with Martin Milner, our very own Mel Anderson, two

years after *Valley*], *The Name of the Game, Hawaii Five-O, The F.B.I.,
The Virginian, Medical Center, General Hospital, The Streets of San
Francisco, Barnaby Jones,* and *Hart to Hart,* but whose real claim

to fame was her appearance in the 1962 Elvis Presley film *Follow
That Dream,* during the filming of which she began a relationship
with The King and visited his home at Graceland after shooting

finished, and that while married to Robert she gave birth to
actress/model Serena Viharo, who has appeared in such TV
shows as *Lifestories, Days of Our Lives,* and *Acapulco H.E.A.T.*)

transfixed by the star (I think we're to believe, based on this
and a suggestive exchange just before the wig scene, that he
and the "old battle-axe" are in love), chorus boys (with pink

and purple feathers in straw boaters, and festive striped shirts)
and girls (in silver headbands and colorful fringed flapper dresses)
in varying degrees of veneration (from *What a star!* to *She's a fucking*

*hideous three-faced fire-breathing newborn-eating monster but when
she belts out a show tune my heart just melts* to *Oh my gosh I can't
believe I'm going on next* [take a look at the blonde standing

behind the director, wringing her hands in anticipation of her
upcoming number—based on the costumes, either the Charleston,
the Shimmy, the Bunny Hug, or the Black Bottom]). Director,

backstage dancers, Anne and Lyon and the whole New Haven
audience, the original sixties audience who sat in darkened
theaters across the land munching popcorn and slurping cokes,

and countless contemporary queens who plop the DVD into
their laptops or desktops or PCs or Macs or Sony or Philips
DVD players connected to flat screen or plasma or HDTVs—

all transfixed by this riveting number? "Not so. Not so."
Anne and I have magically appeared (like Hiro and Ando;
all I have to do is put my hand on her shoulder and she

transports us through time and space; can you tell I recently
watched season three of *Heroes*?) in the wings, as two
of the dancers. "Susan cannot walk an inch," she says, "in

that dress originally designed for the concentration-camp-thin
former MGM goddess of song—you can hear Judy sing 'I'll
Plant My Own Tree' on YouTube, she recorded it before she

was fired from this film—have you guys said that yet?—and
though her voice is all but fried to hell, her version has a raw
edge, a knock-your-socks-off showstopping punch that puts

this candy-coated nonsense Hayward is lip-syncing to shame."
Songwriter Dory Previn: "Judy did endless takes. The final tape
had eighteen splices. All the mistakes were cut out, the breaks

in the voice erased. The track had been altered to appear straight,
but the uneven sound only emphasized the confusion so carefully
edited. There were too many splices in too short a song." Anne:

"Still, everyone would truly be transfixed if Garland was onstage,
mesmerized by the train wreck of her booze-and-dope-sated decline.
My death the same. Susan cannot move a finger without touching

one of God's huge blue plastic teardrops." Anne shakes the fringe
on her flapper dress (red, of course). I fiddle with the pink feather
in my boater. "I planted my own tree," she adds, "a laurel, and lived

in it with wooden legs and O my green green hands." The lights
dim as Helen's ovation winds down; the dancers rush from the wings,
freeze in place onstage. "Your feather's fine, Trinidad. It's showtime!"

(DT)

When you don't know where to start—grasp at straws. Find a new font.
Agent Orange, Ajax Surreal Freak, Alien Mushroom, Betty Noir, Burger
Doodle, Karma Suture, Know Your Product, Little Lord Font Leroy, Soot

Break, Mudshake, or Vulgar Display of Power . . . okay I'm getting warmed
up grab notebook and copy random sentence fragments before the little man
on my shoulder orders me to stop: "overexposed only happens to films,

not people," "petri dish for viral mutations," "it's a pity the world hasn't caught
up with inflatable people," "admonished by authorities we never met in person"
"teeth trouble (okay, loss)," "suburban housewives hovering in battle mode

what have you done to our sons," "Pauline Kael as exterminator (you as cord
cutter)" "full bodied, pear overtones," "they resent being defanged, claws
getting clipped," "drugs didn't ruin my career, basketball did," "a look that is

particularly ludicrous in daylight," "I was too guilty to be mirandized,"
"if you say he's your uncle they're not going to ask for DNA" okay I'm
rocking now go make a cup of English breakfast, switch to Soot Break

for a change of visual pace, now I have no idea why it took me five weeks to sit
down and work on this why the dread . . . the *dread*! The guilt I experienced for
not writing as I watched my *Criminal Intent*s . . . but now, suddenly, the world is

my petri dish! P.S. Above quotes courtesy of Danny Fields, Jim Carroll,
the *New York Times*, and the menu on the Acela . . . (not necessarily in that order).
I recall the email from Mr. Trinidad re: how lucky I am time-wise—the death

of Susan Atkins, the 40th anniversary of the Tate-LaBianca murders, the arrest
of Roman Polanski, the release of Squeaky Fromme—but that in fact was
the *problem*—the perfect opportunity dropped into my lap and I can't manage

to rise to the occasion (sounds very Neely, no?) Instead, I am going to turn
to my informant, John Aes-Nihil, of Littlerock, California. From an email dated
October 13, 2009: "Onto the Sadie fiasco. Legs had everything arranged

we thought. I drove up there and that town is real Hell hole [sic] and extremely
[sic] hot and humid. Went to the prison and since I didnt have a physical press
pass couldnt get in. This turned into having to go back into town since it was

way too hot to stand around out there and had this series of calls between me,
Legs, the guy with HarperCollins and the prison. The prison was faxed a press
card. Now its right before the hearing starts and the prison says you cant get in

period. So I said can you tell me who's taping it and they said I think it was NBC
in Fresno so since that was on the way back I went there. I told them I was with
HarperCollins and couldn't get in on a technicality etc and could I get a copy off

there [sic] tape. The woman said she would call me back which she did and said
No. Then she said that it was being sent to CNN so I told Legs all this. Anyway
I definatly [sic] need an actual press pass or card. Bruce [Davis] was supposed to

have a hearing September 3rd and I can't find any info at all. Patricia
[Krenwinkel's] is in December. That's at Frontera which is the easiest prison to
deal with. On to Roman [Polanski]—I've got about 60 minutes of reports off

TV but missed Debra [Tate] on the *Today Show* but got what she said from
another show. It was certainly Out There, don't know if you heard it. 'There's a
difference between Rape and *Rape* and Roman's a Great guy, and what Roman

and the young lady had was totally Consensual [sic].' Reading between the lines
she's saying *Hey I did it with him when I was 16 and I'm still here so big deal*
Debra is a real nut. In one of the recent documentaries she said No one [sic]

wants to do a documentary on me, no one lets me tell My Story, they just
misquote and distort things. She has also said things that no one ever said
before. She went on and on about the Manson Family Partying at the Tate house

many times. Those people used, the pool, they used the bathroom, many
many times she said. Matthew [the supposed son of Manson] gave me his
number and I'm going to interview him since he threw out that he knows

that Roman had more to do with the murders than Charlie did. Of course
if he were to be extradidted [sic] to L.A. he would end up in the Special Needs
section of Corcoran with Charlie and Phil Spector! Will send more news soon."

(GMC)

So much going on: monsters singing onstage;
Roman Polanski vying for release
in Switzerland; elder artists full of rage;

three collaborators, each with a piece
of the puzzle in his/her head; and now me,
sitting in the Quiet Car again—peace

so hard to come by these days. I see
this typed at bottom of page (a note by/to me?):
"episode 38 of peyton place we

have a pill reference." (For months DT
and I have been watching the first two
seasons/DVDs of *Peyton Place* [the sixties TV

show starring Ms. Parkins and a few
other hot young stars of the day—peach
Mia Farrow and hunk Ryan O'Neal too];

DT is writing a haiku for each
episode, and me, well, I'm just plain old
addicted to this rather slow-moving niche

drama. I think dolls may have a hold
on one of the characters or something—
I really can't remember, truth be told,

at the moment.) It's difficult watching
this short "sexy" scene of *V.O.D.*
(Anne and Lyon finally doing

it). White-washed, vanilla, and flouncy
are adjectives that come to mind. Jackie's book
was way more graphic than this goofy

film, and isn't it weird that *another* book
was the progenitor of Jackie's *Valley*—
Grace Metalious's 1956 book

Peyton Place, the story of three lonely
and repressed women living in a small
New England town. Why are movies

(and their television show spin-offs) all
so watered down? (Barbara Parkins is
Betty in the *Peyton Place* TV show *and* fall-

wearing Anne in *Valley*; she's a real wiz
at the female trilogy thing.) Texts are just,
I don't know, better at sayin' it like it is.

Get the humor? Here's some Jackie wis-
dom from her novel, *Valley of the Dolls*:

"She clung to him. She didn't care about the hurt or discomfort—just to belong to
this wonderful man was the greatest happiness she could ever know. When the
pain came, she clenched her teeth and made no sound. And when she felt his body
go tense, she felt only surprise that he had drawn away from her. But he had
groaned in satisfaction. . . ."

Dear collaborators, I thought you might
get a kick out of this, an event
at the Poetry Project, Monday night,

January 25, 2010:

**Ruthless 24/7 Careerism: How You
Can Become the Most Important
Poet in America "Overnight":**
*The poet is a social animal above all else: the
poet's art comes second to the types of important
connections the poet can make, not just with readers
and an audience, but with editors, curators and
people in positions of institutional power. The poet
owes it to the art and to him- or herself to look out
for #1 at all times. This talk will focus on the kinds
of important community-building that are at the heart of
all things poetic. People can be manipulated much
like a line of poetry, and a poet must have complete
control of those around them. Jim Behrle will
discuss the kinds of behavior that can help a poet
stand out amid the babbling rabble. Poetry can be
the loneliest journey: we'll discuss how to feel the
warmest bosoms of constant embrace.*

For the sake of poetry, for the sake
of us, I hope to goddess this is a joke;
like a luscious wig, let's pray this is fake.

(JC)

My dear, dear collaborators, I have no idea why it took me
almost three full months to sit down and work on this . . .
dread, certainly, there's always that, but mostly just busy

with teaching and other projects. Now that spring has
come to Chicago (or will, officially, in two days, March 20,
2010), my tree has begun to sprout big rotating translucent

buds. Anne, too, sits at her window noting *her* leaves: "born
in their own green blood / like the hands of mermaids." My
leaves, conversely, are born of the assembly line—purple, red,

yellow, blue—and glow like the pegs in a Lite-Brite (electric
toy introduced by Hasbro in 1967—year of our film, year in
which many artificial seeds were planted—that allows lit

pictures to be created). They grow into gigantic tiddlywinks
and orbit overhead. Come fall, they'll pale to pastel Frisbees
that'll detach, sail in air. The other Anne surrenders her Deke

pin, removes her bra (we see a bit of tit from the side—her big
nude scene?), wraps herself in a blue towel, which she lets fall
to the floor before she and Lyon kiss and *do it* in silhouette.

So tame, as JC points out, in comparison to the sex scene in
the book: Anne's great deflowering. Pages 122-127. I once
read those pages at a reading of erotic literature at Beyond

Baroque in the mid-eighties. My pop contribution got tons
of laughs: Jackie's prose is as purple as some of my unfurling
leaves: "She didn't care about the hurt or discomfort—just

to belong to this wonderful man was the greatest happiness
she could ever know." I'm tempted to quote more (for laughs);
wiser, perhaps, to take a machete to the lurid plant. Since

erasure poetry, like flarf, is all the rage in Poetryland,
and since I'll try anything once (Erasure poetry is made
by erasing words from an existing text in prose or verse

and arranging the new text into lines and/or stanzas),
here's page 126 (actual penetration) as an erasure poem:

    being a virgin
    standing naked in the bathroom
    should be sacred

    inexperienced
    fresh tears of humiliation
    he swept her up

    overcome
    placed her gently on the bed
    try to be gentle

    the pain came
    clenched her teeth
    he had groaned in satisfaction

    her happiness doubled
    height of his passion
    moist with perspiration

    ultimate in fulfillment
    to please a man you loved
    important and powerful

Purple, indeed. It doesn't feel like I've erased anything!

    virgin
    naked
    sacred

    inexperienced
    fresh tears
    swept her

overcome
on the bed
be gentle

the pain
clenched
groaned

her happiness
his passion
perspiration

fulfillment
please a man
important

I will hack my way through this purple wilderness alone . . .

(DT)

--- On Tue, 5/18/10, Gillian McCain <GMcFries@aol.com> wrote:

From: Gillian McCain <GMcFries@aol.com>
Subject: from gillian
To: "Jeffery Conway" <jefferyconway@gmail.com>, "David Trinidad"
<trinidad1@ameritech.net>
Date: Tuesday, May 18, 2010, 3:05 PM

i am stuck and depressed and have that feeling of dread whenever i sit to
write.
can you guys throw me an assignment or two? or advice i can put into action?
i feel like i'm failing and it sucks...
love you both
gillian

Prompt for Gillian:

1. Finish Canto Nine, focusing on Anne and Lyon *doing it* in New Haven hotel room

2. Do not use flarf technique or Soot Break (whatever that is)

3. Use the following nine words in your patch: dismayed, queen, flee, Camaro,
bitchin', fickle, button, size, bullshit

4. Address Sylvia Plath's mother (Medusa)

5. Relax and have fun!

"I once had the illusion I could write"
(so says Lyon as he prepares to bullshit Anne)
A good time for an Oxford man to flee

because this is one *fickle* bitch. Barbara Parkins
comments on this scene: "Love is *truly* happening.
Do kids get wooed today? They kind of get right to it,

hey baby. Hmmm Cat Stevens . . . kiss me again."
But would she date him as his current incarnation,
Yusuf Islam? No Camaros, or Allah, for this Size Queen.

"I love this little moment": pre towel dropping to floor
(no awkward buttons), feast for the eyes before lights out,
silhouette. No current cause for dismay . . . that will come

later, when Lyon's statement "I once had the illusion
I could write" proves him wrong. Assignment accomplished,
splice to new poem: Sharon appears, looks at me penetratingly.

"Gillian, I get the feeling you're in over your head." I'm surprised
to feel tears suddenly well up. "I don't know anything about mythology,"
I blurt, "or the classics or the history of cinema.

I feel like I'd need a Ph.D. to keep up with these guys," I exclaim.
Sharon strokes my hair, and then begins unsnarling the vertical clumps
gently with her fingernails. "I haven't bathed in a week," I moan,

"and my psoriasis is out of remission and I can't believe
it's July and I'm still getting chapped lips." Sharon cups my chin
in her hand and gives my face a good hard look. She daintily

picks off a flap of dead lip skin caked in two-day-old MAC Glam.
Flicking it on the floor she speaks to me sternly. "You have lips
that are rapid defoliators. Nothing some walnut scrub, a washcloth

and some Magic Tape won't cure." She continues to examine my face.
"You're staring at my scar," I cry, despising the whine I hear
in my own voice. "It kind of blends into your lower laugh line,"

she states matter-of-factly. "Did you get in a fight with a sharp object
or something?" And thus I begin to recount my story: the three-pronged
carbuncle that took four months to heal; the trip to the doctor

who said simply, "Hmmm, what do we have here?" before opening
a textbook called *Diseases of the Skin* to show me pictures of numerous
other monstrous facial deformities that also came from within.

"We could lance it," he said, "but not only would that be incredibly painful,
it would leave one helluva pockmark. Not that you're not going to have
a very deep scar anyway, but I think it would be better to just let nature

take its course." Sharon's eyes grow wide. "Jesus," she says, running
her index finger along the two-inch indentation. "Good thing you're a writer.
For me that would have been a career-breaker." She leans back, folding her arms

behind her head and gives me a serious look. "It gives you *character*,"
she announces, smiling, reminding me of my two sisters, who given the
circumstance would have said exactly the same thing. "Besides, it's just a *scar*.

You have great bone structure and a beautiful smile.
As my mother always said, 'Pretty is as pretty does.
And if you do nasty things all the prettiness will go out of you.'"

I think back to Ted Casablanca's slightly mocking question
to Ms. Parkins. "Were you reluctant to exercise your power
as the lead?" You can hear the bitterness in Barbara's retort.

"And what? Say something like 'I could use a little more direction,
or wear a little less beige'?" *Pretty is as pretty does.*
Didn't Ted know that she had a mother's mouth to feed?

(GMC)

Canto Ten

Conway, McCain, and Trinidad try to keep up with Neely's "frenzied self-improvement program" by adhering to their "new lines must be written within two weeks" rule. The second Deadly Sin of Neelyism is thus inaugurated, and continues to flourish in both PoBiz and the "career" of Patty Duke.

Patty Duke's fingers crawling toward a shrill-
sounding alarm clock on bedside table
(7:30? You call that early?). Will

we all agree, she isn't even able
to make her *fingers* act in this film (odd,
since she played Helen Keller in *The Miracle*

Worker for at least two years on Broad-
way, and then again for the 1962 movie).
[Anne Bancroft (stern, in dark specs): "It's *waa-*

ter, Helen!"] Duke sits up in bed: "This is Neely's
'Career Montage' sequence. You three might want to
use Wikipedia and insert this basic, rather mealy

definition of montage in filmmaking right into
this kooky mock-epic collaborative
you've been writing for what seems like way too

many years. No? Well, I'd be happy to give:

> **Montage** is a technique in film editing in which a
> series of short shots are edited into a sequence to
> condense space, time, and information. It is usually
> used to suggest the passage of time, rather than to
> create symbolic meaning as it does in Soviet
> montage theory.

You dig, kids? So don't try to read fancy-
ass ideas into every shot. Yeah, I live

a lot of life in just a minute or so, jazzy
music propelling me forward. Pop out
of bed, spit water in shower, gaze into blurry

make-up mirror, apply lipstick and pout
(repeat). Walk in Edith Bunker-esque coat
across back lot (read: NYC street). Express doubt

to spineless boyfriend while exercising bloat:
'Mel, you call this acting?' All this is how I
power my climb." "Jeffery." "Yes, Frank?" "Not to gloat

(as I'm offering a rather astute observation), but why
don't you mention the slight 'Category E' element
at work here?" "I'm listening." "Isn't it i-

ronic that Duke is posing a self-referential comment:
'Mel, you call this acting?'—one the critics will be
all too happy to echo in reviews sent

off to every paper in the country?
Actually, Patty, we call it *bad* acting."
"I see your point, Frank. What else do you have for me?"

"Well, I hate to be the one reminding
you of this, but you did set up an expectation
for the reader way back in Canto Three by pondering

the first of the Seven Deadly Sins—your explanation
of Helen Lawsonism." "Crap! I forgot
about that bit of business." "What about a continuation

of that trope at this juncture—you could say a lot
about the next Deadly Sin, 'Neelyism.' This career
montage depicts Neely's tremendous pot

of ambition." "Good guide, I'm glad you're here.
I've been a little out of sorts, what with my
trip to Chicago to see DT, my dear

friend, for a *D.O.D.* summit; with my
visit to Michigan with Walls, where we
stopped in a supposedly Gay town (my

'gay sightings' count peaked at about nineteen [me
and Wally included]), and spent time in East
Lansing with friends Karl and Lloyd, who couldn't be

any nicer—they took us to Cranbrook, a place northwest
of downtown Detroit. We went to tour the Saarinen
house. (Afterwards, I realized that Elizabeth

Berkley had attended the elite private school located in
the same place. It's called Cranbrook Kingswood. I have a
picture of it on my phone.) And then

we flew here to Pelican Lake in Minnesota."
"Jeffery." "Yeah, Frank?" "Yawnsville." "Well, just fillin'
ya in." "Let's make montage, cut to next shot, *sans* any coda."

(JC)

It's August 9th, 2010, forty-one years later.
I'm sick of this murder stuff but the timing
is too uncanny to ignore. "Gillian," says Sharon,

"Really, there's been so many accounts I'm over
it. Although it *is* ironic that what happened that night
has only been told from the point of view of the murderers.

But *my* point of view is for another day." Yawn. "Just montage
it—the canned story that has been told over and over ad nauseam.
Roman was never a fan of that cinematic device but this Jeffery

character seems to be setting up an assignment, so at least
start it, then you can ditch this popsicle stand and go
back to that damn Nellie Oleson autobiography."

Spahn Ranch, Chatsworth, California. Night
time. Get in car. *Leave something witchy.*
Drive through canyon. Park car.

Cut telephone wires. Walk up hill.
Enter house. Wake up man asleep on couch.
I'm the devil and I'm here to do the devil's work. Girl

walks down hall, woman in bedroom waves. "Gillian,"
Sharon interrupts, "can we please take a break? I haven't
even made my entrance yet and already I'm bored fucking

stiff." She throws on a paisley pea coat, flips her blonde hair out
from underneath the fur collar and grabs her keys. "C'mon, let's go
to Jax, buy some new dresses, then have lunch at The Daisy."

Sharon takes a compact out of her purse, removes lower
lash mascara residue with the swipe of a pinkie.
"And it won't cost us a dime," she says

mischievously, as she looks up from
her mirror and grins. "Jack
Hansen *adores* me."

      (GMC)

My alarm went off at 8:00 a.m.
I intended to get up and write, yet here it is four and a half hours later.
Time lost on the cutting room floor.

I have to write today, as my lines are due by August 31st.
We have a new rule.
JC and I came up with it when he was here for our *D.O.D.* summit.

Once it's our turn, we (me, JC, Gillian) have to write our lines within two weeks.
Gillian sent her new lines on August 17th, so I have until August 31st to write mine.
Today is Sunday, August 29th.

Neely's wind-up alarm clock is ticking.
I guess this new pace is perfect for her Career Montage.
No more lollygagging—nearly a year for one canto!

"A FAST AND FURIOUS PICTORIAL": that's what the *V.O.D.* script calls for.
An alarm jangles imperatively offscene.
Camera pulls back as she sits bolt upright, grabs the alarm, turns it off, jumps out of bed.

Trouble is, I'm exhausted by Neely's frenzied self-improvement program.
So desperate to get in shape for her breakout nightclub act.
Being a certain age, and feeling several lifetimes away from such industrious career
    striving, I want to tell Neely to slow down.

Like Mel, cautioning from the sidelines.
Take it easy, girl, you'll get where you're supposed to go.
Oh, why does *everyone* want to be famous?

I remember how appalled I was when I heard Madonna (I think it was in *Truth or
    Dare*) say, "Who doesn't want to be famous?"
Meaning everyone on the planet wants what she has.
And will rise at 7:30 every morning, lift weights, do cartwheels, and jump up and
    down on a trampoline to get it.

Neely wants, I want.
My guide, too, has finally gotten out of bed.
Her wind-up alarm clock had an electric seizure at 2:00 p.m. (3:00 p.m. Boston time).

Voice raspier than usual.
She was up till all hours smoking cigarettes, fussing with her immortality box,
    grappling with her ambition bird.
I address her plaintively.

"Dear Guide, who at the height of her popularity understood the folly of fame,
    wouldn't it be good enough to just drink cocoa?"
David, David, David.
Anne is in her study, leaning back in her chair, feet propped against the wall like in
    that early photo by Rollie McKenna.

First of all, a truly good cup of cocoa, with a generous glob of real *whipped cream, would
    cost you far too many Weight Watchers points; you wouldn't be happy.*
Better to stick with those Skinny Cows.
*Second, yes, I did understand the folly of fame, the freak show known as contemporary
    American poetry, but I never achieved sufficient distance, while alive, to free myself
    from it.*

*It would have helped if I'd believed in God, had had some sort of spiritual belief system, but
    that was karma specific to that particular lifetime, and that particular generation.*
It was an existential era.
It made more sense not *to believe, having come through the nightmare of World War II,
    having witnessed that particular set of horrors.*

Sylvia really made the most of that, didn't she—she of the Nazi trope.
When I transitioned, on November 4, 1974, I rose nude from my mother's fur coat, from
*   the idling car, from the gas oven garage; rose above the Greater Boston area, mouth*
*   open in gratitude, wide as a milk cup (here I paraphrase one of my best poems), and*
*   arrived at the edge of paradise, which was gauzy as a old ballroom gown.*
Thus I moored my rowboat at the dock of the island called God.

Sylvia was there to greet me, and my Nana, and many others, all my pretty ones, and I
*   very quickly let go of the limitations of that incarnation—famous promiscuous pill-*
*   and-alcohol-addicted suburban housewife Confessional poet.*
And then I knew.
Believe me, God is not some poker-playing graybeard.

Think more along the lines of boundless energy, light, totally impersonal.
(We get to do with it as we like.)
Third, you, David, more than just about anyone, should understand the pressure I was
*   under.*

It may look like I simply wanted to produce, produce, produce.
But it was really the need to experience, as often as possible, the miracle of the poem.
Poems, real poems, despite the proclamations of the intelligentsia, are miracles.

Poets no longer believe in the miracle.
That's karma specific to your particular lifetime, my dear boy, and you have my sympathy.
No more resources, inside or out.

They're all used up.
But you still believe.
"Every poem is a miracle of faith."

I was floating over your shoulder, invisible between strata of light, when you wrote that
*   down yesterday.*
And the nonsense shall pass . . . it always does.
All part and parcel of the business of words.

Lastly, surely you can empathize with those on the rise.
It wasn't that long ago that you were concerned about "making it."
How many years did you fret about productivity, only to see, later in life, concrete evidence
*   that you have written* enough.

And there were periods of not writing, weren't there (remember how depressed you were in
    New York), or not writing much.
But over the long haul, those fallow times don't show.
James Schuyler (who says hello, and wants you to know it's a pink ball gown*) once told*
    you to relax, he was confident you'd be prolific.

But you had trouble believing it for yourself.
How do you tell a young poet to relax?
Writing poetry is hardly a laid-back endeavor!

Then I laugh, my wise ghost-guide laughs, the Unbelief laughs.
Even fame-driven Neely laughs as she exercises herself in two.
And I knew that she knew that I knew.

(DT)

Neely practices musical scales with
fat lady (Mel and pianist look on);
Neely does cartwheel, falls on her frisk-

y fanny, then walks back across lot, don-
ning same dumb matronly coat, rubbing
her rear end, scowling. She kisses Mel on

lips, glances back at record falling
onto player. Close-up of black-and-white
wedding photo; sound of chiming

bells. Shot of the three couples—might
be the only time in film they are all
pictured together: Mel and Neely (white-

clad, of course, and wearing long fall),
Jen and Tony, Anne and Lyon. Cut to
Neely in gray sweat suit (bright red wall

behind) jumping on trampoline. Cut to
a tap dancing double, in ruby slippers,
clicking toe to heel atop table (if you

study the shadow, you'll see that hers
has no ponytail attached to head); when she
jumps to floor—it's Neely, who prefers

to wear *a long ponytail*, tied with chic
silk scarf. Gay dance instructor pops a doll—
offers one to Neely, and it's (as the meek-

ish Mel admonishes from sidelines) the FALL
of N   E   E   L   Y . . . she downs her first
(white) D   O   L   L. (Cantos ago, I decided

to break free of terza rima—which I have faithfully
adhered to from the get-go—at this precise moment.
Good-bye three-line stanzas using chain rhyme

in the pattern of A-B-A, B-C-B, C-D-C, D-E-D,
whose first known use is in Dante's *Divina Commedia*
and may have been intended to suggest the Holy Trinity.

In *D.O.D.* it suggests three gals on the climb.)
Neelyism explodes. Example A:
"Since I am soon off for yet another year of a prestigious fellowship,

I thought it necessary, only thinking of you of course, to let you know
that my second book of poetry is coming out this month, to GREAT acclaim
I may say, and I know you'll want to find out WHERE you can buy it

(see plethora of links below) and just WHERE you can attend the numerous
readings designed especially around my talent (see the other panoply
of links even further below). Oh, and of course you'll need the link

to my blog, to the blog I'm guest blogging for, and also to the various
blogs and magazines and journals in which my poems will be appearing in
the months ahead. And another thing, I ALMOST forgot—

one of my former students, a minion, a protégée, a FAN, has WON
a contest for a darling little chapbook (written entirely under my tutelage)
and you'll want to BUY it, ATTEND the reading, etc., etc., so

here are the links, AWARDS, dates, bios, BLURBS, reviews,
CONNECTIONS, Twitter, grants, blogs,
ACADEMIC DEGREES, Facebook, writers' websites. . . ."

[Email deleted.]
Pop a metaphorical doll.
Breathe. *You never were, never wanted to be, a careerist, a climber.*

My guide, Frank O., says this matter-of-factly. He sits above
my desk, like Endora hanging out above it all, listening in
to one of Sam and Darrin's living room chats.

In fact, Frank continues, *you wrote a whole damn book about the folly
of ambition and awards—that* Phoebe 2002 *thingy. You know the score,
so why do you still get so upset, so defeated over this issue?*

Me: "I don't know."
I never cared about all that shit—I just wrote, and loved art and wonderful men.
Me: "I know."

*What in hell are you doing living in Philadelphia anyway? I had such a time
finding you.*
Me: "I don't know."

*You're such a mess today! Oh—
the moon is in Cancer!*
Me: "I know."

You're inconsolable. This might cheer you up:
"The 15 Most Overrated Contemporary American Writers"
(from *The Huffington Post*, August 7, 2010):

"Are the writers receiving the major awards and official recognition really the
    best writers today? Or are they overrated mediocrities with little claim to
recognition by posterity? The question is harder than ever to answer today . . .
because we no longer have major critics with wide reach who take vocal stands.

There are no Malcolm Cowleys, Edmund Wilsons, and Alfred Kazins to separate
    the gold from the sand. Since the onset of poststructuralist theory, humanist
    critics have been put to pasture.

The academy is ruled by 'theorists' who consider their work superior to the
  literature they deconstruct, and moreover they have no interest in
  contemporary literature.
As for the reviewing establishment, it is no more than the blurbing arm for
  conglomerate publishing, offering unanalytical 'reviews' announcing that the
  emperor *is* wearing clothes. . . .

The ascent of creative writing programs means that few with critical ability have
  any incentive to rock the boat—awards and jobs may be held back in
  retaliation.
The writing programs embody a philosophy of neutered multiculturalism/
  political correctness; as long as writers play by the rules (no threatening
  history or politics), there's no incentive to call them out. . . .
The M.F.A. writing system, with its mechanisms of circulating popularity and
  fashionableness, leans heavily on the easily imitable.

Cloying writers like Denis Johnson, Amy Hempel, Lydia Davis, Aimee Bender,
  and Charles D'Ambrosio are held up as models of good writing, because
  they're easy enough to copy. And copied they are, in tens of thousands of
  stories manufactured in workshops.
Others hide behind a smokescreen of unreadable inimitability—Marilynne
  Robinson, for example—to maintain a necessary barrier between the masses
  and the overlords.
Since grants, awards, and residencies are controlled by the same inbreeding
  group, it's difficult to see how the designated heavies can be displaced.

As for conglomerate publishing, the decision-makers wouldn't know great
  literature if it hit them in the face.
Their new alliance with the M.F.A. writing system is bringing at least a minimum
  of readership for mediocre books, and they're happy with that.
And the mainstream reviewing establishment (which is crumbling by the
  minute) validates their choices with fatuous accolades, recruiting mediocre
  writers to blurb (review) them.

If we don't understand bad writing, we can't understand good writing.
Bad writing is characterized by obfuscation, showboating, narcissism, lack of a
  moral core, and style over substance.
Good writing is exactly the opposite. Bad writing draws attention to the writer
  himself. These writers have betrayed the legacy of modernism, not to mention
  postmodernism. They are uneasy with mortality.

On the great issues of the day they are silent. . . .
They *desire* to be politically irrelevant, and they have succeeded. . . .
We can dismiss the early Pulitzer winners by claiming that a bunch of old white
    men probably decided back then.

But the people deciding today are motivated by similar (though intensified)
    institutional compulsions.
Awards are no substitute for critical judgment. It's also not true that only
    posterity can separate the good from the bad. In the 1920s, perceptive critics
    were aware of the difference.
Readers know when a much-heralded book doesn't satisfy them. They know
    something is missing. But there's the institutional apparatus telling them,
    You're a fool if you don't appreciate this book. . . ."   —by Anis Shivani

[Overrated writers on his list include: John Ashbery, Mary Oliver,
Helen Vendler, Sharon Olds, Jorie Graham, Junot Díaz,
Louise Glück, and Billy Collins.]

Me: "I know. I read it already—DT called my attention to it."
*Don't you think Shivani makes some valid points? Doesn't he help you see things as
    they are?*
Me: "Yeah, I guess. I would've liked it better if the writer's own bio wasn't rife

with 'Pushcart Special Mention'; 'Longlisted for the Frank O'Connor short story
award'; 'listed by Rigoberto González of the National Book Critics Circle as the
best small press book of 2009.' Ya know what I mean?"

*I see . . . that's why you have that Robinson Jeffers poem "Let Them Alone" typed up
and pinned to the wall in front of you: "If God has been good enough to give you a poet /
Then listen to him. But for God's sake let him alone until he is dead; no prizes, no
    ceremony, /*

*They kill the man. A poet is one who listens /
To nature and his own heart. . . ."*
Me: "Amen."

        (JC)

"It's all well and good," declares Sharon, "about your push-card prizes
But while you three are sitting around on your asses 'writing' all day
Neely and I are in training for a race against our god-given sizes

And it's not just 'those five pounds' that makes 'the suits' queasy, a sashay
With just one extra pound is like attaching two servings of ground sirloin
Onto your 'trouble spots' that no girdle, cream or pill (see below) can melt away"

A moment on the lips, a year on the hips was what my mother used to say
"Well, least your mother was slim, Gillian, so it was not quite so unnerving
To watch her eat a sliver of something, or a small serving, or push her plate away

With my mother the contradictions were never-ending
She talked the talk but didn't walk the walk, her fingers always straying
Toward the smorgasbord of sweets that she was constantly tending

Brownies, gingersnaps, seven layer anything, daily baking
To satisfy my father's 'wooden leg' and of course my younger sisters
Who hadn't yet hit puberty, so they hadn't experienced the berating

That came from having taken after our mother, who would whisper
To the Col. *Such a gorgeous face but she's **got** to gain control of her figure
If she wants to start auditioning we'd be horrible to tease her*

*By encouraging those dreams that visualize a future
Of film sets and leading men and mansions in the canyons
Success takes sacrifice, is that not what we have taught her?*

*How could I have known that Sharon's conception
Would force my thyroid into retirement, and create a ravenous
Hunger that made it impossible to resist the temptation*

*Of consuming an entire pan of fudge, but so what I was talentless
My husband was attractive, but always away on assignment
So I put all my hopes and dreams into this thing in my abdomen*

*Which once born, felt like she was bought on consignment
People looked at me strangely, like she MUST be adopted
Which inspired a depression that sucked my serotonin*

For even though her birth had been hell, I had spawned an angel
Who demanded all of my time, and a wide variety of jobs, I adapted
To all the cleaning, cooing, cooking and colic, trying not to strangle

This miracle, this blessing from God that wasn't made of chocolate
The Col. made no comment, but glared at my hair that was always tangled
And the sixty extra pounds that didn't just "fall off" despite the fat

Dissolving promises (see below) that all the magazines suggested
My body grew more and more stubborn, prayers, pills; all a bunch of crap
Until even my preacher agreed perhaps it was time to start a diet

I began with grapefruit and coffee, then experimented with concoctions
Like lemon juice in chicken broth topped with cayenne, I don't suggest you try it
And how was I to know that this extreme dieting would spark off a combustion

Triggering a sluggish metabolism that had always cursed the Willet
Side of the family   Now I'm obese, and I barely eat, and forgive my assumption
*That you're dumb enough to believe these ads, but **please**, put away your wallet!*

LOSE INCHES QUICK ... AND EAT REGULAR MEALS!

NOW YOU CAN HAVE A FANTASTIC *EXCITING* SLIM

FIGURE ... WORKS LIKE MAGIC! ***** REDUCE Unwanted

INCHES;
***** SLIM Unsightly Bulges From WAIST, TUMMY, HIPS, BUTTOCKS, THIGHS, CALVES, etc. you'll love yourself! **REDUCE** measurements! *A SLEEK, SLIM WAY TO NEW FIGURE CONTROL* **MAIL COUPON TODAY!** * enclose $2.00

LOSE WEIGHT FAST!
LOSE YOUR FAT THE EASY SAFE WAY...
LOSE UP TO FIFTY POUNDS A MONTH.

No Drugs --- No Pills, No Hunger, No
Exercise of any kind! Get the safe way
--- be slim the right way --- Only $1

STOP DIETING!
EAT! EAT! EAT!
AND GET THIN

The amazing Models Method is not going to try and reform you. You can still eat your favorite foods, your deserts and even drink beer and still lose, lose, lose, all that ugly fat fast. You will be as trim and slim as a New York model, without exercise or pills of any kind. only $1.00

SENSATIONAL OFFER! STAR SLIM *The Hollywood Diet*

You'll lose up to 12 pounds a week, 50 pounds a month. Be the girl you always dreamed of being—proud, popular and wanted. No more feeling fat and sorry for yourself—no more seeing someone else. Get all the best things in life. Star slim says goodbye to loneliness, hello to happiness.

STARS & PILLS

the <u>real</u> story!

Luciana Paluzzi, Hollywood's hottest young import, checked into Paramount Studios to begin shooting *Chuka* opposite **Robert Taylor**. "A big hand for the little lady," said her producer. "Her weight's down and she's perfect for the camera." Luciana had trimmed off a few extra pounds, as most stars do before shooting a new film, by a diet helped with appetite depressants her doctor prescribed. "But I do not need to continue the pills," she said. "Once I start working the weight melts off. I put it on in between pictures when I relax and get bored. Eating spaghetti is fun. And I love to indulge in all of the good Italian cooking. I know I don't have to worry—for I can drop eight pounds in a hurry if necessary with appetite control pills from my doctor."

According to **Arthur Ellen**, the famed hypnotist of many film stars, "Pills don't arrive at any solution. The need for excessive smoking or eating or drinking is a human sulking pattern. Eventually, pills are no longer effective, but hypnosis can give one the control to develop confidence."

A devourer of hot fudge sundaes, **Tol Avery** declared that under hypnosis he was told a shrimp cocktail would be more delicious and appealing than sweets when he had the urge for something special. At the same time, hot fudge sundaes would taste like mud. And it worked!

(GMC)

It seems impossible, I'll tell you right now, but forty-three years later, Neely's
     career montage is still going strong.
Or rather Patty Duke's still is.
In the last few weeks, I've received (in accordance with the laws of Magnet
     Theory) emails from three "dolls."

The first was from former graduate poetry student Meg Reilly.
"Hi David," she wrote, "I couldn't resist sending you this link.
Have you seen VotD on the big screen lately?

And Patty Duke will be there!
Hope you're having a good semester."
Her link led me to the website of the Music Box Theatre, where I read that on
     September 24th there would be a special screening of *Valley of the Dolls*:

"Academy Award winner Patty Duke, star of the infamous 1967 film, will be
     present for the event.
Camp Midnight kicks off the evening with a wacky, fun filled 7:00pm prime time
     pre-show hosted by Dick O'Day and featuring David Cerda and the Handbag
     Production Players that will include a costume parade, *Valley of the Dolls* sing-
     a-long at the Music Box organ and more.
The 7:30pm screening (complete with interactive audience guide and hilarious
     running commentary) immediately follows.

Patty Duke will appear on the Music Box theatre stage following the screening
     for a Q&A with the audience conducted by *Windy City Times* film critic
     Richard Knight, Jr. (Dick O'Day's alter ego) and Cerda.
Tickets are $14 in advance, $17 at the door (if available).
A portion of the proceeds will benefit the Queer Film Society."

The second email was from poet Suzanne Buffam.
The subject read, "Do you know about this?"
And the actual message, cut and pasted from the *Chicago Reader*: "Originally
     scheduled for Friday, September 24, Patty Duke's personal appearance at the
     Music Box to introduce her 1967 cult favorite *Valley of the Dolls* has been
     moved back to Saturday, November 20, at 1 PM."

The third email, from another former graduate poetry student, Izzy Oneiric,
     again led me to the Music Box website, where I was informed *why* the
     screening has been moved back:
"We apologize, but Patty Duke has gotten the Movie of a Lifetime (Literally, a
     Lifetime Movie).
This event has been postponed due to talent conflicts.

The new date will be Saturday, November 20th, 1pm.
All those with tickets purchased for the September 24th can reschedule or receive
     a refund by calling Brown Paper Tickets at 1-800-838-3006."
Perhaps Patty, in addition to answering questions from the audience, will lift
     barbells, bounce on a trampoline, row a few leagues on an exercise machine,
     and perform cartwheels (landing squarely on her sixty-four-year-old rump).

In *Phoebe 2002*, we likened Duke to the Energizer Bunny: she just keeps going
     and going and going, ceaselessly starring in made-for-TV movies (many for
     Lifetime) and winning Emmy after Emmy for her "work."
But surely this kind of public spectacle exceeds even *her* battery power.
"Miss Duke! Miss Duke!"

DT anxiously waves his hand.
"Yes, you there, in the middle of the front row, sitting next to that strikingly
     beautiful, chain-smoking brunette."
"Miss Duke, I have a question.

Well, actually four questions."
"Shoot."
"Why am I here?

Why do I live in this movie?
Who's responsible?
Eh?"

(DT)

Truman Capote (high society heretic) approaches me and Frank O.
"Tell me, tell me," he spits out, "is that old dyke
Harper Lee still alive and writing?"

"Wow," I whisper to Frank, "he *is* diminutive, isn't he?"
"JC, you go ahead and talk to him," Frank responds. "I'm gonna sneak
a smoke; that little troll never was part of *my* scene."

"I heard that! You're just a . . . just a *poet* anyway!"
I'm left standing in hell, alone with Truman Capote.
What a world. What a world.

"Listen Conway, I wanna know—is Miss Lee,
Miss Nelle as she was to me as a kid, still kickin'?
And if she is, why isn't she doing something to stop

the malicious rumors and counter-rumors about who wrote our masterpieces?
First I wrote *To Kill*. Then she wrote *In Cold Blood*. Now they're saying
she wrote *both* of them!?!" The little man is irate, and to be honest,

I just don't feel like engaging with a crazy, so I shrug.
"Oh my God!" Truman screams. "She's dead, isn't she? She's dead
and you don't want to tell me—oh my God! Oh my God!" Truman

scurries off, back to his hole. "Frank," I say out loud, "it's safe—
he's gone. Come out, come out wherever you are (it's national
'Coming Out Day')." "Perhaps we should get back to the movie at hand?"

[I just clicked *Valley* on my iTouch to check the scene,
and I thought I had the volume off, but that Career Montage music
started blaring into the air of the Quiet Car: dirty looks; a *shhh!*]

"Conway." "Yeah Frank?" "This daily train ride thing is a freak show."
"Yeah, I know. It's *hell*. Get the humor?"
"Humor got. Let's move on."

"O.K., but I think I should mention that Arthur Penn just died."
"Who?" asks a half-interested Frank.
"You know, the guy that directed Patty Duke in *The Miracle Worker*,

both onstage and in the movie. He's sort of the behind-the-scenes
doll doler for Miss Duke as she started her real-life career montage."
Frank: "Oy."

"He also directed *Bonnie and Clyde*, which starred Faye—
it was released in 1967, the same year as *Valley*. So,
he's sort of responsible for the start of Faye Dunaway's

real-life career montage too." "And?" inquires Frank.
"Duh—she ends up like Patty, also unwittingly making
a quintessential camp masterpiece, *Mommie Dearest*."

"R.I.P., Arthur. Thanks for the memories," Frank drolls.
"Wow. Are you that bored with me, with the underworld?"
"Not really. Just a little irritable today. Hell is so damn hot, ya know?"

Medium shot: Neely (in black-tie attire [or is it faux-hobo drag?] and top hat
between two male back-up dancers; they do a kooky dance routine.
Close-up: Neely's face; she winks as she lifts hat from head.

Wide shot: Neely and two dancers jump off a nightclub stage
into an applauding audience.
A (camp) star is born.

                    (JC)

Sharon sighs. "Do you know the famous Faye Dunaway/Roman
story?" she asks. I shake my head. "Well, it was when they were shooting
Chinatown," Sharon begins, "and Faye was driving Roman *crazy*

with all her Stanislavskian bullshit, until finally Roman shouted at her,
'Just say the fucking words. Your *salary* is your motivation.' You can
imagine how well *that* went over. Now, you have to remember that Faye

was *stunning*—porcelain skin, all cheekbone and burgundy lips—
but like many great beauties she was terrifically vain. So every time
Roman yelled 'cut' out came the Blistex, the lipstick and the powder.

It drove him *nuts*. Do you remember the old Ambassador Hotel,
where poor Bobby [Kennedy] got shot?" I nod, but decide against
reminding her that that was also where the jury for her murder trial

had been sequestered. "Well, there was a restaurant across the street—"
I interrupt her: "The place with the dark wood and the red leather
banquettes?" Sharon nods. I had eaten there a handful of times,

once with a bunch of people including, ironically, the director
of *Henry: Portrait of a Serial Killer*. "Anyway, they were shooting a scene
with her and Jack Nicholson, and there was a single strand

of hair that was sticking out of Faye's head and catching the light
and it was driving poor Roman *insane*. He was trying to flatten it
with his hand but she kept shooing him away. So finally he just snuck

up behind her . . . and pulled it out! Well, the shit hit the fan! Dunaway
stormed off the set." Sharon sniffs, a slow grin spreading across her face.
"Guess what the crew gave Faye as a present when filming wrapped up?"

I shake my head. "A huge Blistex tube made out of paper-mâché."
"And I wonder whose idea that was?" I ask facetiously. "Gee whiz,
I have no idea," Sharon replies, stifling a giggle.

(GMC)

From an article in *Southeastern Antiquing and Collecting Magazine*, which has been
     floating in cyberspace since 2001:
"The Celebrity Collector: Patty Duke, a Woman of Many Talents and Interests,
     Has Just as Many Collections"
By Ken Hall

"The Oscar-winning actress for *The Miracle Worker* and former star of *The Patty
     Duke Show* is more than a collector—she's a pack rat.
She's also introducing a line of collectible stuffed bears."
I'll spare you the mundane details (or maybe that's what the handful of
     trash mongers who will actually read this tome really want) and cut to the
     chase:

Almost ten years ago, speaking by phone from her home in northern Idaho ("It's
     the only place I've ever truly felt at home"), where she'd lived for a dozen or
     so years with her husband Michael, a firefighter, and their son Kevin (then
     12), Patty Duke punctuated her little stories with a hearty laugh and came
     across as "somebody who's about as happy as someone can be."
And that's good, wrote Ken Hall, since her battle with the demons of an often
     turbulent childhood and mental illness are well documented.
Hall wondered, reading her resume, where in the world Duke ever found time to
     collect anything.

There was the Oscar (at age 12) for *The Miracle Worker*, the three Emmys, the two
   Golden Globes (*are you tired yet?*), her three-year stint as the star of *The Patty
   Duke Show*, the past presidency of the Screen Actors Guild (*yes, I'm running
   out of breath*), the 72 (a number that's undoubtedly exponentially higher ten
   years later) made-for-TV movies (*I need a doll to keep going*), the work on
   Broadway and in film, and the voice-over work for cartoons.
Cartoons!
I think it's obvious I'm not going to spare you, dear trash mongers, the mundane
   details after all.

And that wasn't counting her work as a best-selling author.
Her autobiography, *Call Me Anna*, followed up with *A Brilliant Madness*, brought
   to light Ms. Duke's battle with mental illness, as well as other personal and
   professional challenges.
And led Duke to spend a great deal of time speaking on the topic of mental
   illness.

In fact, her illness actually inspired one of her many collections.
She was prescribed lithium as a mood balancer in the 1970s, and hated the vials
   the pills came in.
"Just looking at that jar of pills would make me even more depressed," Patty said
   with a hearty laugh.

Hall failed to ask if that might also have something to do with a certain movie
   she once made—no trash monger, he.
"Then one day in California I saw the prettiest little pill box at Bullock's.
So I bought it, as a way to make the pill-taking experience something nicer."

That led to a collection of Limoges, silver antique, and painted enamel Halcyon
   pill boxes.
Which led (nothing *manic* about it) to collections of antique clocks, pocket
   watches, candleholders, John Deere miniatures, silver spoons, vintage linens,
   angels, bears, and pewter.
"I still have most of what I ever came across," Patty said with a mix of wonder
   and amusement.

"The angels thing started about 25 years ago with a pin.
Then came a brooch, a statue, a picture, then more and more stuff."
She said her most prized angel was a Baccarat piece, a present from her husband.

Another gift from Michael, a Steiff bear to keep her company when the two were
    apart, started yet another collection.
"Bears are great—you don't have to dust them," she said.
The Steiff was eventually destroyed by Patty's pet Schnauzer, but it didn't deter
    her from acquiring more bears.

She bought one from an Idaho neighbor, Ann Inman-Looms, who'd been
    handcrafting one-of-a-kind bears for more than 20 years.
The two became fast friends, and Patty enrolled in one of Ann's bearmaking
    classes.
"It opened up a different kind of creativity I didn't know I had," Patty said.

Patty confessed the first few bears she made on her own were "pathetic," but
    when she and Ann put their collective minds to work, magical things
    happened.
They talked, jokingly at first, about going into business together.
The joke got serious the more they chatted and a business plan was drawn up.

And before Helen Keller could say "wah-wah," the Patty Duke Signature Collection
    was born.
The initial collection consisted of three bears: Faith, Hope, and Charity.
Each was 10 inches tall and cost $89.00, and could be purchased online through
    www.annemadebears.com (web address now defunct).

"These are truly collectible," Patty said, back when she was hawking the line,
    which grew to include bears with names like Samuel, Bert, Angelica, and
    Annie, who came dressed in Amish-style apparel based on that worn by Patty
    Duke's character in the 1996 Hallmark Hall of Fame TV movie *Harvest of Fire*.
"You wouldn't want to give one to a child.
Their eyes are made of glass, and each is made from top-quality mohair, with
    hand-stitched noses.

They have little Battenburg bibs, and each one wears a medallion with an image
    of either a rainbow, hearts, or someone in prayer."
Patty said it's the eyes that make the dolls special: "They're so expressive, they
    seem to have a soul."
Perhaps, but the fact that each one came with a Patty Duke autograph didn't hurt
    sales once the line was officially up and running.

This career montage begins with an alarm clock ringing in Bumfuck, Idaho;
   includes Patty peddling her product at bear shows nationwide and making
   appearances on TV shopping channels; and ends with a spread in
   Southeastern Antiquing and Collecting:
"Cuddlier than the Energizer Bunny—and twice as interminable."
She's so expressive, she seems to have a soul.

(DT)

Canto Eleven

A three-ring circus of miscellaneous scenes: West Coast or bust, tryst in Central Park (where the East River flows), and Miriam's overdue telegram. Aaron Smith finally appears as tormented David Arkin (not to be confused with Alan!), Western Union Boy. More bunnies, snow, suicide, etc., etc.

DT, that is so weird that you should write about Ms. Duke's passion for
collecting, since Ms. Wasserman and I were just discussing
that very topic yesterday. I *love* it: "Cuddlier than the Energizer Bunny—

and twice as interminable." Speaking of bunnies, they happen to be the subject
of one of MY collections—vernacular photographs of children dressed as
bunnies, or in the vicinity of stuffed bunnies, or adults wearing bunny costumes,

or the occasional person photographed with a REAL bunny but that is somewhat
straying from the theme . . . a kid posing with a chocolate bunny will make
the cut, and sometimes I even stray from my mission statement and have a kid

or two searching for Easter eggs or simply holding Easter baskets, then there are
the variations: kids dressed as bunnies holding pumpkin trick-or-treat bags;
girls in pastel dresses and bobby socks standing in front of their Easter baskets

clutching a bunny figurine; an adult dressed in a bunny costume (hopefully
NOT a furry) with a bewildered red-headed girl sitting on his lap inquiring
on the health of his elves; a group of *Mad Men*-looking professionals

all wearing suits, cocktail dresses, and bunny skullcaps (my husband, with the
help of one of his blog readers, came to the conclusion that this was an actual
Xmas party that the creator of *Bullwinkle* threw one year for his employees);

I've got one from the fifties of a kid in a typical suburban living room, his hands
pressed against each cheek in a pre-*Home Alone* stance, standing between two
identical daffodil-colored blow-up bunnies (hopefully which will NOT sow

the seeds of a future fetish); and last but not least, perhaps my favorite, one from
the early '60s of a young girl wearing a white dance leotard and matching bunny
ears, voguing in front of a fireplace in her new black patent leather tap shoes.

But to get back to my conversation with Ms. Wasserman, in which we were
speculating on the psychology of collecting and then moved onto the recent
hoarding epidemic, and the human inclination to want to fix things

that are broken, or to recycle, reuse, or create, with the "some day" sigh of the
over-worked American whose serotonin rush could alleviate the stench
of a dumpster dive IF they were to find a snow globe celebrating the Pope's visit

to Halifax in 1985, in perfect condition, with no nicks or scratches, that maybe
won't sell on eBay *this* month but when the anniversary of the invention
of the Popemobile comes along in 2013 . . . *It could be worth. . . .* But meanwhile

you don't see shows about people in Europe dying under piles of their own shit
(figuratively and literally) because they can't bring themselves to throw away
the broken cup they drank from when they were a baby because they hope

to give it to their own child someday. And Mr. Sartre thought HE was living
in a meaningless world (great quote in my Moleskine from Ms. Wasserman:
"I want to live in a post-meaningless state"), drowning in the muck of absurdity

along with his fellow man. Do you think he ever imagined that someday man
would pay to talk to a computer, only to have IT tell HIM, "I'm sorry, I don't

understand what you are saying"? Or that someone would be able to deposit a
check simply by sending the bank a *photograph* of it? A world where people are
willing to give a sales clerk their SS number in order to qualify for a buy-one-get-

one-free opportunity and then react incredulously when they get their identity
snatched? Think about it: it may be okay for you to use the name of your cat as
a password reminder for eBay, but not eBay AND PayPal; although it is

perfectly easy for someone on PayPal to be able to dip directly into your bank
account simply by guessing correctly the name of your favorite
                                        neighbourhood bistro . . .

Which could be the same one that Lyon and Anne will head
off to after the meeting that is currently occurring in his office.
"Actually this is a celebration," says Mr. Lyon Burke—as he hands

cocktails to Miriam (Tony Polar's sister-cum-manager), Mel (Neely's lover-cum-
manager), and then of course Neely, who is looking a bit on edge in Technicolor
blue, that is until Lyon declares, "I've been having conversations with the coast—

they want to test you and Tony out there next week. Matter of fact
I have the scenes right here, and a song"—and, as if an afterthought—
"a really good one"—whereas virginal sweet Anne, decked out in her off-the-rack

fungal ensemble, is unintentionally responsible for interrupting the meeting
when a secretary enters. "Call from your Aunt Amy," she whispers to Anne
discreetly/*Oh tell her I'll call her back later*/"she said it's very important she speak

to you"/*oh, something must be wrong, Mother has not been well* . . . Anne departs
in a mushroom cloud, suitably flustered by potentially tragic news. "Miriam,
here's a copy for Tony—" continues Lyon as he hands an envelope

to Miriam, who is seated elegantly on his green velvet tufted sofa, silhouettes
of skyscrapers peeking through the hazy sheers behind her. "Incidentally,
where is Tony?" Miriam is smoking, automatic signifier of stress,

as she answers, "Well, I know *who* he's with but I don't know *where*—
I can't reach him" to which Neely shrieks,

"Well, find him!"

(GMC)

A celebration, this is—
The end result of Neely's
Career(ism) montage—of

Her and Tony's big chance to
Become movie stars. Neely
Emits a breathless *Oh* at

The idea, bites her lower
Lip. The camera follows
Lyon across the room: bust

(Alfred, Lord Tennyson?), gilt-
Framed portrait of equally
Stodgy literary type

(Browning?), dictionary worn
From looking up words like *star*
And *monster* (to see if they

Mean the same thing), tufted green
Couch (as long as, well, this scene
Is short), Miriam (in checked

Raincoat), nautical wall clock
(I think). Ice cubes in drinks clink.
Anne withdraws with steno pad,

Pencil—*Mother's not been well.*
Life-changing loss awaits; she's
So *beige*, will it affect her?

Big sis knows who little bro
Is banging, just not where. She
Worried they make retarded

Babies. Neely's ambition
Bird swivels its nasty head
(Cf. Linda Blair), seethes

Well find him. There ought, in that
Widescreen row of red books, to
Be a law against Neely.

(DT)

Anne gets a Twitter from Aunt Amy;
Tony sends Jen a text;
Miriam posts on Tony's Facebook wall.

Everyone waits for something.
It's been three years since DT and I
wished Gillian a happy birthday here in *D.O.D.*

We grow older with this movie.
Some I've seen as of late: *Tron* in 3D,
The King's Speech. I also rewatched *Damage*

from 1992. Wally gave me Schuyler's
Other Flowers for Christmas, and four
beautiful glass bowls from DWR.

DT reports watching all of Joan that's available
on DVD to date. I can't find my copy of *V.O.D.*,
had a notion I'd look at this scene again.

Gillian and I are trying to make a date
for coffee sometime soon. Nothing is where
it should be; no one is *here*:

PayPal sent one of my gifts to the wrong address,
my therapist called to change our appointment.
2011 is the year of the metal rabbit.

A post-Christmas blizzard hit New York.
A tiger peed on me at the Omaha zoo!
A conversation occurs among movers and shakers.

Gillian and DT have exhausted this scene—
I've nothing new to add or say. Oh,
I'll be going to Puerto Rico in February.

(JC)

GILLIAN HERE off to Fort Lauderdale tomorrow
Where I will walk on the beach, get my inevitable
Sun rash, go to The Galleria, stock up on socks, watch

Dancing with the Stars with my mother-in-law,
Eat too much Italian food and when I return
To New York hopefully the snow will be intact,

The mayor will be back from Bermuda, the recycling
Will be picked up, and I will be able to smell
The clean air that is currently engulfing Jen and Tony

During their romantic romp through Central Park

(GMC)

Snowbound in Chicago—third
Worst blizzard in recorded
History: 20.2

Inches overnight. Haven't
Seen the likes since my Denver
Fiasco, recorded four

Years ago in Canto Two.
Let's not even go there, raves
Faye in her best performance

Ever, recorded on an
Answering machine and put
On YouTube for all us queens

To replay, replay, replay.
Today we pay attention
To *this* fiasco, what may

Well be the best-performed scene
Yet (feel free to pelt me with
Spoiled fruit), but innocuous

Nonetheless. Gillian, does
The East River run through the
Park? *Meow!* When Jen quotes her

Mother, I think of Doris
Tate, grieving Saint of Victim
Rights, who in '84 looked

In the eyes of the Devil
(Watson's parole hearing) and
Said, "What mercy, Sir, did you

Show my daughter when she was
Begging for her life?" Snow in
Every state 'cept Florida.

Nice. *It's freezing here.* Here, too.
6º to be precise.
Welcome to the new Âge d'Ice.

(DT)

I'm starved for Tony's coat. *Sans* hocked fur, Jen is frozen.
Process screen reveals person walking pup
on path behind clandestine lovers one second, then person

and pup disappear the next second. Wind blows furiously through
Jen's blonde heap of hair, but the bare stick arms
of trees don't budge. I wonder if Elizabeth Berkley

has ever been inside the Statue of Liberty? She could
join Jen's elite group if she has: *Showgirls of the Statue-high Club.*
Foreshadowing Alert: Tony breaking off—*and there's something else . . .*

I've never been able to quite put my finger on it.
Miriam will get a busy signal again and again on Jen's
off-the-hook phone, while Tony, dumb and hung,

does his *pumping, pumping, pumping* on top of Jen.
It's a familiar scenario, one that's been playing out for months.
Jen's mother all the while in the background: *make him*

marry you. In just a frame or two, these lovers will be
in Los Angeles, on the threshold of witnessing new
heretofore unknown *modes of malice*: "ordinary" fraud,

treacherous fraud, incontinence—gross! (Aged
Hollywood stars and industry workers, locked inside
the long-term care unit at the Motion Picture Country House

in Woodland Hills, exchange nervous glances.)
When did Jen ever do what her mother wanted her to do?
Tony's boyish "Aaahh baaaby" would do me in too, girl.

So I say go, *like a pig in a fashionable trench coat* go.
Take him back to your place, yank off his clothes,
let him put it in you. *And you'll like it. You'll like it!*

(JC)

—So I missed my cue as the Western Union Boy.
DT told me I had two weeks to complete
my cameo, to deliver

the telegram to Miriam
while she smokes a cigarette in her dark blue robe
in her light blue chair,

and I fucked it up,
was unable to get the buzzer to ring,
the note delivered on time.

The night after my deadline
I was crawling around boxes
in my new apartment

trying to find my copy of *V.O.D.* What I found instead:
Midnight Cowboy
All About Eve (I thought DT would forgive me

if I included it in this list
[though I really did find it!])
Field of Dreams

Enduring Love (Daniel Craig before all the muscles)
Seasons 2 and 3 of *Alias*
The Comeback starring Lisa Kudrow

(who I think is a "fucking dorky bitch").
I stole that line from one of Peter Davis's
"Tina" poems in *Court Green*. (Is that code for crystal meth?)

Little Children
The Silence of the Lambs, The Graduate, Fight Club
Showgirls (Hi, Jeffery!)

Moonstruck
(Cher!),
but then I remembered it wasn't in a box

but in my teaching bag
because I knew I'd need it after the move
and didn't want to lose it.

According to the book *Extra! Extra! Hollywood's Most Famous Unknowns*,
David G. Arkin (no relation to Alan) had to film the telegram scene 14 times
because he kept forgetting his lines.

He was also supposed to say:
Can I get a phone number with that signature?
but Mark Robson cut the line

because they were running out of time
and still had to film the phone call.
Instead he told Arkin to give Lee Grant "a hungry, lusty look,"

an "up and down" while she signed.
Arkin added the "Thank you"
on his own.

According to IMDb
Arkin killed himself on January 14th, 1991 in Los Angeles.
The word *suicide* is in parentheses beside his death date,

like: oh, btw,
he did it to himself.
He was 49.

I wonder if it was pills?
I have a feeling he used a gun,
or hanged himself like my friend Robert.

It says under Trivia:
"His mother's maiden name was Collins."
I don't know why that is important?

Arkin also appeared in: *I Love You, Alice B. Toklas!*,
Nashville, MASH, Cannonball!,
All the President's Men,

and an episode of *Hawaii Five-O.*
He played the character George Loomis.
The episode was called "Killer Bee" (death! death! death!).

Okay, I made up the book *Extra! Extra!* because I thought
it would be a fun rumor to start,
but I looked on Wikipedia

(which I told my students today is not a valid source)
and saw that his brother is Robert M. Arkin,
a psychologist on the faculty

at Ohio State University in Columbus, Ohio,
and I was afraid he'd sue me
for making up stuff about his brother.

I thought about sending him an email.
His email address is: arkin.2@osu.edu,
but what would I say?

I'm playing your dead brother in the poem version of *Valley of the Dolls*
and I was wondering if you could give me some insight
into his motivation. (See the telegram, be the telegram.)

Did he use his own pen in the scene?
Are there limits to what someone
should do for a poem?

            (AS)

Come to think of it, could that be part
of Miriam's motivation? That if Tony
ever finds out what *could* be in store

for him that he might kill himself? And couldn't
we blame that on the power of *dread*? Dreading
the dread of never really knowing. . . .

Would rather die than experience the dread
of the possibility of becoming. . . .
Someday, will someone in a church basement

inform Miriam, "You're only as sick as your secrets"?
Or that her fringe, lightly dusted over her forehead,
looks like an afterthought that simply doesn't belong?

(GMC)

There's a lot to say about
this bit—Lee Grant's scene-chewing
gestures (pacing, smoking) and

unruly wiggery, and
the contempo Italian
décor of room 14 B

(green shag rug, throw pillows, bric-
a-brac [how many vases
does one chick need?], powder blue

telephone)—but Aaron's guest
spot got me on a tangent
about David Arkin: watched

two other movies I own
in which he appears (*All the
President's Men* [missed him, his

part is so small] and Robert
Altman's [the director liked
him] *The Long Goodbye*, in which

he's good as a half-witted
wannabe thug) and obtained
(via Amazon Prime) *The*

Nashville Chronicles, from which
I learned Arkin wallowed in
great, tragic novels; iden-

tified with Charles Laughton; and
had a self-deprecating
Oscar Levant-ish wit. And

that during the filming of
Nashville, he physically
attacked a journalist from

the *Los Angeles Times* for
calling him Alan: *I'm not
Alan Arkin!* A thorn in

his side: people were always
addressing him by the name
of the more famous Arkin:

*Don't you know the difference
between Alan and David?*
I thought perhaps he was gay

and killed himself because he
had AIDS (so many men died
in the early '90s) or

out of conceit refused to
see fifty. *Not so. Not so.*
He was straight and tormented.

And cute, sexy-angry; I'd
have tipped big, or pulled him in.
He was put on Valium

after the incident with
the journalist, so maybe
David took an overdose

of dolls? Dorothy Parker tells
us that drugs cause cramp and guns
aren't lawful, that nooses give.

However he went, I hope
(to quote the theme song of *MASH*)
his suicide was painless.

(DT)

*Calling Dr. Eberhart, calling Dr. Eberhart—come
in please.* Miriam is desperate. Tony just got married!
What to do? Get the name of another conspiratorial

physician in Los Angeles who, like the esteemed Dr. E.,
will keep the truth from dum-dum Tony—
the knowledge that he's got some super fucked-up disease.

Ya think that Salvador Dalí painting on M's wall is real?
Ya think that treasure trove of crystal highballs is being
hoarded to this day by some sad sack in the south?

And where is that powder blue telephone? Starved.
Easter is coming and Bunnies glitter now on the horizon;
can we all agree to let Tony & Jen's, Mel & Neely's

futures crack open like Cadbury eggs in Hollywood—
oh, and let's not leave out Miriam, whose wiglet flops
atop her head, cascades out over the sides of her head like

giant fluffy brunette bunny ears at ease.

(JC)

Canto Twelve

The poets descend further. "La de dah," drones Ms. Dog. Conway faces his youthful Farrah-do. McCain confronts the face of evil, an associate of the Manson murderers, in a rain of volcanic ash. A teenaged Trinidad blithely water-skis across a river of blood. The climbing never endeth.

It's Easter in the East.
But it's still snowing in
Lawrenceville. At the train

station, Lyon in voice-
over: "I wanted to
come up for your mother's

funeral; why didn't
you let me?" Icy Anne:
"It was my own *private*

grief." A kiss in the front
seat of dead Mom's station
wagon, then off to the

old homestead our lovers
go. They cross over a
~~boiling~~ freezing river

of ~~blood~~ water, known as
~~Phlegethon~~ Nemasket. Some
~~Centaurs~~ agents watch over

young wannabe actresses
and poets immersed just
below the surface. You

can see the occasional
Carrie White-like hand pop
up from the watery

cage. Sad conversation
quickly turns chatty and
jocular: Paul Revere's

hoof beats, scandalous rumors—
pro-British town! Regret
to have missed Aunt Amy—

she's gone to the cousins
in New Hampshire. They stop
in front of a center-

chimney colonial,
white with black shutters. "You
know, everything is better

here. It really is. I
don't know how you ever
left." (One of the dumbest

stints of acting in the
movie is done right here
[42:49-

43:02]—look
at Barbara Parkins
ACT! Roasting chestnuts seems

to mean play autistic.)
As far as violence
against neighbors: oh my

gods! Here in Philly, for
two days now, the people
in the house next door have

been frying *something* in
unimaginable
bad-smelling grease, while tons

of their friends and family
come and go *loudly*, honk

horns, gather in clumps in

the street and sidewalk, scream
and yell like you wouldn't
believe. It's taking all

my spiritual practice
not to go completely
Seventh Circle, First Ring

on their asses. I stare
at the bejeweled greenish-
blue framed picture of Frank

O. that Gillian gave
me recently. It, he,
is calming, centering.

Other photos on my desk
today: Anne at her desk
in Newton Lower Falls,

the late nineteen-fifties.
And me—wallet-sized school
picture, in seventh grade,

wearing my Pop Warner
football jersey (number
forty). My hair is long,

parted in the middle,
feathered like nobody's
business. I'm smiling less

than Frank, who's smiling less
than Anne (a fact that seems
rather disturbing at

the moment). On the back
of the photo, written
in my own teen cursive:

"Robin—it has been good
knowing you these past years.
You're really sweet. I've liked

you ever since your eighth
birthday party. Let's stay
friends, O.K.? Jeff Conway.

P.S., if Lisa D.
is ever back in town,
please call me." I have no

recollection who this
picture was meant for, no
memory of "Robin."

But Lisa D. was my
first girlfriend—in second
grade. Lisa Daniels. She

and her big friend Patty
held me down in the long-
jump sand pit one recess

so Lisa could kiss me
on the lips. She was the
prettiest girl at Dos

Caminos grammar school.
Me of the Cancer moon,
always living at least

partly in the past, still
clinging to the idea
of Lisa Daniels six

years after her family's
abrupt move out of the
neighborhood (and state I

think). I used to ride my
bike in front of her house
when I was seven and

crash into their tree, fall
off, hoping she would see
me from her window, come

outside to check if I
was hurt. She never did.
Probably never saw

me, even though I did
it quite a few times. Sad.
It seems like Lyon is

having better luck with
Miss Welles. She's already
worried, however, what

the neighbors will think: they
saw the car drive up, the
both of them get out and

glide arm in arm up the
front walk, step inside, where
they *all* know there's just one

marriage bed—a marvelous
four-poster (which are great
for tying up lovers).

(JC)

"Gillian, there is nothing I can possibly eat
here," blurts Sharon, throwing the IHOP menu
on the table with frustration. "A Southwestern

Scramble is 1140 calories—and that's one
of the *healthier*-looking choices." "Get a short
stack," I reply. "They're only 540 calories."

"Including butter and syrup?" I shake my head.
"Excluding." Sharon, who has been kind enough
to meet me at a rest stop outside Bakersfield,

is having none of it. "Let's go to the In-N-Out Burger
next door," she suggests. "I can get a double cheese for 640."
"And 370 of it is pure fat." "You're a bitch," she says.

"Yeah, but I'm *your* bitch. Come on, I'll buy you a tee-shirt
when we get there." Sharon is oblivious to all eyes following
her as we exit the building. "Maybe being fat wouldn't be so bad,"

she says, glancing back at a middle-aged woman in lumpy spandex
leggings taking a bite of lemon meringue with one hand and holding
a baby in the other. "Maybe after Paul is born . . . I'll give it all up,

let it all go, become ordinary." She pauses. "Whoops, strike that."
She is quiet while I give a disgruntled employee our order.
While we are waiting, I take a Sharpie out of my purse, cross out

the "B" and the "R" on a tee-shirt before handing it to her.
"In and out urge," she reads aloud. "Charming." I foot the bill
and we sit down. "So, how was the drive here?" she asks, peeling

back the paper of her burger. "I sat in the backseat and wrote notes
for a poem. One that will never appear in tercets." "Break the rules,"
advises my drop-dead guide. "Live a little," she adds, as she gobbles

a fry. "How about I just put it in prose?" I suggest. "Easier for the typesetters."

* California Carrot Express * Slow trucks * Break FAST * Ingredients for life *
Frito Lay * Budget * Vons * HALIBURTON * Runaway ramp * 1-800-get-thin *
Providing California's future * Great American Transport * FOR LEASE 666 *
FOOD GROWS WHERE WATER FLOWS * Live Better * "Expect More Pay Less"
* OPEN FOR FUN * Buck Owen Boulevard * Reduced speed ahead * contract-
free Android * Vagabond Inn Celebrating 41 years * BIG CITY SKATE PARK *
Plasma Center * Rootie tootie breakfast special * Merle Haggard Drive * Without
Trucks America Stops * Stericycle: Protecting People Reducing Risk *

I put down my pen. "Sharon, you know where I'm heading, don't you?"
She nods before going on a tangent. "You've got sixty miles left until Corcoran.
Ever been there? Weird place. Population: 16 500, 3200 of which are employed

by the California prison system. Cow farms. Pistachio trees. Apocalyptic
industrial compounds. I booked you into the Corcoran Country Inn. Fifty
dollars a night and free hot breakfast. Hey, is it true Legs gets off on the fact

that Ring Dings go through no actual baking process?” I nod. We laugh.
I get serious. “You know why I’m going there, don’t you?” Sharon nods
as she takes her final bite of burger, ketchup drooling down her thin wrist.

“To meet your pen pal. The guy who’s trying to get Mr. Manson a new trial.
How long has the old coot been in jail now?” “Altogether, sixty-four years,”
I reply, peeking at her out of the corner of my eye. “You mad at me?” Sharon
shakes her head. “How could I be mad at you? I’m the one who’s leading *you*

into the depths of hell. I mean, it’s just research. You’ve got to get all points
of view.” She sighs. “Besides, he didn’t kill me. Susan Atkins and Tex Watson
did. But aren’t you supposed to be writing about that Gillian Girl going home

for her mother’s funeral?” “Yeah, but Lawrenceville sounds too much like
Florenceville, and as Joe Pesci said in *Casino*, ‘I want to get away
from back home right now.’”

        (GMC)

We laugh . . . The Absurd laughs . . . Me of the Scorpio moon,
Sex(ton) always on my mind. Is there anything else to
say about this nothing scene?

Anything JC, in his semi-synopsis, didn’t touch on, and thereby
exhaust? Try this on for size:
As Anne and Lyon

get in the station wagon, you can see the name of the store
behind them: Super IGA Market. A quick
Google search reveals

that the abbreviation stands for Independent Grocers Alliance.
Founded in 1926, IGA brought together
independent grocers

across the United States to ensure that the trusted, family-owned
local grocery store remained strong
in the face of growing

chain competition. Today, that entrepreneurial family business
spirit is alive and well: globally, IGA consists
of more than 4000

independently owned and operated supermarkets, 1 750 of which
are located in the U.S. In denis408's
Flickr® photostream,

there's a picture of an antiquated store in rural Pennsylvania,
Horace Harrison's, with a "Super IGA Market"
sign identical to

the one in the movie. (Denis Sweeney, God bless him, has 2 369
pics in his photostream: * Tile Pattern * Etched
glass ticket booth

* Squirt gun display * TACKLE AMMO * Exorcism Van * Winchester Shopping
Center * Stan's * Clash of Styles * imprissoned [sic] junk pile * Y not? * 1960 Chevy
Bel Air tail light * grinchy * monkey fez * Celtic Mood Chart * military-style bushes *
corroded mudflap girl * Benzilla * Campbell palm tree * Campbell cactus * Auto
Parts/Machine Shop Service * Warning Keep Out! * flowers * steel and rocks *
Bolted Iron plate * Rivets * Threaded connector * Water Tower Piping * Cambrian
Park Plaza crowd * Robot Furnace * wind chime * papa do sled * super snow * Mrs
Jones * Mary with Flowers and Plastic Lawn Chairs * Rooster *

skull clock * etc.) Anne and Lyon kiss in the car—an equally
earnest and somehow perfunctory
peck.

As they back out and pull away, we see that something—I can't
quite make out what—at the IGA supermarket
is on sale for 69¢.

Sixty-nine: a number that might scare Anne, particularly in her
mother's house. Beef? Is that what's
on sale?

    (DT)

When my parents visited
a few weeks ago, they
passed me a large manila

envelope as we chatted
in their hotel room at the
Washington Square. (DT, their

room had Claudette Colbert and
Garbo on the walls.) Inside

the shabby package were old
childhood photos of JC
(*That's me, baby, remember?*)

They also gave me a large
Ziploc filled with my track &
field medals (mostly blue) from

high school. *Yeah, I was a BIG
track star.* Included was my
sixth grade class photo. I'm in

the top row, Farrah hair, head
cocked a bit, white jean shirt with
patchwork quilt motif on chest.

On the train from NYC
to Philly again. Quiet
Car. A kind of heaven with

the AC pumping this coach
full of cool as inferno
outside blasts 100-plus

degrees of heat against the
steel shell. *It is June. . . .* Lyon
is very self-involved, right?

I mean, Anne is just a prop—her
quintessential New England
family home—she just gives his

"writer aspirations" some
hoity street cred—that and he
expects to bang her. Wait, wait—

nope, she's going to call him a
cab. It's off to the inn with
him. "Dos Caminos Killer

Whales, Grade Six, Mr. Hagen."
Our teacher was older (he
might even be dead now), and

he was beloved. He read *The
Call of the Wild* aloud to
us every day right after

lunch. He had lived in Africa,
smoked a pipe, dressed cool. In eighth
grade, when I had a stint in Drama Club,

Mr. Hagen showed up as
a judge. I thought that meant I
would win for my humorous

expository writing
piece, but I didn't. Instead,
a sophisticated girl

who had moved to our town from
back East won the competition.
She was a pretty brunette

who wrote a story from the
point of view of her feet. Mr.
Hagen smiled and chuckled,

said glowingly afterwards,
*That's the kind of story I
wish I could write!*

She was as smug as Welles. I
should have gotten *something* for
my "Handy Helpful Hints From

Henry" piece. . . . There's always
an Anne waiting *out there* to
win, to out grace, to withhold.

(JC)

There was no "Inn of Florenceville" in my old hometown,
but in my adult years a young man relocated to *his* hometown
of Hartland, fifteen miles south, home to the Longest

Covered Bridge in the World, and birthplace to New Brunswick's
most "flamboyant" premier, Richard Hatfield. I only met the man
once, when I opened the door of my childhood home and there

he was, dressed in a red Adidas tracksuit, inquiring "whether
my mother had a pair of scissors he could borrow," one of the more
surreal moments of my life, much like when I saw a bunny

hopping its way down Thompson Street in the late eighties.
Anyway, this young man moved to Hartland with his lover,
bought the house the premier had grown up in, aptly

named it "Hatfield House," and opened a restaurant/inn
memorializing the life of our late premier, a "confirmed
bachelor," who was said to have attended Warhol parties

and was a friend of Truman Capote's. Though my all-time
favorite Richard Hatfield story came from my late brother,
who said that one day when everyone at his office was talking

about their favorite songs, and Pete mentioned, "I Wanna Be Your Dog,"
a relative of the premier, who just happened to work in the same
office, asked, "Isn't that one of Ziggy [sic] Pop's songs? I remember

Cousin Richard flying down to New York a bunch of times
to see him play." Anyway, back to the inn. It was the only place
within eighty miles that used flavour-infused vinegars

and the food was excellent, and the décor was even better.
Wall-to-wall pictures of Premier Hatfield, from infancy
to death, my favorite one of him drooling on Princess

Diana, an historical event in which he played host to the Prince
and Princess while intoxicated, which was almost as scandalous
as when, in hopes of creating an auto industry in New Brunswick,

he invested provincial money in the ill-fated Bricklin SV-1 car,
or when, in 1984, according to Wikipedia (I know, I know),
"he was charged with criminal possession of marijuana

after thirty-five grams of the drug were found in his suitcase
during a routine inspection of luggage during that year's royal visit
by Queen Elizabeth II." (He was later acquitted on the charges.)

I remember my twelfth-grade and favorite English teacher, the late
Barb Carter, made jokes about that in class, and probably even more
to her friend Helen who visited every weekend, and who on several

occasions invited my parents to their house for dinner.
Once, when Barb vanished from the table, Helen excused herself
and upon return, announced to my parents, "Barb will not be rejoining

us this evening." (Probably the next day was one of those days
whereupon entering the classroom she immediately closed the drapes.)
Barb had gone to college with Anne Murray, wore corduroy blazers

with patches on the elbows, and is the reason I am a writer.
She managed to make *Beowulf* and Chaucer palatable,
and taught *Macbeth* in a contemporary light by comparing

its plot to that of my extended family, which I found hilarious,
but apparently, my younger cousin did not, and years later

a complaint was made. (*Get a life!*) As for the IGA,
that was our local grocery store, owned by the Greens,
whose son Rodney I went to school with from kindergarten

through twelfth, and who in sixth grade was the proud
title-owner of a goat named Farrah, which was the year
he wrote me the following note:

DEAR:GILL
FROM:ROD

THE REASON THAT I HAVE'NT BEEN PAY-
ING ATTENTION TO YOU IS CAUSE EVERY
TIME US BOYS TRY TO HAVE SOMEK FUN
YYOU GIRS AW- ALWAYS GO AND TELL
AND GET US IN BIG TROBLE EXPECIALLY
CINDY I'A NOT MAD AT YOU JUST   T-
hAT   I'AM JUST SICK AND TIRED
OF THE GIRLS GETTING TO DO EVERY-
thing.

love;rod

(GMC)

Isn't this scene meant to convey Anne's coldness, her frigidity?
Much more is made of it in the book—
the icy New England

beauty who melted for the wrong Mr. Right—than in the film. Is it
evidence of Magnet Theory that I recently
found on eBay a

childhood treasure I've searched for for years (please don't laugh):
the coloring book for *The Snow Queen*,
the 1959 animated film

based on the fairy tale of the same name by Hans Christian Andersen,
which "starred" the voices of Sandra Dee,
Tommy Kirk, and

Patty McCormack (she of *The Bad Seed*). It's a truly awful cartoon
(I of course own the DVD, as well as several
posters and stills

that I collected over the years), but I loved it when I was six. Kay,
a little boy, is abducted by the angry
Snow Queen (she

uses ice splinters to freeze his heart) and held captive in her ice palace;
his friend Gerda ("played" by Sandra Dee,
whose voice is

cloying beyond belief), goes on a quest to free him. One day at Thrifty
Drug Store (site of countless childhood
upsets involving

this mass-produced culture of ours) I saw the *Snow Queen* coloring book;
it was my have-to-have. I asked my
mother (stop me if

you've heard this one too many times) to buy it for me, but ice splinters
from the Snow Queen's smashed
mirror had frozen

her heart and she refused. Mothers of America: never, never, never tell
a sensitive, artistic son he can't have
(or watch or read,

for that matter) *anything* his gay little heart (*fairy* tale—Magnet Theory—
get it?) desires—otherwise he'll spend
the rest of his life

looking for it. Said coloring book cost fifteen cents in 1960; in 2011, I paid
fifty dollars for it—its pages brown,
beginning to chip.

*She walked on in the cold and snow. At last she came to the ice palace. There was
Kay! How happy they were to see each other! The Snow Queen
began to melt.*

Fifty: one dollar for every year that had passed since I first saw it at Thrifty's.
The child who originally owned it
colored very few

pages. One that he (lucky fag-boy) or she did fill in is of the Snow Queen
sitting evilly on her ice-throne. Her
dress is magenta;

her face and ice-helmet, orange. The helmet calls to mind Elizabeth Taylor's
monstrous spiked headdress in *Boom!* That's
me, baby, remember:

Is it further evidence of Magnet Theory that Gillian's mention of Anne
Murray carried me, as if in the Snow
Queen's flying sled,

back to the summer of 1970, when her song "Snowbird" was a big hit:
I'm flying from L.A. to San Francisco
for a week-long visit with

my Uncle Jack and his wife Betty. First taste of freedom: a reprieve from my
father's constant belittling. We went water-skiing
(I got up my first try—

what exhilaration, flying over the water) and to a nearby Renaissance Faire.
Jack had a red sports car, which he let me drive
(no license) in the hills

above San Rafael. One of the few memories of pure happiness from my
teenage years: driving with the top off, smoking
cigarettes, Anne Murray's

"Snowbird" (just found it on YouTube, am playing it now) on every channel:
Spread your tiny wings and fly away,
And take the snow

back with you where it came from on that day. A pilot for TWA, Jack was my
mother's cool younger brother. I always dreamed
that Jack and Betty

would rescue me from the fairy tale *I* was trapped in (my father a Snow King
in his own right; *something* had frozen his heart).
No such luck, as

Schuyler would say. On May 18, my father forwarded the following email,
which he'd received from Betty five days earlier
(5/13/11) at 10:47 AM (PST):

Dear friends and family,
Jack flew away in his own private jet to his planet last night. He courageously
fought prostate cancer which he had had since 2006 even though it wasn't
diagnosed until Nov 2010. He was in extreme pain and confused on the heavy meds.
So he definitely wanted out of here. He lost his zest for life. He left the earth
peacefully and his family is devastated. He was our Rock of Gibraltar. He left us
with lots of wisdom and great memories. Hope you all are well.

For six months my father had known that Jack was ill, but had failed to tell me.
The last time I saw Jack was in New York, late nineties; I
was still living with Ira.

He and Betty were in town; the four of us ate lunch in SoHo. Betty commented
on my graying hair. In 2007, Betty and her daughter
Stasia showed up at

a reading I gave at Moe's Books in Berkeley. I was afraid they'd be shocked by
my poems—my explicit sensibility. None of my
relatives had ever heard me read.

Did that stop me from reading what I'd planned to read? *I feel like I've taken off all
of my clothes.* Both courage and shame in that
standing naked.

My guide knows something about this: *This is my* [fairy] *tale which I have told, / if
it be sweet, if it be not sweet, / take somewhere else* [the inn,
for instance] *and let some return to me.*

(DT)

The first time I tried to water-
ski, I fell right after getting
up, and I forgot to let go

of the rope, was dragged behind the
speeding boat for what felt like miles,
ingesting so much water I

needed my stomach pumped. I was
eight or so. Our family's big
Shasta Lake vacation. This heat

(Camp Chesterfield, Indiana)
reminds me of those long days on
our rented pontoon boat, aimless

floating for hours, my siblings and
I fighting over limited
supply of Frescas in ice chest.

I'm here with DT, Tony and
Liz. A little side trip from my
week in Chicago visiting

DT. We all had appointments
with psychics today. I was so
nervous earlier, holed up in

my room at Daleville's Travel Inn,
across from the Denny's and the
Sixty-Nine Liquors store (no lie)—

I felt like Anne, Welles that is, must
have felt at the end of this scene.
Anne, it seems to Lyon anyway,

is afraid of ghosts. And I hope
she *does* believe in ghosts—spirits,
I mean—though, as I now see it,

they are not to be feared at all.
It's July 13, 20-
11: today I had one

of the most amazing, profound
experiences of my life.
I'm not being dramatic, not

trying to shock or sway any-
body, I'm just here to say that
I met the numerologist

psychic at 2:30 p.m.
Patricia J. Kennedy. An
enlightened spiritualist with

a true gift. I was of what I'd
describe as "medium" belief
when I first sat down with her to

begin. That changed completely when
she suddenly said, "Philip (or
Phil?) is here with us!" I looked at

her suspiciously. "Phyllis?" "Oh
yes, Phyllis. She wants you to know
she loves you *very* much, she's so

happy you're here today, she wants
me to tell you she's found peace, she
was met by a male presence—it

could be her father—she wants you
to know she wasn't in as much
pain as people thought at the end,

it's just that she had decided
quite some time before she died that
she was ready to leave, and she

wanted to go. She loves you so
very much! She is so glad you
are here." My friend Phyllis Sklar, born

May 3, 1923, died
January 28 of
2010. Her father had

always been absent from her life,
and I'd often thought that, deep down,
this situation had led her

to a lifetime of struggle with
disappointment and anger. Thanks,
Phyllis, for our wonderful time

together, our conversations,
the drawings and paintings—pure joy
and fantastic color. I've missed

you since you've moved on. DT will
be saying to himself about
now that he had always assumed

I was on the same "vibration
frequency" as he—he'll be so
surprised to read about this new

epiphany, this deep belief,
that has only just now occurred
for me. I've always been willing,

open to this phenomenon,
never any contempt prior
to investigation, but in

Patricia's presence, receiving
messages from the spirit world—
I guess I had to *touch* it for

myself (yes, my Taurus nature).
Other spirits with whom I was
so blessed to have contact with: Tom

Roberts (my uncle) and my long-
dead friend Leonard Canela. (For
you non-believers out there in

Poetryland, I did not say
one word to Patricia about
any of these people before

she began to name, establish
contact, relay messages to
me from these spirits; in fact, I

had never spoken or written
Tom or Leonard's name since each passed
years ago.) Thank you, Patricia,

and DT for guiding me here
to this place and moment. My out-
look on life has changed—another

flash of insight—I suddenly
understand: I know again, in
a different way, at soul

level, that I am one with God.
Patricia told me I'm on a
spiritual journey—one which I

began years ago, at a time
when I suffered from liver pain
(my drinking and dolls), one that I

need to resume traveling to have
a "rebirth of me." I'm at a
"crossroads of inner self." *Just go.*

The next time I am being dragged
behind that metaphorical
speedboat, I will, indeed, let go.

As you should too, Anne, let Lyon
go, out of the inn, out of town,
back onto the train, just let go.

(JC)

I agree with JC, *Anne, give it up!*
Think of some of the words that rhyme with "Dear John":
bon-bon, bygone, dead-on, Don Juan, Teflon, walk-on . . .

And Jeffery, funny you should mention Shasta Lake,
not only because it makes me think of Lake Isabella,
which is the place the LaBiancas spent the day of the night

they were slaughtered, but also because it could be
the most evil place I have ever encountered . . .
Let me tell you a story . . .

Legs and I went there some years ago to look
for someone involved with the Manson case
who lived at an apartment complex for seniors.

We arrive. The building looks vacant. We enter
the lobby and are greeted with a potted plant,
two bought-on-sale-at-Staples armchairs, and a faux

fireplace—employee schedules on easels—water-
cooler—as we begin to make our way down the hall—
plastered with Mod Podged puzzles—we hear wailing:

guttural, supernatural, angst-filled moaning,
only to encounter the source, an elderly lady,
bald, probably three hundred and fifty pounds,

in a white cotton nightgown, sleeveless, legs splayed,
wedged in between the confines of her own doorway,
her arms outstretched to anyone who might help her

and much to Legs's credit, he tries, but what is really needed
is some kind of apparatus. So after finding an attendant,
who is most definitely within hearing distance, and who comes

only begrudgingly . . . who knows what happened next.
We continue to walk past holiday-infested doors
until we find the one we are looking for

knock knock who's there the door opens a notch, the chain
lock still intact, a gnome-like creature pokes his nose out;
Legs pushes me into his viewfinder, hoping a "young"

(middle-aged) woman might entice him to talk to us—
which seems to work, because no more than five minutes
later the guy comes jaunting out of the building—

and yes, I mean, *jaunting*—looking like a totally different
human being: his white hair now tucked underneath
a gingham kerchief, gangster-style, his white beard looking

groomed; his approximately five-foot-two body
casting quite an imposing figure in a black leather
motorcycle jacket. Our encounter

was brief: he despised Legs, and possibly my true age
was evident in the late afternoon light—Paul Frank
tee-shirt and Converses aside, I was probably thirty-

five years too old for him (thus the reason for his recent—
nudge-nudge wink-wink—incarceration). Have you ever
been in the presence of evil? That was my first time.

As I feigned interest in his proselytizing—standard
be-here-now sound-of-one-tree-clapping shit—the sky
became gray and the cinders from Legs's cigarette

began to swirl all around me—I was just about
to reprimand him when I realized that it was actually
raining ash. Something about a volcano, okay,

question answered, but it was *eerie*, and understandably
our older friend wanted to seek refuge inside—
asthma got worse during his confinement, etc. etc.

But before exiting he made me promise
to read two books: *Stranger in a Strange Land*
and a tome by someone named David Icke.

I will never forget walking out of the local Borders
with a shopping bag filled with my homework
assignment and seeing people casually coming

and going, like robots, or zombies, oblivious
to the gray matter, dandruff-like, falling from the sky,
dusting their hair and clothes. I returned to our motel

happy to have something to do. Tucking into bed,
I started reading Icke, which seemed to me standard
conspiracy kind of stuff—but no way—here it goes:

Bohemian Grove . . . a lady who'd been raped by Reagan
and whose teenage daughter had been raped by Bush Sr.,
how the masters of the universe and the hoi-polloi

kidnapped women like herself, and gave them five minutes
to run beyond the hills of Shasta Lake before they became
target practice. Which I probably could have slept

after, but when I got to the part about Shasta Lake
being the center of the occult scene in the U.S.
and how much of it revolved around the local

country music scene—*Merle Haggard was playing the next day!*—
I ran out, knocked on Legs's door, and announced, *We're out of here.*
It was about nine p.m. and he happily agreed.

The ash continued to descend as we drove out
of the city limits, the only grumbling
from Legs came because he thought we should wait it out

until the gnome agreed to give us an interview:
I told him that we would probably hear from him
in a week when we were in a different time zone,

and I was almost right, one night, staying at an inn in Oregon,
Legs's cell phone rings and it was the goblin, asking for me
by first and last name, saying he'd gotten a premonition

that I might benefit from some spiritual guidance.
I put my head under the pillows, and tried to exorcise
the ickiness into oblivion.

     (GMC)

Dear Anne, thank you for the moment of reckoning . . . I've always wanted to
write, so I'm going back to England. . . . And so Lyon dumps
Anne, leaves her to read his "Dear Jane"

letter (I've always thought it was a "Dear Jill" letter, but Wikipedia strikes
again: "The reverse situation [of a 'Dear John' letter], in
which someone writes to his wife or

girlfriend to break off the relationship, is referred to as a 'Dear Jane' letter")
leaning against her black station wagon (with the fabulous
wood siding and red interior) in

front of an antique barn and snow-covered cemetery. She's devastated.
She'd bounded into the inn as if a night alone in her
mother's bed had changed her mind—

"I want to fuck now!"—only to find Lyon gone. "Shall I write you a poem
called 'For My Lover, Returning to England'?" my guide
whispers (after all it is noon [or four

minutes past, to be exact], that ghost hour, on Tuesday, July 26, 2011) from
Oblivion. The sun stands fire there, and the clouds are
as small as puppies . . . it is always

summer afternoon. Ms. Dog sunbathes nude in her backyard—she doesn't
care if UPS sees her parcel. La de dah. The angels
pull their cloud-curtains back. Ms. Dog

talks to God, but he floats with his belly up, that is, he gives her both of his
buttocks, two gold records rolling off toward Liverpool.
Did I say Liverpool? What England means

to me, this summer at least, is the British Invasion, "a term used to describe
the large number of rock and roll, beat, rock, and pop
performers from the United Kingdom who

became popular in the United States during the period from 1964 through 1966."
One of my obsessions this summer. Yes, there is a
world outside my closed blinds, a world

where Pulitzer Prize-winning suburban poets lay buck-naked in their backyards
or skinny-dip in their swimming pools (paid for by
this or that literary grant), but this

summer I know it not. (At Camp Chesterfield, Patricia advised me to be more
physical—I've been so mental the last three years,
working on Tim Dlugos's collected poems

and my own new and selected, not to mention essays about Sylvia Plath
[Anne calls from Oblivion: "I was the living Plath!"]
and God knows what else—and I will,

I will, I will strive for balance . . . but do I have to be physical today?) In May
I started listening to and compiling songs by sixties
girls: "Blame It on the Bossa Nova"

by Eydie Gormé, "Popsicles and Icicles" by The Murmaids, "I Have a Boyfriend"
by The Chiffons, and so on (something I'd done back
in the eighties when, obsessed

with girl groups, I was writing poems like "Meet The Supremes," but those
cassette tapes are long gone), which reacquainted me
with two songs by Evie Sands—"I Can't

Let Go" and "Take Me for a Little While"—that I played incessantly in the
sixties, poor tortured pubescent gay boy up in his bedroom,
curtains shutting out the suburban

summer afternoon. Of course I knew nothing of Ms. Sands then, except the
ache of heartache and longing in her soulful voice
(Dusty Springfield went on record

citing Sands as her favorite female singer). But thanks to Wikipedia, I learn
that Evie Sands is a Brooklyn-born singer, songwriter,
and guitarist, whose career began as

a young teenager in the mid-1960s (she wasn't much older than me when she
recorded the songs I sighed to). But stardom was
to prove elusive. In 1965, Sands signed

to the Blue Cat label and recorded the single "Take Me for a Little While." Prior
to its release, a test pressing of Sands's recording
was stolen by a Chicago-based

producer, who shopped it to established Chess Records recording artist Jackie
Ross, who was coming off the major pop/soul
hit "Selfish One." Ross—who

was unaware of the duplicity involved, and who left Chess shortly afterwards—
and her producers loved the song, and recorded,
pressed, and released the record

within 48 hours, beating Sands's version to the street by a week. Backed by
the marketing and promotional muscle of Chess
Records, and with Ross's name

attached, this version unsurprisingly received the lion's share of airplay.
The subsequent legal struggle set back Sands's
young career before it had had

a chance to get started. By the time Chess withdrew the Ross single from the
marketplace, Sands's version would only
break through in the few

cities (like Los Angeles: lucky me) that had thus far stayed "on the fence,"
waiting to see which version to play. You
can listen to both—Ross's and

Sands's—on YouTube and decide which you like best. (I'm of course biased,
and tend to favor the underdog.) You can also
see a strange mid-sixties group

called The Koobas perform the song. It was also recorded in the sixties by
Cher and by Vanilla Fudge. So the song got
around, though it should have

been Evie's hit. Her follow-up single, "I Can't Let Go" (which I loved then
and love now—it's a sublime song), was lost amidst
the post-"Take Me" chaos, leaving

British Invaders The Hollies clear to score a hit cover in the spring of 1966.
I listened to The Hollies' version on YouTube.
It's more upbeat, more pop than

Evie's rendition. This is what kicked off my interest in the Brits. A click-
through suggestion on the right of the screen led me
to a clip of The Hollies performing

"Look Through Any Window," a terrific song I wasn't familiar with. The
music was great, but what really grabbed me was
the black-and-white innocence of the period,

how the band and the fans look so fresh and clean-cut and handsome, and
look like they're having such fun. I was especially
taken with lead guitarist Tony Hicks,

the epitome, in my opinion, of sixties boy beauty. Only nineteen or twenty
years old, he seems to be having the time
of his young life. And so

cute! If it's still up on YouTube by the time this tome is published, go to
http://www.youtube.com/watch?v=0CfH-FAGc88
and see for yourself. He's

the one on the far right. Unblushingly, he meets the camera's gaze then
looks away: this is new, he's getting used to the
attention, but clearly ready

for his fifteen minutes. I re-bought *The Hollies' Greatest Hits* (a CD I once
owned but must have forfeited when Ira and I
got "divorced"; it irked me to

have to buy it again) [I just took a break, walked out in the summer sunshine
to mail three letters, so there—I did something
physical today] and basked in

their "hook-heavy pop sensibilities": "Bus Stop," "Carrie Anne," the afore-
mentioned "Look Through Any Window," "Stop
Stop Stop," and "King Midas in

Reverse"—my faves. Plus the ripped-off-from-Evie "I Can't Let Go,"
which isn't on the CD. For weeks the British
have been invading my iTunes:

the biggies (The Beatles, Herman's Hermits, The Dave Clark Five, and
The Hollies [came across a great song by them
I'd never heard of: "Have You Ever

Loved Somebody"]), the lesser groups (Freddie and the Dreamers ["I'm
Telling You Now" has always done something
special to me], Gerry and the

Pacemakers, Peter and Gordon, The Fortunes, The Searchers), some new
discoveries (The Merseys' "Sorrow" and Chris
Farlowe's cover of "Out of Time"),

and the ladies (Marianne Faithfull, Lulu, Petula Clark, and Dusty Springfield).
Is there anything more heavenly than this vintage
b&w video on YouTube: her blonde

hair in a huge bouffant, wearing a chiffon dress and heels, Dusty lip-syncs
"I Only Want to Be with You" as she dances in
and out of a spotlight

on a pitch-black stage—like she's shimmying circles around a full moon,
or like she's the moon herself, as in the
Bashō haiku (translated by

Robert Hass), the harvest moon walking around the pond all night long.
Did I ever tell you that in 1983, when I was newly
sober, I heard Dusty Springfield

tell her story at an AA meeting in Hollywood? One of The Four Tops gave
her her first drink, vodka, backstage before a
performance. It was like warm oil,

magical, relaxed her enough to make the grind enjoyable. A few years later
I was seated behind her at a meeting in
West Hollywood. With my foot

I touched, ever so surreptitiously, the leg of her chair, thinking some of her
stardust might rub off on me. Evie
Sands, by the way,

eventually saw chart action in 1969, before mostly forgoing live performance
in 1979 to concentrate on writing and production.
She experienced a fashionable,

Brit-led surge in cult popularity beginning in the 1990s and returned to live
performance in mid-1998. She is still actively
recording and performing today.

Earlier this year, in February, she sang "I Can't Let Go" at The Echo in
Los Angeles. Watch it on YouTube. God bless
Evie Sands, and may the angels

throw open their cloud-curtains and assuage any pain from the way fate
denied her superstardom, let her let it go.
Fame lasts but an instant

(Lana Turner has collapsed—who she?), but denied your rightful spotlight—
that climb lasts an eternity. *Thank you
for the loveliest winter of my life.*

"The end of the affair is always death." It doesn't look like Lyon's departure
will touch Anne very deeply. She would cry, if she
had the tears. It took me

eight years to let go of my first lover; as soon as I did, a door opened: a friend
walked in, suggested I accompany him to an AA meeting.
Hurry up please it's time.

This canto ends with me still climbing.

(DT)

About the Authors

Jeffery Conway's books include *Showgirls: The Movie in Sestinas*, *The Album That Changed My Life*, and two collaborations with Lynn Crosbie and David Trinidad, *Phoebe 2002: An Essay in Verse* and *Chain Chain Chain*. His work can be found in *Dream Closet: Meditations on Childhood Space*, *Rabbit Ears: TV Poems*, and *This Business of Words: Reassessing Anne Sexton*. He lives in Philadelphia.

Gillian McCain is the author of two books of poetry, *Tilt* and *Religion*. With Legs McNeil she co-wrote *Please Kill Me: The Uncensored Oral History of Punk* and co-edited *Dear Nobody: The True Story of Mary Rose*. She is the former Program Coordinator and Board President of The Poetry Project at St. Mark's Church. She lives in New York City.

David Trinidad's books include *Notes on a Past Life*, *Dear Prudence: New and Selected Poems*, *Peyton Place: A Haiku Soap Opera*, *The Late Show*, and *Plasticville*. He is also the editor of *A Fast Life: The Collected Poems of Tim Dlugos*. He lives in Chicago, where he is a Professor of Creative Writing/Poetry at Columbia College.

Made in the USA
Monee, IL
07 July 2026